the
real
jazz

revised and enlarged edition

the
real
jazz

by hugues panassié

new york: a. s. barnes and company, inc.
london: thomas yoseloff ltd.

to
madeleine gautier

look, you don't pose, never.
that's the last thing you do, because
the minute you do you're through as a jazzman.
maybe not as a musician,
but jazz is only what you are.

louis armstrong

preface

Reader of my first book, *Hot Jazz*, may be surprised in reading this new book to see that I have changed my mind about
certain musicians and certain questions of general approach.
Perhaps they will accuse me of being inconsistent. For that
reason I feel it necessary to offer a few explanations, to give my
reasons for changing my opinions.

Since jazz is a music created by the colored people, it is very
difficult and, in fact, almost impossible for a white man to get
to the heart of it at first shot. A period of slow assimilation is
required, and this period may well extend through several
years. I had not yet achieved the necessary degree of assimilation at the time my first book was finished in 1934. It should
be confessed that I had had the bad luck, in a sense, to become
acquainted with jazz first through white musicians, through
the recordings of Red Nichols, Frankie Trumbauer, Bix, Ben
Pollack, whose music, because it differed enormously from that
of the great colored musicians, could not give an exact idea of
authentic jazz. As a consequence, while I scarcely knew Louis
Armstrong, Duke Ellington, etc., and was barely learning to
like them, I still retained too great an attachment for the white
musicians who had introduced me to jazz. I did not realize
until some years after the publication of my first book that,

from the point of view of jazz, most white musicians were inferior to colored musicians.

Let no one imagine, however, that I have a categorical prejudice in favor of colored musicians. You will see in the pages that follow that I do not hesitate to praise some white musicians abundantly. But the number of white musicians who have succeeded in assimilating the musical inspiration of the Negroes (and that is the real spirit of jazz) is far smaller than I believed a few years ago.

For the same reason, you will see that I praise certain colored musicians whom I criticized in my first book. I made the mistake of judging these musicians unconsciously by standards acquired from the white instrumentalists I had heard first.

Another explanation of the modifications I have had to make in certain judgments may be found in the fact that when I wrote my first book, I had not been able to hear enough of certain musicians, their records having been very hard to find.

Furthermore, in the mass of information gathered for the first book, certain facts turned out to be inexact, and have led me to commit various succeeding errors.

In spite of all that, some people will undoubtedly attribute my changes of mind to my inability to judge with consistency and discernment. To them I reply that to change one's mind indicates more intelligence and sincerity than is found with those who cling to the same opinions from birth to death. For the human spirit is too imperfect to grasp the truth in all its nuances at first attempt, and must strive to bring it constantly to a finer point.

In any case, I would rather be contradictory, or appear to be, than persist in an opinion which I realize mistaken. Only little minds are afraid to contradict themselves. I should like to quote here a clarifying passage from Marcel Proust: "There is no man, however wise, who has not at some time in his youth said things or even done things whose memory he would wish to see expunged. But one does not receive wisdom; one must discover it for himself after a voyage which none can make for us, and which no one can spare us, for wisdom lies in our own point of view about things."[1]

[1] A l'ombre des jeunes filles en fleurs, Tome III, page 137—French edition.

foreword
to the
revised
edition

The manuscript of the present book was sent by Clipper to the United States in 1941. It was badly watersoaked in transit from France and was damaged by the time it reached the translator's hands. Miss Anne Sorelle Williams did her best to recreate a number of parts of my book in her translation, for it was impossible at that time, and for several years after, to correspond between the United States and France. A number of errors crept in, some of them rather important.

I myself worked on the present edition, made the necessary corrections, and brought the book up to date. I wish to point out to my readers that this new edition is the first one I feel entirely responsible for, as previous editions did not accurately reflect some of my opinions.

It would not, therefore, be fair to reproach me, from now on, for the involuntary errors in the previous editions of THE REAL JAZZ.

H. P.

foreword
to the
revised
edition

contents

the
real
jazz

1 true and false jazz

More than half a century has elapsed since the birth of jazz. Much has been spoken about it; many books have been written about it; and still the layman has no idea of what this music really is.

One of the chief reasons for this lack of understanding is that vastly different sorts of music have wrongly become associated with the word jazz.

There is no point in starting a quarrel over words. Words may be loosely used. No more is required to render discussion completely hopeless than for one person to understand a word in a different sense than another. So it will be useful once for all to understand what we mean by the word "jazz."

The word jazz (and this is a historical fact, unchallengeable and unchallenged) originally described the music of the Negroes of the South of the United States, and it seems logical to keep the original meaning. Of course other words were used to describe authentic jazz—such as "hot jazz," "swing music." But experience has shown that these terms create confusion. The expression "hot jazz," which I first thought would be a good one to use, seems to imply that there are two varieties of authentic jazz in existence: hot jazz and some other kind. In reality there is only one real jazz. As for the term "swing music," it has been too frequently used to designate a new form of jazz when no such new form existed. Thus it has been possible for Benny Goodman to be described sometimes as the creator of swing music, when in fact he has created nothing of the sort. *En outre*, the word "swing," to be perfectly understandable, should never be used as a noun or adjective but only as a verb, as I shall try to demonstrate a little later.

For all these reasons, it seems preferable to stick to the original designation and to reserve the expression "jazz music" for the one and only authentic jazz.

The case of jazz is so unusual in the history of music that only by examining the psychological roots of that music can we gain an appreciation of all the elements in their true values, and at the same time demonstrate the true significance of jazz. That is why, in spite of the books which have been written in the past by others and by myself, I propose to take up the question here as though it had never been dealt with before, observing it from several new angles.

Above all it must not be forgotten, as it too often has been, that jazz was created by the Negro people—more precisely by the Negroes of the United States. And of course, there is as much difference between a United States Negro and a Senegalese or Martinique Negro as there is between a Frenchman and a Russian or a German.

We have here the reason for the extraordinary lack of comprehension authentic forms of jazz have had to battle against, on the rare occasions when jazz has succeeded in reaching the public at all: it is the music of another race, and when confronted with this music, the white race has found itself completely bewildered. This does not mean that white people are unable to understand jazz. We know that there are good jazz musicians belonging to the white race. But in general the

Negroes prove more gifted, and while the Negro masses among themselves have an instinctive feeling for this music, white people approach it with resistance and assimilate it slowly.

Some white people once said: "What do we need Negro music for? We who are civilized, why should we interest ourselves in the music of savages?" Let us assume—merely for the purpose of argument since it is certainly not the case—that Negroes are savages. In what way would the music of savages be inferior to that of civilized men? At the risk of stirring up many prejudices one cannot refrain from saying that there is no reason why civilization should necessarily imply progress so far as music is concerned. Those who have such preconceptions show that they have misunderstood the true nature of music. For music is, above all, the cry of the heart, the natural, spontaneous song expressing what man carries within himself. A man who ignores all musical theories but who is endowed with extraordinary creative gifts and who sings alone in the desert can be more sublime, can be a greater musician, than the author of the most complicated symphonies and quartets if the latter is less inspired. The role played by culture in music is secondary. Inspiration without culture can produce beautiful works; culture without inspiration is incapable of doing so.

We must go further and say that in music primitive man generally has greater talent than civilized man. An excess of culture atrophies inspiration, and men crammed with culture tend too much to play tricks, to replace inspiration by lush technique under which one finds music stripped of real vitality.

Thus there is no valid reason to condemn jazz because it was created by the Negroes. Far less can we reject it by virtue of the fact that jazz implies an entirely different conception of music from that of classical European music. There is no reason why classical European music should be the only good music. And it may not even be the best music!

It would, however, be absurd to represent the American Negro as consciously inventing a musical form destined to supplant other music. What characterized the extraordinary creative flow produced by the Negroes at the beginning of the twentieth century was that it was spontaneous—unconscious of its novelty, untarnished by the slightest design. Jazz did not issue from the individual efforts of one composer, but from the spontaneous urge of a whole people.

If jazz is a new musical form, it is by no means the result of an effort to reject traditional musical forms. It was, rather, created by a people to whom classical music was unfamiliar. There is no point in supposing here that the American Negro was cut off from all the influences of white men's music. Actually, the music of the Negro plainly owes much to the songs of the white missionaries. Furthermore, instead of using instruments of their own invention, the Negroes adopted the instruments of the whites. By this much their music, far from being an anachronism, takes place naturally in our epoch. But the creators of jazz were unaware of the main points of "classical" music, and used the little that did reach them as a springboard to fledge the very rich musical resources they themselves possessed.

Further, the originality, the true novelty of a music lies far less in the material than the way in which it is used. In itself, the material of music is very limited; there are a limited number of notes and harmonic combinations. It is only in the new utilization of the material that a new musical form can be born.

It has not been sufficiently realized that the appearance of jazz in our day was a phenomenon. Far from representing "the nerve-wracking life of our century," "the noise of the machine," and other foolish theories which have been brought forth from time to time, jazz represents the reappearance of such a primitive[1] musical conception as had arisen many centuries ago among the people of Europe and elsewhere. It is music in which creation cannot be separated from interpretation; collective creation dominates the individual effort and everything stands or falls on the auricular tradition.

A glance at the conditions under which jazz was born will help to explain this phenomenon. As a consequence of the ostracism to which, in the United States, the whites had subjected the colored people, the Negroes lived apart, among themselves, and did not participate in the prevailing cultural stream, but formed a society of their own. The music which flowed from such a social grouping could not fail to present the characteristics of "primitive" music. But, being created in a country like the United States, it was possible for the music to be widely disseminated—and that is what happened—unlike the music of the scattered African tribes which was unknown to all but a few explorers or planters.

One of the most striking characteristics of primitive music is the absence of the line of demarcation between creation and execution, such as distinguishes European music of the twentieth century. In the beginning, before written music had been invented, a man seeking expression would sing or play what was on his mind. Creation and interpretation were as closely united as possible—were really one; the distinction between conception and interpretation with no direct connection was then unknown.

Thus during the nineteenth century, the American Negroes

---

[1] "Primitive" is not taken here in a sociological meaning but in the artistic sense, such as applied to primitive painters.

who sang the blues would improvise the music and words themselves, except in those cases where they had heard and remembered blues sung by someone else. These blues, it is true, had an extremely simple, invariable harmonic form, upon which the improvisation was based. I shall later study the blues, the origin of which still remains obscure. What is important to remember for the moment is that a Negro singing the blues cannot be compared to a Frenchman humming a song. The Negro, even when he repeats someone else's blues, creates something new by the freedom and originality of his interpretation, his numerous improvisations, his inflections, and the modifications in rhythm and melody. He does not seek to reproduce exactly what he or others have already sung; he abandons himself to the inspiration of the moment.

In a certain sense the Negro liberates himself when he sings the blues. It has been said that the blues were the cry of the black man's soul under the oppression of the whites. Hence the plaintive quality, the often hopeless accent. But let us make no mistake; when a Negro sings the blues, it is not to give way to his sadness, it is rather to free himself of it. He has far too much optimism and too vivid a sense of life to permit himself to do otherwise. That is why the blues, in spite of their nostalgic mood, have nothing to do with whining—but rather express a confidence, a tonic sense of vitality. The Negro has no time for that sentimental, languorous touch which is the scourge of so much music, notably of the phoney commercialized type of jazz. Furthermore, when the blues are sung in fast rather than in slow tempos, they can assume an even joyful note.

Originally blues were sung without accompaniment. Later, most blues singers accompanied themselves on a guitar. Finally the blues were interpreted on all sorts of instruments, notably the cornet and clarinet. Having no sheet music, the musicians had to improvise, guiding themselves by the rigid harmonic frame we have already mentioned. They played their instruments in a style like that of the singers, that is, they *sang the blues on their instruments*, reproducing the inflections, the cries of the human voice. Thus were the early orchestras formed. Besides melodic instruments like the cornet, trombone, and clarinet, they included instruments like the banjo, drums, and string bass which furnished the rhythm and harmonies. Jazz was born!

It was, quite naturally, dance music from the very beginning. Not music composed specifically *for* dancing, nor music to which one *must* dance—but simply music to which one could and did dance. As with primitive music, creation and interpretation were one, so with primitive people were music and dancing inseparable, being but two different means to express the same series of movements. Early blues singers instinctively translated with the rhythms of their bodies the movement of the music they were singing. Later, jazz musicians would do the same thing. Speaking of them, the celebrated conductor Ansermet well said: "They are so entirely possessed by the music they play that they cannot keep their bodies from dancing, to such an extent that their playing is a real spectacle." Those who listened to blues, just as those who later listened to jazz orchestras, felt the urge to dance—or at least, if they did not dance, to follow the rhythm with movements of their hands and heads, and with all sorts of gestures. And, when the first orchestras were engaged to play in cabarets, the clientele was made up chiefly of dancers.

In order to vary their repertoire, jazz musicians were not satisfied with playing blues; they drew from very diverse sources, notably from spirituals (whose style of interpretation was, with the blues, the main inspiration for jazzmen), from ragtime and from certain tunes recalling the French polkas and quadrilles, which came from the very notable French influences in New Orleans, the homeland of jazz. The method of interpretation and improvisation born of the blues and spirituals was applied to these bits. The music thus developed scarcely differed from the blues themselves, more or less the way an Englishman trying to speak French, although he may use French words, gives the impression that he is speaking English because of his intonation and accent. Thus the jazz musicians repeatedly incorporated into their music various sorts of material, different from their own basic material.

In view of the preceding observations, it is easy to understand how fake jazz, the commercial product, was derived. It lost no time in supplanting real jazz in public favor. With the success of the first Negro orchestras, white orchestras imitated it in New Orleans and other Southern towns. Since the white musicians were not familiar with the original blues, the inspiration they derived from the Negroes was superficial. At best these white orchestras of the South, being in contact with the best colored orchestras, sometimes came very close to playing real jazz. But by the time jazz had reached Chicago, and then New York, there had already been considerable distortion. The white orchestras did use the repertory of the Negroes, for the most part, but since the Negro style of interpretation was scarcely familiar to them, they did not know how to play with the same accent. So the ragtime numbers, one-steps, and other numbers, executed by white musicians in a style without real affinity with the blues, were but faded and hackneyed versions of the real article. In short, these white orchestras, if they used the same instruments and often played the same numbers as the colored orchestras, did not at all create the same kind of music. The public, who did not look into the matter too closely, lumped the whole together under the name jazz.

Naturally, the white orchestras pleased the white public far more, since that public did not understand the style of the Negroes, so different was it from the music they were accustomed to hearing. Once this lack of understanding became apparent, numerous people set to work organizing the commercial exploitation of jazz. The white public was, of course, by far the richest and most important. Certain white bands, deliberately turning their backs to the style of the colored orchestras, offered the public the kind of music most calculated to flatter its taste, and at the same time preserving a superficial resemblance to jazz for its "novelty" value. Instead of improvising, they used arrangements and played them with the utmost softness. Since these arrangements were often fairly complex, as with Paul Whiteman's orchestra, the term "symphonic jazz" began to appear, an expression which shows how far afield the music in question tended to go from real jazz. In the light of such examples, sometime later the colored orchestras in their turn fell into commercial ways in order to make more money.

Here lies the cause of the misunderstanding which, even today, makes difficult my discussion on jazz with people insufficiently informed on the subject.

2 jazz and classical music
the difference

To understand jazz thoroughly, it is necessary to revise the narrow and distorted concept so widespread in our day concerning music in general.

For our contemporaries there are two distinct kinds of music, "classical music" and "light music." They believe that the first alone offers any real depth, produces any intense emotion, or is worthy of careful study. They turn to the music of the great composers, classical or modern—the Bachs, Mozarts, Wagners, Debussys and Stravinskys.

The other, the "light music" comprises all forms of popular music, dance music, and comic operettas, which have the reputation of being occasionally diverting but poor in substance and unworthy of "true" musicians.

In sum, this concept implies a belief that collective music is inferior to personal music, that dance music is inferior to music not written for the dance, and to a certain point, carries with it a discrimination between improvised music and "composed" music. Above all, this concept implies a poor understanding of the importance of interpretation as compared with creation.

Such a concept is entirely European—or, to be more exact, is the view taken by the white race. It should be observed again that three or four centuries ago the whites themselves had a very different concept of music.

Some will perhaps assert that the present theory of music must inevitably be the good one because of the superior culture of the white race and the historic need for growth and progress. I have already observed in the preceding chapter my reason for believing that culture does not necessarily imply any musical superiority. As for the dogma of progress, it is worth tarrying over a few minutes.

No one would dream of denying the existence of a continuous progress in the material world. In numerous branches of scientific knowledge the result of a discovery, which has been made and verified by experiment, is a definite acquisition; the scientists who follow, profit by that discovery and in turn further extend the domain of scientific knowledge.

Though it is legitimate to speak of perpetual progress in the sciences such as physics or chemistry, the same cannot be said of the arts. Here it is no longer a question of a purely intellectual knowledge—knowledge which may be verified by experiment. In music, as in painting or poetry, the creative gift is essentially incommunicable. When an artist of genius dies, his gifts die with him. Those who come after can admire his work and find inspiration in it, but if their gift is not as great, they can never equal him. The notion that progress is inevitable in the domain of inspiration and artistic creation is not realistic.

Instead of leading toward progress, the development of musical theories, which are often erroneous, has, on the contrary, a tendency to muzzle inspiration, to restrain and cripple the creative effort of the great artist who thus loses much of his spontaneity. That is why musicians who are untrained in musical theory and who have no preconceived notions often express themselves with a naturalness which, granted an equal talent, makes them far more interesting than the cultured musicians who are more or less consciously victims of the theories of their age. In general, such independence is impossible except in a primitive music and then only in the beginnings of that music. Later we will see that after thirty years of existence jazz itself could not escape the inhibitions created by the "artistic conscience." Unfortunately this led many musicians to modify the natural style of earlier times.

The worst musical error committed today lies in composing the musical work without thought of its performance and independently of its interpretation. Certainly it cannot be denied that such a work will conserve its intrinsic beauty in spite of the most execrable interpretation; but who then can boast of having fully understood, or, to be more exact, fully *felt* the beauty of the work? Only an excellent interpretation will permit us to *know*, in the fullest meaning of the word, a musical work.

What is too often forgotten is that a score is not music, but only a sheet of paper covered with signs which determine the musical pattern. Music is *the sound*. It is the note heard by the ear, not that seen on paper. To affirm, as some people do, that one can gain as much pleasure from reading a musical work as from hearing it is ridiculous. How could one ever read a work of music if one had not previously had a notion of the different sounds represented on the paper? And how could one acquire that notion if not through the ear?

The objection may be raised that in reading a book one can penetrate the author's thought equally well whether the book is read aloud or silently. That is true, but the comparison is inaccurate. Words, whether heard or seen, are only *signs*. They represent a conventional idea—that is to say, men have agreed that a certain grouping of sounds is to represent a specific idea or object. Without a knowledge of this conventional agreement, without the key to the word, this grouping would have no meaning. This is demonstrated, for that matter, in a person's inability to understand a foreign language without previous study of that language. It is clear then that language does not address itself only to our ear but also to our intelligence, as the latter's use is indispensable.

The same does not hold in music. What one hears necessitates no previous knowledge. No previous education is required in order for the notes to signify what they were intended to signify. Music addresses itself to our sensibility and not to our intelligence—which fact, contrary to a current prejudice, in no way detracts from the music's nobility and grandeur. A ready illustration of this difference between language and music can be seen in the fact that a language can be understood only by the people of one country, whereas music is international. The cinema was international before the invention of the talking picture because its language addressed itself directly to the eye—it was not a language of words but one of gestures and pantomime.

It follows then that, in comparison to the note that is heard, the written musical note plays the role not of the written word as compared with the spoken word, but the role of the word, either written or spoken, as compared to the idea behind the word. That is to say that the notes of written music are symbols, but not the "heard" notes.

Thus in reading a score, one can imagine the music as it is indicated by the notes, but one cannot enjoy it fully, as the ear, which is the only proper organ for the perception of music, is not reached.

Musical writing offers the tremendous advantage of permitting us to conserve musical works. However, it has the disadvantage—which is scarcely taken into account today—of being unable to preserve those works against the inevitable deformations of interpretation. From this point of view the oral tradition in music is a far surer means of accurate preservation of works. We live, it is true, in a time when music has so lost its living quality that it would be almost impossible to perpetuate it through the oral tradition.

Far be it from me to contest the importance of musical literature; however, it has assumed too great a place and we must be sure to remember that it is not the music itself. We must, above all, rise against those who in its name condemn improvisation and, generally speaking, scorn all music based on tradition—music which is actually the most direct and most natural.

If it is necessary to convince still further the champions of written music, I will quote here a few lines of Pierre Lasserre whose alliance with classical music is well known:

> The essence of an idea (in music) lies not in the elements of musical diction which the composer has been able to note down on paper, in the letter of the melody and harmony, the values, the measure, the mathematical duration of the beats and the nuances of *piano* and *forte*. All that can be performed with irreproachable exactness without the essential idea being in any way expressed and without the very basic feelings which were intended being transmitted to the listener. The vital essential is lacking. That essential, one might say, is that which is not written and it is the goal of what *is* written (which it is necessary furthermore to respect scrupulously) to suggest to a true musician that same vital quality in order that he may imbue his interpretation with it. It is a question of a succession of indefinable inflections, seemingly instinctive, which reproduces the palpitations of the living surge and which,

from a passage either quiet or agitated according to the mood, raises one after the other, in the auditory memory of the composer at work, the successive notes which make up the theme. To release this imprisoned quality, the performer must identify himself psychologically with the original creative impulse—I do not say that this is an identical psychological action, it is only analogous—from which that quality originally sprang and which is throbbing throughout the music. The succession of notes follows the line of evolution which that creative psychological action unfolded. When this is brought out by the performer, the public naively translates it by saying "he plays or sings *with feeling.*" It is important to emphasize that this expression is not merely an addition which supplements the realization of the idea, but is the idea itself—the *soul of the idea.*[1] And when it is absent the concept of the composer is not only diminished; it is completely destroyed.[2]

From all this evidence, we can see how necessary it is to have artists who live the music they are to interpret, and as a general rule we can expect nothing from the musician for whom music simply represents bread and butter. In the symphony orchestra of today, with the exception of a few sincere artists, how many musicians are there who play only to make a living? However, let us suppose that all are real artists. Could one hope to find among these forty or fifty musicians, a simultaneous psychological action analogous to the creative psychological action, as outlined by Pierre Lasserre? Here we touch the very ginger of the advantages of all primitive music. The only musicians here are those who feel a need to create music, or at least a need to make themselves heard, those who have something to say and who feel the need of expressing what is singing within them. Among these musicians the performer

[1] Our italics.
[2] *Philosophie du goût musical,* pp. 131–133.

is also the composer, and he finds it far more natural to play his concept than to write it on paper for others to play. That this concept of music should appear inferior to us today can only mean that we have lost sight of the very essence of musical art.

It is interesting to find that we have fallen into the same mistake on the subject of the spoken word as compared to the written word. Certainly the comparison cannot be perfect since spoken words are signs as much as are written words, but it is nonetheless true that we are less easily moved by the reading of a sermon or a discourse than we are by the delivery of that same sermon or discourse if the speaker makes all that he says intensely lively. The warmth of his conviction will be communicated to us through his voice—a phenomenon similar to that of the interpretation in music. Today the power of the spoken word has been increasingly underestimated; we have been filled with prejudices which prevent us from realizing that the written word is not the final expression. Let me quote here the words of R. P. de Grandmaison:

> Both the written word and pictorial illustrations have supplanted oral gestures—the spoken word—for which they are ordinarily only a *handy substitute*.[3] In the Occident, this substitute has so imposed itself on us and the conventions upon which it rests have become so familiar to us that it is difficult for us to conceive of a society of men in which writing plays only an incidental role, or none at all. Indeed it is a fact that such a social state, relying almost entirely upon the spoken word, has existed for thousands of years among certain peoples even using collaterally the written word.[4]

[3] Our italics.
[4] *Jesus Christ*, Tome I, Chapter II, Note C, p. 203.

This same fact has been true of unwritten music.

Under such conditions, music did not tend to be, as it is today, an individualistic art but was rather a collective occupation. Instead of a lone composer writing his work in solitude, composing was a collective art. This method has again reappeared with jazz. Here the musicians generally improvise on an extremely simple theme, or, when pure improvisation is not relied upon, the ideas of the various players are united in a common work. These ideas, far from being firmly established once and forever, can be modified and improved upon after the results of each performance have been studied. All these revisions and inventions are arrived at through the ear alone. A musician will hum or play a phrase on his instrument as it comes to mind; the others retain it in their memory and pick it out on their own instruments. But this does not exclude written arrangements in jazz; however, we will see further on why such arrangements do not offer the same limitations as the orchestra parts used in classical music.

It will be asked, "Doesn't individual music have numerous advantages over collective music?" The solitary composer can carefully weigh the value of an idea, correct the weak parts of the work at leisure, and finally attain a better structure and greater depth. Moreover, once the work is finished, it is set once and for all and can brave the deformities of time.

Undeniably the principal advantage of such a written composition is that it may be gone over and cleaned of its faults. For my part, I would never question for a second the validity of such a procedure. But from all sides I hear people denying the value of a collective musical creation, and I feel that it is imperative to show here the strong points of collective music as well as point out the shortcomings of individual composition.

Primarily the collective creation has the incontestable superiority of insuring an ideal interpretation of the music since the creators themselves play what they have conceived. The objection will be raised that the music of these actor-creators will die with them, since it cannot be recorded on paper. But this is not precisely true—here oral tradition intervenes with all its force—for whenever a musician leaves the orchestra, his successor is trained by the other musicians on the part he is to play and the *manner* of playing. Thus all the virtues of the original interpretation are indefinitely perpetuated. Should this interpretation be modified over a period of years, according to the temperament of the new musicians in the orchestra, can there be any harm done? These newcomers will in their turn create something new so that the same composition is in a continual process of creation. As a result jazz, like all other primitive music, is a music which is perpetually in motion, a *living* music which will never fall, for an instant, into the funereal sleep of so many *chefs-d'oeuvre* which often give the impression of having been imprisoned in a pickle jar. Speaking about jazz, the celebrated symphony conductor, Ansermet, said: "The importance of the writer in the creation of a work is well balanced by tradition as represented in the performer. Though the work is written, it is not *fixed*, and can only be completely realized in execution."

Remember too that the invention of the phonograph now permits us to preserve recordings of all original interpretations. Of course many people, even today, feel that listening to a recording in no way gives the satisfaction of the original interpretation, and moreover that a recording cannot be relied upon for judgment. Undoubtedly the original performance is incontestably preferable to the recording, but this does not lessen the latter's importance. Later I will attempt to show the many advantages of a recording as a means of preserving musical work. In any event, who would dare uphold, for a second, the idea that it is better to conserve music on paper than on a record?—for the latter offers the incommensurable advantage of speaking directly to the ear as well as giving us at the same time both the interpretation and the musical score itself. Furthermore the record is the only means of conserving improvisations, which hold so tremendous a place in jazz.

This leads us automatically to the question of improvisation, one of the points where collective creation is so strongly at variance with individual composition in the classical sense. Too many people consider improvisation as synonymous with superficial music. They are too ready to suppose that improvisers are musicians who hide the poverty of their musical ideas under a display of brilliant instrumental virtuosity, and they assume that improvisation implies the use of numerous clichés. They claim that the improviser does not have the time to consider carefully his next step and must as a result use fillers each time he is caught short of ideas. Briefly their contention is that all the beautiful discoveries are only accidental and are the exception.

Such reasoning only shows that modern musical theories have caused us to lose sight of the real nature of improvisation. Certainly this method possesses disadvantages—for example, it is impossible, when inspiration fails, to wait for a better moment in order to correct weak passages—but we neglect its trump card, which is so valuable that it more than compensates for the inconvenience mentioned above.

The principal trump card is the incomparable stimulant which the support of an entire orchestra, or even that of one or two accompanists, can give the improviser, for music acts on the sensibilities with a greater intensity than can be found in any other art. Sounds striking the ear of the musician who is about to play exercise an immediate and profound impression on him which warms and provokes his inspiration. In turn, his improvisation will excite the other musicians to greater and greater heights. They once again will feed the soloist's inspiration even more abundantly (for this reason, as experience shows, most improvised interpretations are more beautiful at the end than at the beginning). An uninterrupted exchange is thus created between the members of an orchestra which improvises, an exchange whose effectiveness proves, in a shining example, the all-powerful virtues of collective music and improvisation.

It goes without saying, that the inspiration of a musician under such conditions often depends upon the worth of the musicians with whom he plays. A great improviser may find it impossible to create something interesting if he is surrounded by mediocre musicians who remain frigid, do not respond to his call, and who, instead of provoking his inspiration, annihilate all his efforts. In jazz this is a frequent phenomenon of which the public, through ignorance, is totally unaware but which explains the ups and downs of numerous famous musicians. However, when an improviser of merit is well supported, when the other members of the orchestra follow him in his flights and are one with him, the highest peaks may be reached.

Here then is the strength and weakness of improvisation. The result is that the music will sometimes be thoroughly mediocre, whereas at other times it will be of a beauty surpassing that of any "composed" music.

The composer who works apart may have sublime ideas but only with difficulty can he achieve the heights reached in a collective improvisation where several musicians express themselves in a perfect community of inspiration, playing with a warmth which can be equalled with difficulty by the best interpretation of a written work.

Some would have us believe that improvised music cannot be as well balanced, as well constructed, and as logical as composed music. This might be true of an individual improvisation not based on a theme or harmonic suite, but in jazz, as we saw in the first chapter, the improvisation is always founded on a specific theme. Nor could it be otherwise. Without a theme no collective improvisation would be possible, since the musicians would have no base upon which to coordinate their various roles. With a theme to guide them in improvising, the musicians "knowing the voice which is assigned them in the harmonic ensemble and conscious of the role their instrument is to play" (to quote the excellent words of Mr. Ansermet) can balance their various voices. Thus this theme guides and helps balance their creation. But do not imagine, because of this, that the theme limits the musicians' invention—far from it, for they are in no way obliged to follow the melody line of the work and need only guide themselves on the basic chords, and they can inscribe on them a melody line which has no relation to the original.

In the final analysis, however, the greatest advantage of improvisation over the written composition is the fact that conception and execution are inseparable. While improvising, the musician may create not only by the ideas which come to his mind but also by the way in which he performs one or two notes—and that is what jazz musicians often do. There can be no doubt, moreover, that a musical phrase as played by one performer will leave the listener untouched, while this same phrase played by another musician will bring him to the point of tears. Obviously then "to a certain degree execution is creation" as Pierre Lasserre asserts.[5] As much might be said perhaps for the interpreter of a classical work who brings the written phrase to life, but how much closer to the heart of music are those who not only conceive but express their own thought, so closely coordinating the musical thought and its expression that they cannot be disassociated, nor separated from one another. In reality these musicians do not conceive the musical phrase as a separate identity but think of it as *it will be performed*. Being interpreters, their creation is based on their own style of playing and it is around this style that they work. Such a method of composing must necessarily be far more alive than that of the composer who is not an interpreter and who must conceive his work through an intellectual process. Of course such a composer may have in mind an ideal interpretation of his work, but he is powerless to indicate it on paper.

This is the eternal weakness of written music. The musical signs can express to a certain extent the thought of the composer, but they are powerless to express the thousand nuances which make up the interpretation. The composer's complete thought can never be conveyed to the performer. Let us bear in mind that musical writing is no more than an easy way of preserving the ideas.

Improvisation and collective creation were the first mode of musical expression because they were the most natural and most direct method. In distant times, when a musician was to learn the work of another, it was not by reading a paper—he learned it by ear, thus knowing the composition as it was interwoven with the interpretation—that is, he learned living music. Briefly, all music was created, learned, and reproduced through the ear alone—*its proper organ*. The *creation* as well as the exe-

[5] *Philosophie du goût musical*, p. 94.

cution was not individual but collective, but today we have
largely overlooked the extraordinary possibilities of collective
creation.

A further characteristic of primitive music is that it is dance
music—a music in which the tempo never varies in a work.

Today music with an unchanging tempo has been discred-
ited to a certain degree. It is said to be monotonous and to
restrain the creator, but what has been forgotten is that the
music of Bach, his contemporaries and predecessors, relied on
a continuous and unvaried rhythm. The gradual disappearance
of musical works with an even tempo, far from reflecting
progress, as some would have us believe, far from opening a
gateway to unexplored territories which would allow one work
to express many diverse feelings, on the contrary seems to me
a sign of weakness. Richness of form has been substituted for
richness of depth. Instead of *developing* the music, a superficial variety is organized in a more or less artificial way, and
sentiments and images are sought rather than holding to the
pure musical idea which expresses nothing at all—at least
nothing which can be defined by words.

Actually music with an unchanging tempo is more natural
and is a direct reflection of life. Such music recalls the pulsa-
tions of the human heart which give life to the entire organism;
it conforms to the essential laws of life and is born of nature
itself out of the laws of the universe. Moreover the continuity
and uniformity of tempo puts the melody into extraordinary
relief by establishing precise and luminous relationships between the notes of each phrase, bringing out the direction of
the development and underlining the smallest nuances of the
work. That steady pulse helps lead up to the climax through
an imperceptible development of ideas in such a way that the
audience is unaware of the approach of the climax whereas

music with a varying tempo, by sudden changes and brusque somersaults, seems to warn the audience, "Look out, here comes the grand finale."

As to the reproach of monotony levelled against this kind of music, one might possibly accuse the listener of inability or an unwillingness to investigate the internal development of the musical idea. Modern music—by that I mean music since Bach or if you wish Mozart—has gradually departed from the purely musical idea and has encumbered itself with harmonic effects and values whose interest though often great is not essential; and the modern listener, accustomed to these de luxe effects, has a tendency to feel that music stripped of all such ornaments is dry and even monotonous.

Attempts have been made to debase jazz by accusing it of being dance music, as though that could be a mark of inferiority. On the contrary, it is a mark of vitality. Music and dance are two arts which complement each other, in fact one might say that they are two facets of the same art. I doubt that the so-called "serious" music has gained much by further breaking away from its alliance with the dance during these last two centuries. But unfortunately as the presumably "civilized" world has degenerated, the notion of the grandeur of the dance has further and further declined. Today, for example, it is assumed that dancers must have musicians, but no one imagines that the musicians themselves need the dancers. There is no understanding of the perpetual exchange between the orchestra and the dancers which stimulates and inspires both: an orchestra is not at its best when working with poor dancers, just as the dancers cannot fully express themselves when working with a poor orchestra.

Likewise many feel that it is ridiculous for Negroes to clap their hands, dance in their seats, sing and cry when listening to an orchestra. (Haven't we heard enough about these supposedly "hysterical" Negroes who are subject to "attacks of epilepsy"?) To me the most ridiculous spectacle is the sight of a concert hall filled with hundreds of spectators who sit statuelike in their seats listening with a lugubrious expression to solemn music which is served up to them in massive doses. There is nothing quite as distressing. Ennui seizes you by the throat and crushes you. It could hardly be foolhardy to state that such an audience lives and enjoys its music far less than the man who accompanies music with gestures and voice. One cannot listen to music as one reads a treatise on philosophy!

Music puts our senses and feelings into play—it is motion. Of course one can enjoy it while remaining completely immobile—the Negroes themselves do this occasionally—but it is only normal for our bodies to translate the sonorous language which our ear receives, to dance in our seats if nothing more than that. Yes, jazz is dance music and this is precisely one of its greatest attributes.

3 "blues" and "swing"

We saw, in the first chapter, the important role the "blues" played in the birth of jazz; therefore it is well to study closely the form of the blues since the essential elements of jazz, from the point of view both of musical material and interpretative style, are to be found in these works and in their rendering.

The particular melodic style essential to the blues and the harmonic form growing out of that style depend upon the alteration of certain notes of the scale, the third and seventh degrees—that is, the mediant and the leading notes. Musicians call these "blue notes." In the scale of C major these blues notes would be changed to E flat and B flat. However, during the same interpretation the E and the B might be found natural as often as flat. From this style there arises in the mode of the work an ambiguity which has been stressed by one of the rare personalities of the classical musical world who cared to study jazz music, Michel Andrico, Rumanian composer and professor at the Royal Academy at Bucharest, who said:

> "If jazz is surely *tonal* (using a normal scale of seven notes), it is not always *modal*. By this I mean that major and minor are not always clearly differentiated. There exist works in both minor and major key; however those in the major key, which are more frequent, offer several interesting peculiarities.

44

We assume that the major key is only *relatively* major, whereas the minor retains a more stable character. We know that the mode notes of the scale are always the 3rd and the 6th. Thus, a major scale will have, without exception, a *major third* between the 1st and 3rd degrees, and a major 6th between the 1st and 6th degrees. In the minor mode, the intervals become minors.

This difference, absolute in the classics, less so in folk music, *has no importance in jazz*. Frequently works written in the key of C major, for instance, will have a more or less mobile 3rd, that is to say moving between E natural and E flat.

This fluctuation of the actual "nervous centers" (especially the 3rd) is enough to remove from the scale its character as an absolute major. Add to this the fairly frequent omission of the leading note (7th degree) from the descending scale and you will readily see what profound modifications the scale undergoes. The essential characteristic of this style, then, is the interchange of modal notes in the same phrase, now altered, now natural, then vice versa.

Thus our conceptions of mode are confused because the major includes in its sphere the minor mode from which it borrows its melancholy and sorrow. (This interchange does not apply to the minor mode.)[1]

These characteristics of jazz in its present form can equally well be applied to the "blues."

What is the origin of these alterations? Of these "blue" notes which give such a characteristic modal variety? Personally I am inclined to believe that they grow out of the style of interpretation of the Negro singers. These singers, in translating their lamentations, use frequent glissandos of a quarter tone, or a half tone, or of an even broader interval. Leaving the normal note, they finish on an undetermined note which surprises any ear accustomed to classical music. This quality can

[1] *Jazz Hot*, September-October 1936.

be heard even now while listening to singers or jazz orchestras —the "blue" note is sometimes attacked directly but frequently it arrives at the end of a long inflection.

We can see how inseparable are the composition and the interpretation in the blues. A blues singer makes no pretense at an accurate rendering of the work of another, but attempts to express himself with all possible effectiveness, making no distinction between the basic musical material and his own interpretation.

The blues, in pure form, consists of twelve bars divided into three parts of four bars each. The harmony, which scarcely changes during the first four bars, turns toward the sub-dominant which serves as a fundamental base during the fifth and sixth bars, then returns to the tonic during the next two bars, and as conclusion goes into a diminished 7th on the dominant during the ninth and tenth bars, finally returning to the tonic. A more shifting form of the blues introduces the harmony of the sub-dominant quietly during the second bar without prejudice to less important embellishments. This is the essential structure of the chorus. Sometimes a verse, somewhat more variable in form, but generally twelve bars in length is used.

All the twelve-bar blues contain the same harmonic succession. Upon this harmony each singer or instrumentalist improvises the melody he wishes. However, do not suppose that this harmonic succession is the point of departure for the blues; it is but the result of certain melodic constancies native to blues singers.

The development of the melody is strictly bound to the lyrics; therefore the singer always repeats the words of the first four bars from the fifth to the ninth bars, the musical phrase being changed only by a few unimportant variations in inflection. During the final four bars, however, words and music are different.

But a blues singer does not necessarily limit himself to the twelve-bar blues; he uses longer works occasionally, as well as numbers with a different structure which contain here and there similar harmonies. If the singer sings these songs with the same accent and the same mood one may justly say that he is still "singing the blues." It is thus that such songs as *Baby Won't You Please Come Home, Careless Love Blues*, and many others may be qualified as "blues." This should be sufficient evidence to show that all numbers including the word "blues" in their title are not necessarily twelve-bar blues.

To return to the previous discussion, it should be noted that in the majority of instances the phrase that is sung, instead of occupying the entire four bars, extends over the first two and ends lightly during the third. From there to the end of the fourth bar takes place what is called a "break" in which the accompanist, if there is one, can improvise according to his inspiration, answering and echoing the singer. We can find such instances in innumerable blues records. If the accompanist is a good musician, this method gives magnificent results as can be seen in the splendid recordings of Bessie Smith with Louis Armstrong playing trumpet, *St. Louis Blues, Cold in Hand Blues, Reckless Blues, Sobbin' Hearted Blues*, etc. This style of accompaniment played a large part in giving birth to jazz.

As was said in the first chapter, the jazz musicians, even when playing music other than blues, employ the style of interpretation to which the blues gave birth, that is, they scatter their phrases with "blue" notes, rendering their instrument as flexible as the human voice by employing frequent glissandos and an intense, rapid vibrato, similar to that used by singers.

It would be well to say now a few words about *swing*, that impalpable element which is the soul of jazz music.

Much has been said about swing; many have attempted to define it and have been naively astonished at not being able to do so. The truth is, however, that all words are not equally susceptible to precise definition. One can define accurately objects which belong in the domain of science; one can likewise define material objects such as a table or a chair, but it is impossible to similarly define things which belong exclusively in the domain of emotion, and swing belongs in this last category.

Rather than muddle through a vain effort to find an impossible definition, let us examine the manner in which this thing called "swing" comes to life and how it affects us.

In jazz, as opposed to other kinds of music, the weak beats are accented—the second and fourth beat of the measure. Why this peculiarity? No one knows, but it seems to go back to the most distant beginnings of jazz. Negroes have told me that while listening to religious sermons which the preacher sang rather than spoke, the believers as an accompaniment clapped their hands on the afterbeat, that is on the weak beat.

While a person accustomed to European music will never fail when listening to jazz to mark the strong beats by motions of his head or body, a manifestation which is instinctive with him, a Negro, when he hears a jazz orchestra, will naturally mark the weak beats. The difference of reaction would be enough in itself to explain the white man's lack of understanding of jazz. Obviously a musical understanding cannot be achieved without an understanding of accents, for it is through them that music takes its melodic and rhythmic value.

It is not enough merely to accent the weak beat; it must be well accented. The existence of swing depends upon the manner of doing or suggesting this accentuation. A comparison taken from the province of the dance illustrates this. Two couples both dance in perfect rhythm, yet one of the couples is greatly applauded while the other is looked at with indifference. Why? Because the first couple's ease and suppleness contribute something to the music. In other words the correct but mediocre dancers are content to follow the music, while the good dancers live it, inventing with it in such a way as to become an incarnation of the music to the spectator. And one hardly knows whether it is the dancers who are inspired by the musicians or the musicians by the dancers, for it is sometimes true that the dancers inspire the musicians as well as be inspired by them.

That which makes the great dancer is also that which makes the great jazz musician. Where there is stiffness, dryness, or tension, there can be no swing. Where the accents are marked or *suggested*—and the latter is very frequent—with ease, nonchalance, suppleness, and naturalness, swing will naturally break out.

Swing is that constant vibration, a delicate pulsation, which enlivens a music with a regular tempo, prevents it from becoming monotonous, makes it alive just as the pulse of the heart regulates the life of the human body.

Although theoretically swing in the music can be distinguished from swing in the dance, actually a single and unique principle animates both—the swing of the music attracts the same swing in the dance, and vice versa.

Perhaps now it will be understood why the author suggested in the first chapter that the word "swing" should not be used as a noun but only as a verb. Truthfully one cannot properly say that a musical text or a dance step "has swing"—neither has it unless the musicians or the dancers create it in their manner of playing or dancing. In other words swing is not embodied in the music or in the dance step but only in the performance of the *interpreter*. Therefore, it is absolutely accurate to say "this musician swings" or "this musician does not swing," for it is the musician's interpretation which causes the listener to experience the sensation called "swing" and it is up to him to accustom himself to *feeling* swing. One cannot define it for him just as one cannot describe the idea of the diversity of colors to a blind man.

Of course, a composer having a feeling for jazz will be able to write a musical text which will lend itself to a swing execution—that is what all good arrangers do—but accurately speaking one cannot say that the text swings. One can only say that there is "possible" swing (this is what is meant in saying of a fine arrangement that it swings by itself), but it depends entirely upon the musicians to bring this swing into being.

The idea was well expressed by the great band leader Duke Ellington who said: "No notes represent swing. You can't write swing because swing is the emotional element in the audience and there is no swing until you hear the note. Swing is liquid and though the same group of musicians may play the same tune fourteen times, they may not SWING until the fifteenth time."[2]

Originally the jazz musicians, when they used the word "swing," used it not as a noun but as a verb, saying, for example: "And now we are going *to swing* St. Louis Blues for you." This statement expresses perfectly the idea that swing depends upon the interpreter and not upon the music itself. "To swing" means therefore "to play," with the additional

[2] Cited by the *Melody Maker*, July 15, 1939.

nuance that one plays in a certain manner. The "swing fad" in vulgarizing the use of the word swing as a noun or an adjective has enormously obscured the idea of swing.

Therefore, if one wants to understand jazz music, one must keep in mind constantly the fact that the number played, the musical text, is nothing if there are no interpreters capable of swinging it, and at the same time that an excellent interpreter can swing a work of insignificant appearance and give it exceptional merit. Here is what was written by one of the great jazz musicians, the pianist Jelly Roll Morton: "Jazz music is a style not a composition. Any kind of music may be played in jazz, if one has the knowledge."[3] It is evident from these words "may be played in jazz" that Jelly Roll Morton means to say "may be swung." There could be no better way of pointing out the negligible importance of basic material to jazz music; the quality of the material can never be an obstacle since when swinging the music the musicians completely transform and transpose it into the language of jazz.

I said earlier that the accentuation of the weak beat—which creates the feeling of swing—could be marked or simply *suggested*. The rhythm section, particularly the drummer, is called upon to emphasize the accents almost continually— that is its principal role. The musicians who carry the melody need not preoccupy themselves with that alone; they play phrases to be enriched and put into relief by the rhythm section. One might say that the melodic section *suggests* the rhythmic accents more than it marks them; suggests them by contrast, playing in such a way as to create an intense need and an irresistible urge for these accentuations. It is this imperious need which creates an extreme feeling of swing.

Just as the musicians and dancers stimulate each other, so

[3] *Down Beat*, August-September 1938.

do the various musicians within the orchestra. The musicians of the rhythm section and those of the melodic section stimulate and respond to one another. The rhythm section by its accentuations both supple and powerful puts the soloists at ease and gives them a sure springboard. The melodic section by its phrasing calls up the accents; reinforces in turn the assurance, the precision and the suppleness of the rhythm section.

In this manner, a great musician when he is feeling inspired may awaken an entire orchestra otherwise badly disposed. This is what is meant by saying of a musician "He swings the whole band."

The question of *tempo* is paramount to swing. For a style of interpretation or for a particular number, a single tempo must be set. If the orchestra begins in a tempo that is a little too fast or too slow the execution will be stiff and the musicians will feel ill at ease and incapable of playing with abandon. The public at large and even the so-called enlightened lovers of jazz are ignorant of this question of "right tempo." When a good orchestra plays badly, one frequently hears listeners attack the song played, saying "On such a poor number, it is impossible to do anything interesting." Of course, a good musician will be more or less inspired by the tune itself, and prefer to improvise on this or that number, but there is not a theme, however wretched, on which he will not be able to work miracles if he is sustained by good musicians and if the right tempo is found. Suffice to mention one: *The Merry-Go-Round Broke Down*— a poor affair, in the hands of Jimmie Lunceford's orchestra became a splendid interpretation simply because the perfect tempo was found.[4]

As a general rule extremely fast tempos are not favorable to

[4] Recorded by Decca (original catalogue No. 1318).

a good interpretation. The musicians are forced to use considerable effort to play at the desired speed; are strained and hence do not have the ease which is indispensable to swing. To a lesser degree, the very slow tempos only rarely give a satisfactory result except for the blues. Here the orchestra feels burdened down; the execution as a result has a tendency to be too languid and draggy. It is in the moderate tempos (fairly slow or fast) that a band swings the most.

When the perfect tempo has been found and the orchestra is playing with complete abandon producing an intense feeling of swing, it is said that the musicians are "in the groove." That notion conveys that there is a complete ease and perfection in the interpretation. A musician who is "in the groove" need make no effort in his improvising for his ideas flow naturally and easily.

Only those with a profound feeling for jazz can understand this phenomenon. This is the point when good dancers abandon themselves and feel as though they were carried by the music. This is the moment when the sensitive listener experiences an irresistible urge to mark time and call out an occasional "yes yes" to underline passages which are particularly beautiful. It is at such moments that one reaches to the heart of jazz music and feels its grandeur.

How far away we are, in such moments, from the too intellectual conception of music, which is the product of a century atrophied by a poorly digested civilization; how far from the "intentions" of composers who lack spontaneity, from the systematic research into an overcharged music to which one listens with bewilderment or a yawn and which does not give for an instant this impression of expansion, of *joi de vivre* which a sane and natural music should not fail to give.

One will easily understand from what has preceded that a

jazz orchestra is far more at home at a dance than on a concert stage. Not that it is impossible for jazz musicians to play well on a stage; it has happened frequently. But jazz concerts should be the exception. The swing of an orchestra is nourished by that of the dance; therefore the surroundings at a dance are far more apt to inspire the musicians to find the "groove," and to improvise with insouciance, while in the frigid atmosphere of a stage each musician feels enervated by the implacable curiosity of thousands of eyes levelled at him; is intimidated by them and is prevented from abandoning himself to his natural style.

But much as musicians who are "in the groove" are a pleasure to the connoisseur, people who are little sensitive to jazz, judging from the exterior, do not feel an instinctive need to mark the weak beats in listening to a fine interpretation and are incapable of vibrating to the discoveries of these musicians. And how astonished they are to see jazz lovers prefer an interpretation lacking external brilliancy but which is in the "groove" to other interpretations which are more brilliant and have a greater virtuosity but which are not executed with the ease and the abandon which are the secret of jazz.

4

jazz— from new orleans to the present day

In its early years, jazz grew up throughout the various Southern states in America. However, New Orleans soon established itself as the most important center because of its many fine orchestras and the exceptional ability of its many musicians. Here jazz developed slowly from its embryonic beginnings to jazz as we know it today. But it was not until several years after reaching this development that jazz came to the attention of Chicago, Kansas City, and New York which were to become eventually the leading centers.

The famous New Orleans style, of which so much has been said, is none other than the original and primitive jazz music— the style from which all others have sprung. We will see in the following pages what characterizes this style through a description of the first New Orleans orchestras and their manner of playing.

Generally these orchestras were composed of six or seven musicians (at that time large orchestras of fifteen men were unknown). The melodic section ordinarily consisted of a cornet, a trombone, and a clarinet, occasionally supported by a violin. The rhythm section was made up of drums, a bass, and a guitar or a banjo. No piano was included for the simple reason that it only proved an encumbrance since the orchestras frequently played outdoors and were constantly moving from place to place. This does not mean that no piano players were to be heard in New Orleans; and it should be remembered that the first great jazz pianist, Jelly Roll Morton, who was a native of New Orleans, played there towards the beginning of the twentieth century.

The first orchestras relied entirely on pure improvisation and "head" music since the majority of the musicians were unable to read music and had to play entirely by ear. Though many of the men were self-taught, relying only on occasional criticism from some more advanced musician, do not suppose that they were poor musicians. On the contrary, many of them acquired a considerable technique for they felt it necessary to master their instruments in order to achieve complete freedom in improvising. As a result the cornet and trombone players, because they were called on to play music of far greater intricacy than that played by the brass section in a symphony orchestra, soon developed an instrumental style infinitely superior to that of the classic musicians.

The mechanism of improvisation was this: The cornet, since it dominated the other instruments, led the melodic section, pointing out the melody and sometimes embroidering on it in a sober vein. The clarinet, which most of the time played in the high register, provided a countermelody of a mobile character opposed to the more sober cornet. Finally, the trombone supplied the low part of this melodic trio, although in general it did not create a melody line but filled in the other two parts and at the third harmonized with the cornet. Such a well-balanced ensemble produced a collective improvisation of clarity and order. Moreover at this period the ensemble work predominated—there were scarcely any soloists.

The rhythm section supplied the harmonic and rhythmic background to the performance. The drummer strongly accented the weak beats on the snare drum, the cymbal, or some other percussion instruments. With his foot he marked out the strong beats, or sometimes all four beats, on the bass drum. Ordinarily the string bass played on the strong beats, while the banjo continually marked all four beats—accentuating no one particularly as in the blues on slow tempo—occasionally very lightly accenting the weak beats, and more rarely the strong beats.

The saxophone was absent from these early orchestras; its use did not begin until about 1920, a period when New Orleans had practically ceased to be the jazz center. For that reason no "New Orleans style" exists in which the saxophone plays a part, whereas all the other instruments were used.

Another characteristic of the New Orleans style is the fact that all the melodic instruments, especially the cornet (or the trumpet) and the trombone, played on the beat, for the New Orleans musicians were accustomed to rest their phrases solidly on the beat, principally the strong beat. Certainly this was not always the case, for syncopation was quite frequent, but whatever detours the melody line might take it always fell back on the beat and returned to it regularly, which would seem to prove that this was quite certainly its base. This was strengthened by the regular return of the string bass notes to the strong beat and by the drummer's steady marking of the beat on the bass drum.

That all these musical parts should rest solidly on the strong beat was not only logical but even necessary. Since jazz is a music based on the accentuation of the weak beat, the latter would be lost if it were made by the entire orchestra. In resting on the strong beat the cornet and the other instruments made an intense appeal for an accent of the weak beat which surged forward an instant later from the snare drum, or the cymbal. Thus we can say that the accentuation of the weak beat is "suggested."

The last chorus of *Willie the Weeper* played by Louis Armstrong and his orchestra is an excellent example of the above[1] When, after several guitar chords, Armstrong begins his trumpet chorus, he places the majority of his notes on the strong beat, while on each weak beat Baby Dodds answers him with a crash of the cymbal. They swing together with perfect ease.

As the popularity of jazz spread over the United States, many New Orleans musicians, following the natural trend, went up the Mississippi. Some played on the riverboats while others sought their fortune in Chicago, where engagements were far more lucrative than they had been in New Orleans. The first arrivals from New Orleans soon invited their former colleagues to join them in Chicago. Thus by 1920 Chicago had become the capital of jazz.

As their engagements took the jazz orchestras more and more frequently into permanent spots such as night clubs, the piano had come into general use; as a result the rhythm section was augmented to four members, the pianist marking the strong beats in the bass with his left hand, and with his right hand marking the weak beats by smashing chords in the higher register. This method of marking all four beats in regular alternation was called "boston."

Soon afterward the saxophone made its appearance in the jazz orchestra. Sometimes it was added to the three other instruments of the melodic section; sometimes it replaced either the clarinet or the trombone.

Nor was it long before many white musicians began to take an interest in jazz. A number of white orchestras attempted to

[1] "The Louis Armstrong Story," Vol. 2, Columbia ML-54384.

assimilate the interpretative style of the Negroes and a few of them were to some extent successful, notably two celebrated New Orleans orchestras. One was the Original Dixieland Jazz Band which included at least one good musician—the clarinetist, Larry Shields. The second was the New Orleans Rhythm Kings which numbered among its members three fine musicians, Paul Mares on trumpet, Ben Pollack on drums, and especially Leon Rappolo on clarinet. Nonetheless these orchestras could not compare to the good Negro groups of that period, such orchestras as that of King Oliver.

But unfortunately the majority of the white musicians paid little attention to the style of the Negro orchestras; they took over the Negro repertoire but played it in their own style, and as we have seen, the repertoire matters little in jazz music. Numerous songs had been incorporated in the Negro orchestras' repertoire because the musicians played them in a manner which resembled the blues and other works of that type; the blues themselves could lose all character if they were not correctly played. The white musicians then, in adopting the repertoire and the instrumentation of the Negro orchestras while neglecting the interpretative style, adopted many accidental elements of jazz and missed the essential one. Such music can in all justice be called false jazz music.

Moreover the whites didn't hesitate to modify the instrumentation. Though they left the rhythm section unchanged they augmented the number of instruments in the melodic section. Likewise since the musicians could read music, the use of musical scores was substituted for improvisation, which was considered unimportant. Under such conditions a reduced instrumentation was unnecessary; in fact, it was preferable to harmonize the melodies for several instruments. Consequently the melodic section was made up of three saxophones, dou-

bling on clarinet, two trumpets, one trombone, and even three
trumpets and two or three trombones. The saxophones carried
the theme while the brass executed an accompaniment, or the
brass would expose the theme with a saxophone accompaniment. What was supposed to be "jazz" was nothing more than
a ridiculously jumpy conglomeration.

Since the public found it much easier to follow the melody
played by these saxophone or brass ensembles than to follow
the complex counterpoint improvised by the Negro orchestras,
the white bands soon gained a greater popularity. As soon as
the orchestra leaders whose interests were purely commercial
discovered that the public was interested only in the melody,
the "song," they began offering melodies which they hoped
might become hits and played them with the sentimental
sweetness of a languorous waltz. They even added several violinists to the orchestra to achieve a sweeter interpretation.
Thus "commercial" jazz was born and triumphed under leaders such as Jack Hylton, Paul Whiteman, Guy Lombardo and
the like, and their music was accepted by the public as authentic jazz.

Nevertheless this evolution had an indirect influence on the
destiny of jazz music. After hearing the white commercial
groups, the Negro orchestra leaders decided that they could
create real jazz by using a larger instrumentation and harmonized ensembles. Fletcher Henderson, whose orchestra played
in New York, was one of the first to try this new formula. At
first he employed commercial arrangements identical to those
used by the white orchestras, but little by little he turned to
arrangements with a style similar to that of the small jazz
orchestras, arrangements which could be swung. Of course,
the question was no longer one of counterpoint but of musical
phrases with an excellent harmonic style. The phrases were

harmonized for the saxophones with a countermelody or an accompaniment for the brasses or vice versa. The entire arrangement was broken here and there with improvised solos. Following Fletcher Henderson's success, many large Negro orchestras were formed which soon outdistanced the popularity of the small combinations. These large orchestras could produce richer and more varied orchestral effects than could be achieved by the small orchestras who had to rely on improvisation.

Nevertheless the small bands who improvised were still destined to see many great days. From 1920 to 1929 Chicago, with its concentration of great New Orleans musicians, was truly the center from which shone the pure jazz music of the early years. Here in the bosom of the small orchestras jazz evolved little by little and developed in an excellent manner, for the same men who had participated in the first steps of this music were also those who guided its evolution. Improvisations became more audacious; numerous solos were interspersed in the ensemble passages, but the whole remained steadfastly based on the discipline of the New Orleans style.

Of course, many New Orleans musicians left Chicago and either toured the United States or established themselves in New York. Musicians from every region came into contact with them and were profoundly inspired by their style. In fact all the really gifted musicians who formed their style on that of New Orleans became great artists and continued to play the most authentic jazz.

It was this period which saw a notable growth of solo work at the expense of the ensemble playing, for the solo gave a musician a greater latitude for improvising than could ensemble work. The soloist need not preoccupy himself with adjusting his part to that of the other instruments of the melodic section, but need only consider the base harmonies marked by the rhythm section. With this freedom the soloists began playing more complicated melody lines with great exuberance.

Remember that the term "solo" improvisation is entirely relative. Although the other melodic instruments are silent while the soloist improvises, the rhythmic section continues to play. This means that the improvisation may still be considered collective: the soloist may play in such a way that the drummer is compelled to swing in a different fashion, or may sometimes lead the guitarist or the pianist to modify some chords, but similarly the rhythm section may, by its playing, drive the soloist down a path he had not originally foreseen.

Another style of solo work was known as the "stop chorus," which today has been completely abandoned. Here the rhythm section ceased continual playing and only marked beats here and there; for example it would accent the first beat every two bars. Such conditions made it difficult for the soloist to improvise, for he could no longer rely on the constant stimulus of the rhythm section. Naturally an occasional musician of great ability succeeded in creating magnificent effects with these "stop choruses," as for instance in the chorus of *Potato Head Blues* recorded by Louis Armstrong.[2]

During this same period the cornet was abandoned by most musicians in favor of the trumpet. The large orchestras were probably responsible for this innovation, for the trumpet could make a more brilliant and powerful effect in a large ensemble. Some musicians, generally those from New Orleans, tried to retain the cornet which they preferred because of its softer and feltlike resonance, but in a large orchestra they were obliged to adopt the trumpet to avoid being eclipsed by the

[2] *The Louis Armstrong Story*, Vol. 2, Columbia ML-54384.

power of the other two trumpets. Moreover the orchestra leaders seemed to object, perhaps for esthetic reasons, to the presence of a little cornet alongside the larger trumpets.

Between 1922 and 1925, under the influence of the New Orleans musicians, a style was born in Chicago, known as the "Chicago style," whose importance has been greatly exaggerated, and I am afraid that I was in part responsible for this. This style was created by a group of white musicians of more than average merit who had attempted to assimilate the methods of the best Negro musicians of New Orleans, but they succeeded only partly. In reality the Chicago style was nothing more than an offshoot of the New Orleans style and had only two distinctive features. The first was the substitution of the tenor saxophone for the trombone as the third melodic instrument, in trio with the cornet and the clarinet. Such a change considerably altered the balance of the ensemble, creating a more liquid and less majestic sound. The second feature was the influence which the celebrated white cornet player, Bix Beiderbecke, had on a number of these musicians. This influence prevented them from playing in the same style as the New Orleans Negroes, which was to their great disadvantage. Not all these men felt Bix's influence. Such musicians as the trombone player Floyd O'Brien, the clarinetist Milton Mezzrow, the cornet player Muggsy Spanier, and the drummer George Wettling remained free from Bix's style and played in the New Orleans manner. They may be classed in the same category as the Negro musicians. But Jimmy MacPartland (cornet), Jess Stacy (piano), Frank Teschemacher (clarinet), and Bud Freeman (tenor saxophone) were variously marked by Bix's personality and to that degree were divorced from the New Orleans style. The latter were the veritable representatives of the Chicago style, if this style may be defined as a mélange of Beiderbecke and New Orleans.

The year 1929, bringing with it the great financial crisis and the ensuing depression, marked a turning point in the history of jazz.

Until then Negro musicians had been able to earn their livelihood with authentic jazz music, by playing almost entirely for their own public—the Negro audience which loved and understood their music. When they recorded they had been allowed to play whatever they wished in the style they wished, since the records were bought almost entirely by the Negro public. However, after the crash, the only musicians and orchestras who could find work were those who made concessions to commercial demands and who had a wide appeal. The recording companies, hard hit by the crisis, considerably reduced the recordings of authentic jazz since their sale, which was only fair in normal times, was now very poor. Thereafter any orchestra of worth that came to record was forced to make numerous commercial concessions. The dilemma of the sincere jazz musician was great—either he must commercialize or stop eating, and of course he chose the first.

But the financial crisis was not the only factor responsible for the commercializing of true jazz musicians. The growth and spread of radio to the four corners of the United States during those years had a disastrous effect on jazz music. The Negro public, who had till then a passionate love of their blues and their own fine orchestras, slowly lost their natural taste for their own virile and strong music as a result of hearing numerous ridiculous Broadway tunes sung by languorous and saccharine white singers over the radio. The youth was especially corrupted, for it had not been immersed in the atmosphere of the blues and true jazz for numerous years, and consequently was more quickly contaminated.

An additional reason for abandoning his own music in favor of the sentimental twaddle of the whites was the Negro's inferiority complex, a complex for which white oppression is entirely to blame. For years the Negro had watched the whites reach the most important positions, had felt the oppressive domination of this famous "civilization" and had listened to the whites proclaim their superiority from the rooftops. What could be more natural than his assumption that the things which the white man liked must necessarily have a greater value than those he liked? And certainly to imitate and assimilate such influences was to share, in a limited way, with the dominant culture. Therefore he wanted to share the white man's taste for music, and as a musician he sought to conquer this "superior" race by conforming to the methods of the successful white artists. That is how some Negroes tended to lose their own native qualities. But what they didn't see was that it was an unrestrained publicity rather than personal merit that had brought to fame the most mediocre white orchestras and singers, not only in the United States but throughout the world.

For these reasons a great singer like Bessie Smith, nicknamed "The Empress of the Blues," whose magnificent records had had a tremendous sale from 1922 to 1929, declined in popularity after 1930. With one exception she made no recordings after 1931. On the same score, the proportion of interesting jazz recordings diminished from this time on.

But all of these factors were more or less external causes of the decline of authentic jazz music. The internal factor was not long in appearing, and the so-called "artistic conscience" took hold of the jazz musicians, doing their art great harm.

For years jazz musicians had played as much for their own pleasure as to make a living. They enjoyed playing at dances and provoking the enthusiasm of the dancers and any musicians who came to hear them. They played by instinct, without thought of technique, and felt elated when the orchestra was "in the groove." To borrow the terms of Mr. Ansermet, it would be impossible to say

> whether these artists made it a duty to be "sincere"; whether they felt that they had a "mission" to fulfill; whether they believed in the "nobility" of their art or whether they had that sanctified "audacity" and sacred bravery which the guardians of musical custom require of our European artists, or whether they were animated by some "theory"; but they had a very precise notion of the music they enjoyed and a feeling of pleasure in communicating it to the listener with an irresistible force, a pleasure which drove them to outdo themselves constantly in order to enrich and constantly improve their work.

But when jazz orchestras began to appear in theatres as "an attraction," when the magazines and reviews began to speak of jazz as an art, and when white musicians, conscious of artistic theories, began long discussions on the nature of jazz seeking to establish its relationship to other musics, the Negro musician became increasingly aware of his own importance, or at least of the importance of his music. That music which had been up to then an amusement took on the aspect of a fine art. And the inevitable occurred. These musicians who had infallibly played in a perfect manner, and had never digressed for an instant from the pure tradition of their art as long as they blindly followed their instincts, now swerved from their tradition and began to reason and to "improve" their music.

The greatest source of trouble was in comparing jazz music

with the classics. Since classical music had already proved itself and was held in universal esteem, some Negro musicians
attempted to get closer to it, not realizing that jazz could not
obey the same laws. Since classical music, at least during the
last two centuries, turned toward harmonic research, they
concentrated on looking out for extensive harmonic effects.
The soloists, when improvising, used harmonies of the base in
a complicated fashion in order to render their melody line
intriguing and strange. The instrumental technique of the
classics was reputed to be "polished" and "refined"; therefore
the musicians must force themselves to mitigate the rudeness
of their instrumental tones, and refine the orchestrations.
Classical music was "composed"; all works had a definite
"form"; therefore improvisation must be relegated to second
place. Jazz must be harnessed to give it a clear and orderly
appearance. More "thought" must be given to the music,
therefore it should not be improvised. Thus reasoned many
jazz musicians.

Unfortunately, this program was to some extent realized.
Overworked arrangements were produced, but their harmonic
effects, new to jazz, were of a puerile insignificance compared
to those of the classic and modern composers. The instrumentalists refined their tone, succeeding thereby in losing a
large part of their purity and character without acquiring the
tone of the classical musicians. Among jazz musicians it became current to say with admiration of an arrangement or a
solo, "Isn't it wonderful? One would think it was Debussy."
Perhaps the work in question vaguely approached Debussy,
but it had most surely lost the authentic jazz flavor.

The other big mistake made by some jazz musicians was to
believe that there is, in art, a constant, a necessary progress.
They asserted that the musicians of the twenties played very

well "for their period" but that a recording made in 1925 had become in 1940 obsolete and hopelessly outmoded. "It's not modern" was their disdainful cry when they listened to an old recording or to an excellent musician who had not modified his style for several years. And if one were to object that an interpretation which had so profoundly moved them in 1925 could scarcely have lost all its beauty, as if it were enchanted, during the passage of fifteen years, they would reply by saying that it was similar to the case of an automobile judged superb in 1924 but now grown grotesque and useless in 1940. That good musicians could judge music as though it were a mechanical apparatus shows to what foolish lengths this reasoning process had led them. But I will not dwell further on this absurd notion of inevitable and necessary progress, having previously examined its falsity in the second chapter.

This superstition about progress, allied to a desire to dazzle, was the cause of still another misfortune. Many musicians, possessed of fine instrumental technique, stressed that technique to the detriment of their strictly musical work. They attempted to play the greatest possible number of notes with a maximum speed and tried to increase their range to abnormally high registers. While improvising, a trumpet player no longer worried about creating beautiful phrases or even about swinging, but thought only of proving that he could reach G above high C whereas another player could not pass F above high C. Briefly, virtuosity became too often an end in itself, instead of remaining only a means. It is only too easy to see what harm such an unfortunate conception could have on jazz music.

We can see then why jazz, under the influence of these various factors, began after 1930 to lose some of its purity and became injected with foreign elements which could only do great damage. Nevertheless, improvisation continued to occupy a large place in many interpretations. The best-known large bands, such as those of Duke Ellington and Fletcher Henderson, gave as prominent a place, and sometimes a more prominent place to improvised solos than to arrangements. These orchestra leaders proved thereby that they still considered improvisation a vital element in jazz music, and had no intention of abandoning it. But the good small orchestras became increasingly rare. However, their kind of jazz still had a part-time existence in "jam sessions" as well as in the recording studios.

A "jam session" is a reunion of musicians, outside of their regular work, at which they play the music they enjoy with complete liberty. This is the music they are not permitted to play in the large commercial orchestras which they have been forced to join to earn their living. But the music boils on inside them, and they have an irresistible urge to liberate this creative pressure. Frequently a trumpet player, after finishing work in his orchestra at three o'clock in the morning, will go to a night club where he knows he will probably meet a pianist, a drummer, a saxophone player, or some other musicians anxious as he is to free themselves during several hours of improvisation. The group will take some theme known to all and each in turn improvises on it. Those among them who feel "in the groove" will not only improvise on the chorus once, but will play it over two, three, or four times and more. The jam session overflows and is carried away with an enthusiasm for which one would search vainly elsewhere. During these hours, the musicians play out of a love of music, without attempting to create a "work" but simply because the music makes them feel intensely alive. Here certainly music is returned to its natural state and is delivered of all preparations and artifice.

Likewise certain recording companies, instead of calling a

regular orchestra, will assemble a small group of musicians especially for one occasion. One of the musicians selects the others, taking from one orchestra the clarinet and guitar players with whom he feels he can work best, from another orchestra the trombone player, from still another the bass player, etc. Such an orchestra, formed for one or two sessions of recording, brings together the very best musicians whom it would be almost impossible to keep together in a permanent orchestra because of the exorbitant expense. Since the orchestra generally does not have an opportunity to rehearse before the recording, improvisation occupies a major part of the interpretation.

Thus by one means or another, improvisation still plays a large role in jazz, a role which is doubly important because of the fact that the arrangers take their inspiration from the original melodic style and sonorous effects discovered by the improvisers. As a result the written arrangements are fed by the spirit of improvised music, and are thereby held within the bounds of true jazz music. Actually the term jazz music is not synonymous with improvisation but simply implies a certain interpretative style which, although born out of improvisation, may be brought to life through arrangements prepared in advance, as long as those orchestrations can be swung.

Unfortunately the style of the improvisers, already spoiled by an excess of instrumental virtuosity, partly lost its plainness with the disappearance of the great New Orleans musicians. Some died; others fell into obscurity; many could not or would not conform to the so-called "modern" conception of jazz, and as a result achieved no success whatsoever and finally ceased playing rather than play under unfavorable circumstances. Those whom fame continued to follow, such as Louis Armstrong, have been rare.

Nor did the younger generation of musicians have before them, as their seniors had had, the example of primitive jazz style, the style of New Orleans which was the most genuine music. They could, it is true, have studied the older records, but as we have already seen, the musicians listened only to recent recordings and scorned the older works, and in addition most musicians seldom study from records preferring, quite legitimately, to listen to the actual orchestra playing in a night club. The younger generation imitated those who had originally been inspired by the New Orleans style but who had more or less involuntarily departed from it because of later influences and developments. But it was those later developments which, because they probably seemed more "modern" to the younger musicians, retained the latter's interest and impregnated their playing.

The trumpets ceased playing on the beat, for it seemed to them an oversimplification. The trombone players began tackling choruses as rapid and difficult as those of the trumpet. The drummers, with the help of the "high-hat" cymbal, began to sound as if they accented the strong beats instead of the weak beats. There resulted a disunity in group work, particularly in small orchestras. In the New Orleans orchestras the instruments were combined in an excellent balance from the point of view of tone as well as accentuations. Each member of the group, while free to improvise, knew his own role in the ensemble, and each man's discipline added its stone to the edifice. Each part called to the others and in turn leaned on them. However, in the later days, too many players follow their own fancy, and do not consider the other parts; bastard styles strike against one another, contradict each other, and there is too little ensemble playing.

It is no wonder, then, that the best jazz created after the

New Orleans golden era was that of the big bands, thanks to the arrangements which, when written by good arrangers, introduced new ideas and effects.

The big bands' vogue started to grow in 1935, when an incredible publicity was given to a white band, that of Benny Goodman, who was pompously titled "King of Swing." Although Goodman's band was inferior to the best colored orchestras, which he imitated (in fact, Goodman's main arrangers, such as Fletcher Henderson, Jimmy Mundy, and Fred Norman, were colored musicians), its success trained the public's ear to noncommercial jazz—"swing," as it was called at the time—and this, in turn, helped the great colored bands led by Chick Webb, Fletcher Henderson, Count Basie, and others to get the recognition that some of them had spent years waiting for.

This was what has been called the "swing era." Until then, the public had not been acquainted with the word "swing" as it was used by and among jazz musicians. When publicity agents started plugging Benny Goodman by calling him the "King of Swing," the public thought that "swing" was a new kind of jazz, the kind played by big bands only. This was the beginning of endless misunderstanding. Finally, all post-New Orleans jazz of the thirties and early forties was referred to— very improperly—as "swing."

The "swing fad" had some advantages. It put many good musicians who were having hard times back to work and it permitted them to play more often the music they wanted, instead of spending most of their time in commercial, sugary bands. This fad brought a period of fine recordings, and it was a creative era for big bands. Besides Duke Ellington's and Fletcher Henderson's orchestras, which were already great before the thirties, an incredible number of wonderful big bands were to be heard in the thirties and the early forties: Jimmie Lunceford, Count Basie, Chick Webb, Erskine Hawkins, Earl Hines, Benny Carter, Cab Calloway, and later on Lionel Hampton and Cootie Williams. There were some nice small groups too, such as John Kirby's, Louis Jordan's, Fats Waller's, and a few others. At this time, too, Count Basie and his great blues singer Jimmy Rushing brought the blues back into the limelight and gave them a new life. Also, Count Basie's straightforward arrangements, full of good riffs, magnificently swung by the band, gave back to the music a simplicity, a freshness that was needed.

Sometime around the early forties, a group of young colored musicians started suffering what we will call a complex of "modernism," of "serious music." They studied the works of European modern composers and then tried to inject into jazz music some of the harmonic alterations used by the so-called "serious" composers. By doing so, they became prisoners of the harmonic difficulties they had to face; they lost the freedom of inspiration which had been the privilege of improvisation, and their playing lost its ease and abandon and sounded like monotonous exercises. The creative element in them was choked up, buried under complications, and little by little, it died. Different names were given to that new trend: be-bop, cool, progressive music.

Whatever name may be given to the experience, it finally proved to be a failure, and despite all that has been said by the "intellectualists" on the subject, *be-bop music is not jazz*. This is no mere opinion. This is fact. Facts prove that bop music deliberately turned its back to the jazz tradition. The bop musicians, instead of learning to express on their instruments the feeling, the emotion, the accents of the human voice, went to study the "classical" technique in conservatories, in acad-

emies such as Juilliard. The drummer ceased to be the heart of
the band (as he should be by giving a regular pulse), introduced Afro-Cuban rhythmic figures on bongos, and played as
soloist rather than remaining a support to the whole group. As
a matter of fact, *all* the members of progressive bands were
soloists: consequently the basic rhythm went to pieces. So,
while jazz music had always been a *dance* music, bop and
progressive music could not make the grade: the colored
people would not dance to progressive bands and the "Savoy"
in Harlem as well as other dance halls would not book progressive bands.

It is quite absurd to pretend that be-bop is an improvement
on jazz music; the comparison between these two kinds of
music is impossible to make. Many jazz musicians have pub-
licly stated that bop is not jazz; it is well known, for instance,
that Louis Armstrong said it a hundred times, and he was far
from being the only one. Here is what Lionel Hampton wrote:

> I've been asked by a lot of critics, who seem to be con-
> fused, about bop, progressive music, jazz. . . . As far as I'm
> concerned, I am a *jazzman* and, in my way of thinking, I
> don't think that any one can coin a phrase and say it is be-
> bop or progressive music. One critic said to me, "You're
> playing flatted notes." In all numbers such as the blues
> and jazz phrases, flatted notes have been used for years.
> As far as bop and progressive music are concerned, Brahms'
> and Debussy's compositions scooped the music world
> years ago.
>
> Let's bury be-bop and progressists and "Vive le Jazz."[3]

As for Buck Clayton, here is what he declared:

> On response to several questions I've been asked and in
> reference to articles written on my opinion as to whether

[3] A photoprint of this letter has been published in the *Bulletin du hot
club de france*, No. 33, December 1953.

or not be-bop is jazz, I would like to make this clear to all.

True jazz was born in New Orleans several years ago. Be-bop was born in New York City only a comparatively few years ago. Be-bop is not, never was and never will be true jazz if it has a beat or not. This has been my opinion in the past and will remain so in the future.[4]

Not only jazzmen insisted on pointing out the difference between jazz and be-bop, but also the hero of "progressive music," the celebrated Charlie Parker, who himself declared: "Bop is no love-child of jazz. Bop is something entirely separate and apart. It has no continuity of beat. . . . Jazz has." [5]

Statements by such authorities from both sides, by musicians talking of their music, are a hundred times more valuable than the affirmations of those self-appointed critics who keep on trying to make the public believe that bop is the new and better jazz that makes the older one obsolete.

In every domain, there is always a way to remain sensible and fair—and a way to twist facts and realities so that almost everyone is plunged into the greatest confusion. Life is no problem in itself, it's just that men make it so. As far as progressive music is concerned, there would be no problem at all if no one called it "jazz." What is suspect, in my opinion, is the loud way progressives insist on calling "jazz" a music that has nothing to do with it. Real jazz musicians and bands do not have to specify heavily at every move they make the kind of music they are doing: Duke Ellington does not present his "JAZZ Orchestra," Count Basie his "JAZZ Band," Louis Armstrong his "JAZZ All Stars." So why must progressive groups specify that they are the "JAZZ Messengers," the "Modern JAZZ Quar-

[4] A photoprint of this letter has been published in the *Bulletin du hot club de france* No. 33, December 1953.
[5] *Down Beat*, September 9, 1949.

tet?" Such an insistence is suspect to the utmost. If people appreciate the music made by the boppers, fine, let them enjoy it. But why confuse the public by presenting progressive music under the "jazz" label? Why not use the right name and say "Bop Messengers," "Modern Cool Quintet?" Might it be that the progressives are ashamed of the music they are doing, of having turned down the jazz musical tradition?

In fact, progressive music represents no progress, as some still pretend, but a regression, not only in jazz especially but in music in general. It brought no novelty in the music field because it was only an imitation (often very poor) of the European music of earlier times. The music to bring novelty and open new fields during our time is jazz music, the real jazz which has remained rooted, from its beginnings to the present day, in the tradition of the Negro music of the United States of America.

5   the trumpets

The earliest of the great New Orleans trumpet players made no recordings; therefore their music remains lost to us forever. Such is the case of Buddy Bolden, whose power was such that Louis Armstrong stated, "On a still day, they say, you could hear him a mile away"; of Emanuel Perez and Buddy Petit. Others, such as Bunk Johnson, were recorded only at the end of their careers, after having gone years without playing, so that they were unable to blow as once they had when they were young and their lips were in good condition.

The two oldest of the great New Orleans trumpet players who have been recorded quite extensively are Freddie Keppard (born 1883) and Joe "King" Oliver (born 1885). But it is said that Freddie Keppard's records, made only a few years before his death (1932), can give no real idea of his ability. He was described as having a clear, big tone and as blowing with such power that "the walls trembled when he played," as some musicians jokingly stated.

Anyway, Keppard's importance cannot be compared to that of Joe Oliver. Keppard's only disciple of note has been Natty Dominique, who sounds very good on the slow blues but is not in a class with King Oliver's disciples.

King Oliver's playing is a perfect example of the New Orleans style. It is solidly based on the beat, very melodious, and has a fine singing quality; the phrases are both simple and rich, and Oliver swings with a maximum of intensity. On the slow blues, his playing has that "lazy" feeling, that "low-down" accent which closely resembles the moving nostalgia of the great blues singers. During the years 1920–1926, when Joe Oliver was playing in Chicago, his fame grew constantly. Then it gradually declined and, in 1938, Oliver died in poverty.

Sidney Desvigne and Mutt Carey, born a few years after Joe Oliver, play in a rather similar style. Mutt Carey is well represented on records, thanks to the fine performances he waxed with Kid Ory's band in 1944–1946.

But the great disciples of Joe Oliver are Louis Armstrong and Tommy Ladnier. Louis Armstrong being by far not only the greatest of all trumpet players but the greatest of all jazz musicians as well, I shall elaborate fully on his development.

Louis Armstrong was born on July 4, 1900. In 1922, King Oliver called him to Chicago to play second trumpet in his orchestra, the "King Oliver Creole Jazz Band"—that orchestra which was probably the most extraordinary in the whole history of jazz. Then in 1924, Louis went to New York to join Fletcher Henderson's band. His style amazed the musicians there, for New York had not yet heard, as had Chicago, the typical New Orleans style. In 1924 he returned to Chicago. There, under his own name, he began to make a series of marvelous records with a small orchestra. Finally he became in 1927 the leader of a permanent orchestra at the Sunset Cafe. Although famous among musicians, he was still little known to the general public. But from 1929–1930 on, as Louis Armstrong began to tour the United States, his popular success grew by leaps and bounds and has never ceased growing. Louis' growing success was due to both his prodigious showmanship and musical genius.

Louis Armstrong is a musician of such extraordinary ability that he is above all possible praise. From a creative point of view, his improvisations show an abundance of ideas and an inspiration that is so lofty that any other musician pales in contrast.

From the point of view of execution, he possesses a dazzling technique, due in part to his surprising physical make-up. He is capable of playing in the high registers with incredible ease. Although many jazz trumpets succeed in forcing out an F above high C, or a G above high C, it is frequently in a dry and strangled manner; whereas Louis Armstrong produces these notes with the fullness and roundness of a unique tone.

In every register, Louis' tonal quality is unique; it surpasses in power that of all other jazz trumpet players; it is full and majestic, both fierce and polished, but at the same time it is heartbreaking and soothing. His incisive vibrato, so filled with emotion, makes his tone unforgettable.

But all of these qualities are of minor importance in comparison to Louis' feeling for jazz. In the shortest passage, in the individual note itself, he swings so much that he seems to become a veritable incarnation of the music.[1] His unrelenting attack, his tremendous tone, the power and supreme ease of his playing, and the greatness of his ideas create a whole so impressive that to compare his style with that of other musicians is like comparing a monumental cathedral with a gray city dwelling.

Louis' style is as thoroughly New Orleans as that of King Oliver, which certainly doesn't mean that their styles are similar—far from it. This can only go to prove that although

[1] "Louis really blew with every dancing molecule in his body." Mezz Mezzrow, *Really the Blues*, Random House, 1946.

numerous musicians have played in the New Orleans style, their personalities have in no way been hampered or limited by it.

There are several distinct periods in Louis' style. The earliest period begins in his youth (1916) and extends to the year 1927. At this time Louis resembled externally many of the other great New Orleans trumpets. But even then his playing was not so *dragging* as that of King Oliver and his contemporaries. Armstrong's style was more brilliant; his solos, while basically sober, were infused with excursions into the high register, and filled with rapid phrases requiring the most intricate execution. Then during the last years of this period, toward 1926 and 1927, the full melodic lines of the next period began to appear.

This second period extends from 1927 to 1931. Louis' style still remained solidly rooted in the New Orleans technique, but the traditional surface forms were shattered. The creative impulse which boiled in Louis sent him into highly imaginative improvisations in which he gave free rein to the almost frightening fluency of his technique. He employed vast and grandiose phrases, and used the most audacious and unforeseen melody lines. Here one feels that his invention is indeed limitless, that nothing can stop it.

Though still pursuing the same trend between 1931 and 1935, Louis Armstrong got his kicks in playing abundantly in the upper ranges, hitting twenty high C's in a row, crowning them off with an F above high C with the utmost facility. Such amazing displays of virtuosity, such exceptional strivings for effects, such an unbelievable technique nonetheless left his inspiration as pure and fine as ever.

The last period, his fourth, which began in 1935, is very different from the preceding ones. Except on rare occasions, Louis no longer strives for dazzling phrases; he no longer varies and embroiders the melody so as to make it unrecognizable. He states his theme simply, modifying it here and there with touches that give the most uninteresting phrases a beauty which transfigures them.

Throughout his entire development Louis' tonal quality changed little by little. From somber it became brilliant (when he abandoned the cornet for the trumpet in 1926). Then towards 1932 he adopted a beautiful "cloudy" tone. But finally, in an inexplicable fashion, he united all the seemingly contradictory nuances and resolved them in a tone which is both low and flamboyant, vermilion and gold. And as the years pass that tonal quality becomes increasingly beautiful.

There has been a great deal said about Louis Armstrong's so-called decline. Critics who do not understand jazz but who have appointed themselves authorities delight in proclaiming that since 1931 Louis Armstrong is no longer the great musician of other days. They criticize his effects in the high register and claim that the sober style he has adopted during the last years indicates a loss of creative power.

A word should be said here about playing in the very high ranges. Obviously such effects when created only to startle the listener with one's instrumental virtuosity are uninteresting from a creative point of view. But unfortunately an unreasonable prejudice has developed about passages played in the very high register of the trumpet. When the interpreter seeks to create phrases of real musical richness, there can be no reason for not employing the high register. Listen, for example, to *Jubilee*,[2] recorded by Louis Armstrong in 1938. Here Louis plays almost constantly in the upper register, but he does so to create a sober and enchanting melodic line which is in the most classic New Orleans style.

[2] Decca 1635.

Moreover, the objection that Louis' creative power has declined could only arise from a total misunderstanding of the great trumpet player's evolution. If Louis, since the mid-thirties, has not used so exuberant a style, it is because now, in one or two notes, he concentrates all that he said earlier in a long phrase. In his youth he was a man who seemed to enjoy the battle and triumphed over all with enthusiasm; a man who amassed difficulties in his path in order to conquer them. Louis is now a man who has no need to fight, for he dominates all and *knows* all. Today he does not enjoy the battle, for he has reached so high a place that he is *above* the fight. It is in fact this very thing that gives his present style such a *detached* and sublime touch.

Compare Louis' three choruses in *Sugar Foot Stomp* recorded with Fletcher Henderson in 1925,[3] with his three choruses in *Dipper Mouth Blues* recorded with Jimmy Dorsey's orchestra in 1936.[4] In both cases he took his inspiration from King Oliver's celebrated solo in the same number, recorded in 1922,[5] and Louis plays both numbers in much the same way. What makes these two solos so different is the *manner* in which they are played. In Fletcher Henderson's recording, one senses a young man who is filled with ardor and exuberance, though he is already a master of himself. Whereas, in the more recent recording one finds a man who conserves the freshness of youth but has arrived at a perfect detachment after grappling and triumphing over life. Hence Louis' playing is more solemn, imposing, and full in the later version.

If a proof should be needed of Louis' actual ability to create

[3] Columbia 35668 Master No. 140.639. Do not confuse this *Sugar Foot Stomp* recording with those made by Fletcher Henderson in 1931.
[4] Decca 906.
[5] English Brunswick 2200 (same solo on *Dippermouth* UHCA 77-78).

magnificent phrases, one need only listen to the two versions of *Two Deuces*[6] recorded at a thirty-year interval: Louis reveals just as great an invention in the recent version.

The truth is that nowadays Louis' creative power overflows in each note, even in what would otherwise be the most uninteresting melody. Many people do not realize that in jazz a beautiful melodic idea is frequently less important than slightly delaying or anticipating a few notes which, when done rightly, may swing a whole orchestra.

Louis has always surpassed other musicians in the manner in which he places and rests his notes. At all times his playing has been perfectly established and balanced, producing a sense of complete ease and nonchalance, and a freedom which is the secret of jazz interpretation. Likewise, Louis has always been able to swing an entire orchestra, even a mediocre one, by the power and ease of his style as well as by the power of his inspiration. Even when accompanied by mediocre musicians, he has proven himself capable of playing magnificently—a capacity which is extremely rare. And all of these qualities, far from disappearing, have been enhanced during his later years.

Far from thinking that Armstrong has declined, I am prone to believe that he is greater now than he was. However, his playing has been so perfect since his debut that it is indeed hard to make any strict differentiation. That slight suggestion of detachment, which was mentioned earlier, has only added something more to the basic Louis.

The only concession that can be made is to say that since 1931 the orchestras with whom Louis has recorded have not always been as fine as they should have been. But that has

[6] Old version: Columbia ML-54385 (*The Louis Armstrong Story*, Vol. 3). New version: Decca DL-8607 (*Satchmo—A Musical Autobiography of Louis Armstrong*, Decca album DX-155).

nothing to do with Louis' own value; it only reveals that even when he is given rhumbas, or Hawaiian melodies, or other such numbers, Louis can interpret them in such a way that he draws the most authentic jazz music from them—something very few other musicians could do so successfully.

If Louis can play the most mediocre number magnificently, it is doubly evident that his genius lends itself even better to the blues. Here the pathetic and poignant expression which emanates from all of his interpretations is intensified. He plays the blues with an emotion which completely stirs the listener. Although he uses more execution than King Oliver, he plays them in just as "lazy" a fashion. His use of "blue" notes is orthodox and at the same time strictly personal. Whenever possible he makes abundant and audacious use of these "blue" notes in all types of music. This is just another proof of his great genius for melodic invention and sense of harmony—a purely instinctive feeling, for Louis' musical studies were little more than elementary. Another outstanding characteristic of his melodic style is the long repetition of one or two notes on different chords; far from shocking the listener this only makes the ensemble interpretation more intelligible.

Likewise Louis Armstrong is a marvelous singer. He surpasses all other singers in the same measure as he surpasses all other trumpets. His vocal style is substantially the same as his trumpet style, and everything that has been said for the latter is true of the former. His throaty, veiled voice touches one by its beautiful tone and by that same intense vibrato which he uses on trumpet. His diction is excellent, but he is never hampered by the lyrics in improvising on the melody. He will repeat certain words, or add others of his own invention when he wishes to create a longer musical phrase. Other times he will sing the same few words on different notes, completely transforming the melody thereby. His singing swings as much as his trumpet. He was several times asked to record some spirituals. He sang them splendidly and swung them from the first to the last bar; his was a veritable jazz interpretation.

Of course Louis Armstrong's influence has been immense. Not only have most of the trumpet players and singers been directly or indirectly inspired by him, but the trombone and saxophone players, and even the pianists, have attempted to copy and adapt his style to their respective instruments. Even the arrangers have felt his influence. There are numerous arrangements in which a sequence of phrases was borrowed from one of Louis' solos and harmonized for the entire brass section. Without any exaggeration, it is safe to say that Louis Armstrong's personality has impregnated the whole of jazz music, and that without him jazz would have undoubtedly evolved in a different and probably much less fortunate manner. As Milton Mezzrow, the great clarinetist, once said, "Louis Armstrong has given so much to the world that it will take them years to realize it."

Next to Louis Armstrong, Tommy Ladnier is probably the greatest of all trumpet players. He was born in the same area as Louis, and in the same year (May 28, 1900). Moreover his beginnings were similar. He came to Chicago when he was about 20; he played with King Oliver; then he was a part of Fletcher Henderson's group in New York for a year (1926–1927). However, he went to Europe several times and remained there for a few years. Consequently his fame never reached the same great heights in the United States. When he finally returned to America, the wave of commercialism so disgusted him that he left New York to play in various small and obscure orchestras. It was only in 1938, when most musicians no longer believed him capable of playing well, that he returned to New York. Again he called attention to himself with a magnificent series of records with Mezz Mezzrow. But unfortunately he died of a heart attack on June 4, 1939.

Like King Oliver and Louis Armstrong, Tommy Ladnier is a perfect representative of the New Orleans style, though, unlike Louis', his style completely reflects King Oliver's. His nonchalant expression, his melodic structure, and his inflections in every way recall Oliver's. However, he has a more powerful tone and many personal ideas.

Of all the jazz trumpets, Tommy is the closest to equaling Louis Armstrong, both in his power and his ability to swing. The boiling ardor of his solos, his sensitive and effective vibrato indicate a fiery temperament. His somber tone, both ample and massive, is one of the most beautiful one can hear.

Tommy's evolution was much the same as Louis'. Leaving the classic New Orleans style, he turned progressively toward more daring improvisations. They were sharp and violent but always extremely beautiful from a melodic point of view. When he reappeared in 1938, he had returned to the more sober style of early New Orleans. In fact his style was even simpler, if possible, than that of his youth. Like Louis, he no longer sought for so many original embroideries, but looked instead for a *solidity* and a profound and intense expression. Consequently, in his last records his playing is as solid as a rock, and has a steady tempo which seems to guide and fortify the musicians of the rhythm section. These musicians were irresistibly drawn on by his perfect conception, were carried on and restrained by him at the same time. But throughout he dominates them with his great musical stature.

There are few musicians—no matter what their instrument —who play the blues with the sensibility and raciness of Tommy Ladnier. From the first years of his musical career, he was known by many in Chicago by the nickname "King of Blues." Though his blues were externally less brilliant than those of other musicians, his interpretation was wonderfully hard, powerful, and "lazy."

Another trumpet player, who greatly resembles Tommy Ladnier, should be mentioned here, Joe Smith (who died in 1937). Joe Smith was not a native of New Orleans. Tommy Ladnier and Joe Smith played side by side in Fletcher Henderson's orchestra during 1926 and 1927, and it is a curious thing that their styles were very similar although they had never heard each other until that time. Joe Smith's phrases were similar to Tommy's; he too had a beautiful and ample tone which took on the quality of a trombone in the lower register. But Joe Smith's playing was much softer than Tommy's. In fact his was probably the softest of all those which jazz has produced. Like all New Orleans trumpeting, his music is perfectly balanced on the beat, though with a certain lightness. He swings a little less; his execution was somewhat less powerful but it was so delicate and tender that it drew tears from his listeners. His vibrato was just as sensitive as Tommy's but it was less pronounced and lighter. He had a unique and moving way of exposing a melody with broad inflections which were full of melancholy. However, when Joe Smith played with full power and when Tommy bridled his ferocity, their phrasing was so similar that for the moment the two could easily be confused.

Returning to the New Orleans trumpets, the next in importance is Lee Collins, a powerful and lyrical player, who was inspired by both Joe Oliver and Louis Armstrong and who, at times, sounds very close to the latter. In fact, when Louis Armstrong was asked once which trumpet player most resembled him, his answer was: "If a trumpet ever sounded like me, I think that's Lee Collins." (Lee died in July 1960).

Another good New Orleans-style trumpet player (although he was born in Louisville) is George Mitchell, whose playing is close to that of Joe Oliver; he is perfect as a lead man for collective improvisations.

Charlie Creath, from St. Louis, belongs to the same musical family. He was one of the greatest blues players on his instrument.

Other New Orleans trumpet players are Henry "Red" Allen, "Kid" Rena, and Guy Kelly. Allen has a considerable reputation but it would be a mistake to classify him as a New Orleans-style player. His style undoubtedly has some tie with New Orleans jazz but he does not play firmly on the beat, as typical New Orleans musicians do, and he is not too good a leader for collective improvisations: his playing is too erratic for comfort. Even when he solos, his musical thinking often lacks continuity, and some beautiful phrases are followed by poor "clichés." However, Red Allen has imagination, plays with a lot of fire, and is a brilliant technician of his instrument.

Before leaving the New Orleans-style trumpet players, I must quote the names of Eddie Allen, whose smoothness reminds one of Joe Smith; Johnny Dunn (nicknamed "triple-tongue Johnny"), a flashy player who made very effective use of mutes; Bob Shoffner, Punch Miller, Dave Nelson, Ward Pinkett; and three white trumpet players from Louisiana: Paul Mares, Sharkey Bonano, and Wingy Manone, the latter being the best.

Among the white trumpet players who are not natives of New Orleans, two musicians assimilated the style especially well: Muggsy Spanier and Max Kaminsky. Muggsy, first inspired by Joe Oliver and mainly Tommy Ladnier, soon turned

to Louis Armstrong's style (the Armstrong of the mid-twenties) and it is certain that no other trumpet player succeeded
in approximating Louis Armstrong's style of that period as
successfully as Muggsy, both in phrasing and intonation.

Unlike Muggsy, another white cornet player, Bix Beiderbecke (who died in 1931), did not play entirely in the New
Orleans idiom. Though he took some inspiration from Louis
Armstrong, Tommy Ladnier, and Joe Smith, Bix was also influenced by white musicians (chiefly, it is said, by a trumpet
player named Emmett Hardy who never made records). This
was unfortunate, because Bix undoubtedly had more inventiveness and greater musical gifts than most trumpet players.
The Bix of the early years, the one to be heard in *Big Boy* (recorded by the "Wolverines"), swung more and practiced a
purer jazz than the later Bix. In addition, Bix was a good pianist. He recorded a solo of his own composition, *In a Mist*,
which had a fine and original quality. However, most of his
piano compositions (such as *Flashes* and *Candlelights*) are
reminiscent of Debussy and thereby reveal some of the influences which separated Bix from the musical spirit of the colored people.

There is a trumpet player who is never mentioned among
the New Orleans men and who, in fact, is not from Louisiana
but whose playing is so full of the spirit of New Orleans jazz
that he has been mistaken, in some records, for King Oliver: it
is Bubber Miley, a native of Aiken, South Carolina, who died
in 1932. Bubber is known mostly for his admirable technique
of the wa-wa mute, his "growl" and "preaching" style which
was featured in *Black and Tan Fantasy*, *East St. Louis
Toodle-Oo*, and other Duke Ellington masterpieces of the late
twenties; he really made his trumpet "talk" and created solos
full of either dramatic or humorous atmosphere. But he also

played beautifully without the mute, and then his sober, powerful, on-the-beat phrasing was identical to that of the great New Orleans men. He was able to lead collective improvisations as perfectly as King Oliver or Louis Armstrong: for proof, listen to his recording of Jelly Roll Morton's *If Someone Would Only Love Me.*

After the New Orleans period, which can be said roughly to have declined after 1928, came a new and prolific generation of trumpet players born around 1910, all taking their main inspiration from Louis Armstrong and yet very different from one another despite their common source. Louis Armstrong's personality is so rich that each could take from him certain ideas and, starting from there, develop his own personality.

Among those trumpet players are Jonah Jones, Sidney De Paris, Rex Stewart, Cootie Williams, Bill Coleman, Buck Clayton, Lips Page, Ray Nance, and Roy Eldridge.

Jonah Jones has been nicknamed by some musicians "Louis Armstrong the Second," and not without reason. He was inspired by the Louis Armstrong of 1929 to 1931, and acquired the volume, ampleness, and freedom which characterized the great Louis. Gifted with a superb technique, Jonah Jones does not hesitate to throw himself into difficult phrases which he executes with astonishing precision, admirably articulating each note even in the most rapid passages. Jonah Jones plays solidly on the beat, and in my opinion his trumpet swings the most next to Louis Armstrong and Tommy Ladnier.

Sidney De Paris was so much inspired by Louis Armstrong and some other New Orleans trumpet players that he often comes very close to expressing himself in the pure New Orleans style; the only difference is that he does not play as firmly on the beat. There is a deep, moving feeling in his playing. His joyful, "talking" choruses please by their spontaneity and absence of effects. Sidney De Paris is not a "flashy" player but his soulful music always tells a story. His use of mutes, especially the plunger and the hat, is extremely original and effective.

Rex Stewart's playing, solidly on the beat, has been much influenced by the New Orleans style in general and Louis Armstrong in particular. His instrumental technique is unusually brilliant; he rises into the high register, and descends into the very low register, and he surpasses most other trumpet players in his fingering which permits him to play phrases of an incredible speed. Rex's style is fiery and impetuous. In fact during his early musical career his principal defect was the fact that he abandoned himself too much to this natural ardor and sometimes played in a somewhat disorganized fashion. However that defect disappeared little by little during the years. Nonetheless his playing has remained vehement and his vibrato is still fiery. During recent years Rex has frequently used an unusual procedure to obtain excellent effects. He plays certain notes with the valves depressed halfway, in such a way that the note comes out muffled instead of clear. In *Boy Meets Horn* which he recorded with Duke Ellington's orchestra, Rex plays many passages in this manner. The influence which Bix Beiderbecke had on Rex, particularly from the viewpoint of melodic elegance, can be seen in Rex's admirable solo *Kissin' My Baby Goodnight* recorded with Duke Ellington's orchestra.

Cootie Williams gained his fame largely through his "wa-wa" solos when he was in Duke Ellington's band, in which he took Bubber Miley's chair. True, along with Bubber, Cootie is the greatest exponent of the "wa-wa" and "growl" style (the way he uses the mute is quite different from Bubber Miley's). But Cootie is perhaps even more astonishing when he plays open. His tone is extraordinarily warm and powerful—the most powerful probably after that of Louis Armstrong and Tommy Ladnier. His playing has an unbelievable clarity for he articulates each note with incomparable precision, hardly allowing the slightest crack in execution. (Cootie is moreover one of the few jazz trumpet players who practically never cracks a note.) Like his tone, his style of improvisation is in some ways massive and heavy. In slow tempos his solos have a grandiose accent, while on fast tempos he swings more through the power of his breath than from the movement of his rather tight melody line.

Bill Coleman's style is almost opposite to Cootie's. His tone is not voluminous and he compensates for his absence of power by an extremely mobile playing. He employs long, rapid phrases of great melodic richness and exquisite sallies into the high ranges—a register which he uses abundantly. While Cootie gives the impression of a tremendous, slow-moving mass, Bill seems to skim over the earth with a constant motion. Cootie's is a hard and imposing trumpet; Bill Coleman's is an elegant and incisive trumpet which enchants you by its grace and lightness. What seems curious is the fact that both these musicians were influenced by Louis Armstrong, but in opposite fashions. In Cootie there is something of Louis' amplitude and force; in Bill Coleman there is something of his mobility and mordant flights. Here are two great trumpet players with almost opposite techniques. While Cootie "sends" a band by the very power of his playing, Bill Coleman, lacking that force, carries it by his indomitable mobility.

Buck Clayton's style is full of the Armstrong spirit. Buck is one of the most inventive trumpet players jazz has known. His inspiration is free of the unevenness that plagues so many improvisers. Buck's accuracy shows most clearly in the way he uses the chords to build beautiful phrases, so logical that they seem to flow one out of the other. He has a fascinating richness of imagination, yet there never is any harshness in his music, his solos are always fluent, and he plays with an enchanting ease. There is in Buck's playing some of the delicacy and smoothness of Joe Smith, who had quite an influence on his style.

On the other hand the playing of Lips Page (who died in 1954), takes its cue from Louis Armstrong's strength and brilliance. Lips Page was one of the most powerful trumpet players jazz has known, with a big, round, "thick" tone that was beautiful to hear. And no one ever played the blues better than he did. He would make his trumpet really "talk" on the blues, using terrific glissandos and other devices that would make his horn sing just like the blues singers. In fact, Lips Page also was a great blues singer, with a moving husky voice, not unlike Louis Armstrong's. It must be added that Lips Page had few peers in the use of the "growl" and the "wa-wa" mute.

Ray Nance (who in Duke Ellington's band took the trumpet chair occupied earlier by Bubber Miley, then by Cootie Williams) somewhat resembles Lips Page in that he is great on the blues and also with the "wa-wa" mute. He has the same kind of warm, big, "thick" tone as Lips Page and Cootie Williams and, like theirs, his playing embodies a lot of typical Armstrong phrases. But his melodic line is more sinuous, has a more "gentle" approach, at times reminding us that Ray Nance is also a violin player, one of the best jazz has known. He is, as well, a good singer and a wonderful dancer and comedian.

Roy Eldridge, after building his style on that of Louis Armstrong (mostly the Armstrong of 1930–1932), developed ideas of his own, and by the mid-thirties he was becoming one of the major influences in the history of jazz trumpet. In fact, with the exception of Joe Oliver and Louis Armstrong, no other musician had so big an influence on trumpet players.

Roy has a superb technique which allows him to play extremely difficult phrases with a powerful execution and a terrific drive. At times he plays almost as fast as the saxophone players. In fact, Roy was influenced in his melodic ideas by two of the greatest saxists, Benny Carter and Coleman Hawkins, from whom he borrowed the custom of using more chord changes than usual in his variations. It is a pity that Roy has a tendency to display his technique too much because he has great creative gifts, and when he relaxes and gives way to his natural inspiration, he is able to swing as few trumpet players do (a good example of Roy at his best is his recording of *Dale's Wail*). He is one of the most uneven of the notable jazzmen, and disagreements about his real value often arise from misunderstandings, as some judge him through his best performances while others do it through erratic renderings. What is beyond doubt is that Roy plays at times in a very unattractive way but that he has all that is needed to be one of the jazz greats.

Roy's influence, not surprisingly, shows the same dualism. It has been a good one for some musicians, bad for others. It has been bad in inducing many young trumpet players to strive for fast runs and pyrotechnical effects rather than real musical ideas and soul. The best example is Dizzy Gillespie, who started as an Eldridge imitator and tried to play faster, higher, and all kinds of "-ers," often succeeding. Dizzy Gillespie is an amazing virtuoso and a gifted musician as well. But his desire to play things that had been unheard of made him leave the jazz idiom, and his numerous disciples left it as well. Of course,

Roy Eldridge can in no way be considered directly responsible for such deviations.

On the other hand, an example of Roy's good influence is Harry "Sweets" Edison, who has been emulating what was best in Eldridge's style. Neglecting the fireworks, fast runs, and other flashy effects, Harry Edison retained Roy's simpler phrases and assimilated his "drive," which was quite different from the Armstrong way of swinging. One of the things that makes Sweets Edison so nice to listen to is that he plays with a total simplicity and ease, never trying to do too much and always telling a story. Although he does not express himself in the New Orleans style at all, he plays very often on the beat— one of the few trumpet players of his generation to do so.

In turn, Harry Edison had considerable influence on the trumpet players of his generation, who were attracted by his perfect patterns and the intensity of his swing. However, it is quite difficult in many cases to tell whether certain trumpet players were influenced more by Harry Edison than by Roy Eldridge or vice versa, the more so since Louis Armstrong's influence is to be found also, combined with that of Edison and Eldridge, in the style of many musicians. Take, for instance, Taft Jordan, a first-class trumpet player. He started as a 100 per cent Armstrong disciple. Later he put some Rex Stewart and Roy Eldridge phrases into his choruses, but when he used them he sounded closer to Sweets Edison than to Roy, so it is hard to determine exactly the shares of each.

Joe Newman, one of the best trumpet players of the younger generation, has gone the same way; the essence of his style is a mixture of Roy and Sweets, and his way of swinging is halfway between both.

There is a very great trumpet player who came up about the

same time as Harry Edison, around 1937–1938: it is Charlie
Shavers.

Shavers is one of the most amazing trumpet virtuosos in the
history of jazz. He has a complete mastery of his instrument. I
say "complete" because some so-called virtuosos are only fast
performers; but speed is not the alpha and omega of instrumental technique: tone, attack, vibrato, and other elements
are just as important. And Charlie Shavers has everything: a
beautiful tone, a biting attack, an equal command of all registers, speed, and—what is the most important—a real creative
mind to make the best of such an exceptional equipment.
Charlie Shavers has a vast imagination, an outstanding musicianship, and a sense of humor that has seldom been equalled
in jazz; and he can put plenty of soul into his solos, too. Stylistically, he stems more from Louis Armstrong than from anybody else but there is some Roy Eldridge in his playing too.

Another amazing trumpet player of about the same age is
William "Cat" Anderson, who is known for his unbelievable
power in the upper register of the instrument. And he really is
unequalled in this specialty. But too few people are aware that
Cat Anderson also is a telling trumpet player in the medium
register, where he is able to play beautiful Armstrong-type
solos as well as "growl" choruses with mutes in the best Ellingtonian "wa-wa" tradition. Cat Anderson is a much more accomplished and a greater trumpet player than most people
think.

The trumpet being the instrument of the largest proportion
of first-rate soloists, there are still many musicians worth mentioning: Bobby Stark (who died in 1945), a real "soul man,"
who was close to Louis Armstrong and to the New Orleans
tradition; Sy Oliver (better known as an arranger—he was
Jimmie Lunceford's main arranger) who plays a straightfor-

ward, on-the-beat style and was an outstanding exponent of
the "wa-wa" mute; Adolphus "Doc" Cheatham, known as one
of the best first trumpet chair men in jazz but who is a powerful, inventive, fluent soloist as well; Edward Anderson, a robust, straightforward Armstrong-style man; Joe Thomas, another Armstrong disciple, noted for his easy, relaxed playing;
Emmett Berry, whose vigorous playing has something of Armstrong and something of Eldridge; Dud Bascomb, a very inventive and swinging trumpeter who also was influenced by
Louis and Roy; Walter Williams, who has a tremendous drive
and is, with Sweets Edison, the best of the Roy Eldridge followers; Teddy Buckner, one of the best men in the pure Armstrong style, who learned a lot about the New Orleans tradition through years of playing with Kid Ory's band during the
late forties and the early fifties; Jabbo Smith, whose case is
strange: in some records he shows an amazing fertility of
melodic invention while in others his improvisations lack
musical continuity and he does not seem to control what he is
doing.

Harold Baker is different from most trumpeters. He has a
suave, warm tone and expresses himself in a smooth, melodious style, at times reminiscent of Joe Smith.

Another peculiar case is Benny Carter's. Most of the time
he plays alto sax, but when he takes the trumpet, he sounds as
great as the best specialists of the instrument. His chorus on
More Than You Know (recorded with his own band—originally released on the Vocalion label) is one of the most beautiful, inventive trumpet solos ever waxed.

Other good trumpet players are Peanuts Holland, who at his
best is the equal of the great ones; Walter Fuller (whose playing is full of the Louis Armstrong spirit); Freddie Webster
(said to be very good but whom I do not know well, since he

died young without having been featured much on records);
Pat Jenkins (especially good on the blues); Johnny Letman,
who really "fills his horn," as Roy Eldridge so well puts it[7];
Eddie Tompkins (a very inventive musician who died young,
in 1943); Erskine Hawkins, an amazing technician; Herman
Autrey, Reunald Jones, Louis Bacon, Ruben Reeves, Snooky
Young, Luis Metcalf, Jimmie Cobb, Frank Newton, Edwin
Swayzee, Wendell Culley, El Baron, Harry Jackson, Joe
Wilder, Nelson Williams, Eddie "Moon" Mullens, Francis
Williams, Lou Jones, John "Bugs" Hamilton, Gerry Wilson,
Alvin Alcorn, Jack Butler, Bill Dillard, Shad Collins, Gus
Aiken, Henry Goodwin, Merrill Stepter, Taps Miller (better
known as a dancer), Shirley Clay, Charlie Gains, Paul Camp-
bell, and Johnny Morton (Jelly Roll's nephew), whose play-
ing is simple but full of feeling.

Among the white trumpet players, besides those previously
mentioned, the best are Bunny Berigan (who died in 1942), a
very gifted musician (when he was right, few could touch
him); Harry James, who can play good jazz besides being a
virtuoso; Bill Butterfield, an underrated trumpeter while
Bobby Hackett is much overrated (Bobby is a good technician
but a poor swingman); to say nothing of Red Nichols, whose
music is the corniest ever. England has a fine trumpet player
in Humphrey Lyttelton, and France an especially good one in
Guy Longnon. The younger white trumpet players of value, in
the States, are Johnny Windhurst and—chiefly—Ruby Braff,
who has become during recent years one of the best musicians

[7] Last-minute note: I have just heard some new records with Johnny
Letman (who never had his chance on discs before he was 40 years
old) which show him playing with such terrific power, swing, and
inventiveness that there is little doubt he must be ranked among the
very greatest. He is full of the Louis Armstrong fire and spirit, with a
touch of Roy Eldridge's biting drive.

the white race ever gave to jazz. His style owes more to Louis Armstrong than to anybody else but he has assimilated ideas from several sources and has perfectly integrated them within his own personality.

I will not discuss, of course, the "progressive" trumpet players as they do not belong to jazz music. No one who has the slightest knowledge of what jazz really is can think for a minute that Miles Davis and his disciples are doing the same music as Louis Armstrong, Jonah Jones, Roy Eldridge, Buck Clayton, Cootie Williams, and the other great jazz trumpet exponents. However, I must mention Howard McGhee and Benny Bailey because they proved themselves to be excellent jazzmen during their early days, before making a switch to Gillespie and bop music; Ernie Royal, an accomplished trumpet player; Ray Copeland, who although he has fooled around with progressive combos seems to have everything that is needed to be an excellent jazzman; Willie Cook, who, despite his having borrowed some phrases from Gillespie, is most of the time a jazzman and a truly good one; and the formidable Clark Terry, who has been too often described as a bopper. True, Clark Terry has been influenced to some extent by Gillespie, but this influence is more superficial than deep. Clark Terry differs from bop trumpet players in almost everything: he has a warm, beautiful tone; he swings; he makes his instrument "talk" and "sing"; he has melody and feeling, and instead of playing scales and other exercises he creates real melodic variations. Of course, one has to listen to him with Duke Ellington's band (for instance in such recordings as *Star Dust, Stompin' at the Savoy, In the Mood*) or with other jazzmen, not with a bunch of boppers.

Some people once said that all young trumpet players were playing progressive music, so that there was hardly any future for jazz. This simply is not true. I have already mentioned Ruby Braff, a young trumpeter who belongs to the authentic jazz tradition. But he is far from being alone. The truth is that the young men who do not play progressive music seldom get due recognition in write-ups or by being recorded. There is, for instance, a young colored trumpet player from New Orleans, Wallace Davenport. He is a great jazzman, full of soul and imagination, fully worthy of his seniors. But he had to go to Europe with Lionel Hampton's band to be really featured on a recording date. This took place in 1955. Since that time, Wallace Davenport has returned to the States and has been playing in New Orleans, but nobody has done anything to bring him into the limelight.

6   the trombones

Like the trumpet players, most of the first great New Orleans trombonists, the Roy Palmers, Eddie Atkins, Zue Robertsons, Eddie Vincents, are not well known to us, having been recorded very little and in disadvantageous circumstances. Among the trombone players of this generation only Edward "Kid" Ory and Honoré Dutrey have done any considerable recording.

As I said in an earlier chapter, the trombone was first employed in jazz as a sort of bass. It filled in the gaps of ensemble improvisation, and harmonized occasionally with the trumpet at the lower third. During the entire first epoch of jazz, the trombone was scarcely considered a solo instrument and was treated as a supporting instrument whose frequent and large glissandos provided punctuation for the phrases played by the rest of the melodic section.

"Kid" Ory is a living incarnation of this manner of playing. He has an admirable sense of ensemble work; he knows where to place his notes and executes glissandos and short phrases beautifully. Indeed it would be difficult to find another trombone player capable of providing such an intelligent part in ensemble improvisation. Some people do not consider him a great soloist, because he uses phrases of an extreme simplicity. But that is forgetting what jazz music really is. Kid Ory does not even try for complicated variations. What he likes is to give to the few notes he is playing a maximum of strength and expression—and that is what he succeeds in doing. To expect from Kid Ory fast trombone phrases with a lot of chord changes would be just as stupid as criticizing a blues singer for not doing vocal fireworks of the Jon Hendricks-Anne Ross-Dave Lambert type. In his style, Kid Ory has never been equalled, especially when it comes to playing the blues: no trombone has ever swung a simple riff on the blues and made it "sing" as beautifully as Ory.

In broad form the style of Honoré Dutrey (who died in 1935) was similar to Kid Ory's, but Dutrey liked to hold certain notes for a long period in ensemble work, thus creating a singing bass which was very agreeable to the ear. Likewise his playing was not as powerful as Ory's.

But the trombone player who has had the greatest influence on all others was a musician who did not originate in New Orleans. His name is Jimmy Harrison. He was born in Louisville, Kentucky, in 1900. And though his earliest style was probably similar to that of the New Orleans trombonists, he was greatly influenced by King Oliver and Louis Armstrong when he heard them in 1922 or 1923, while on his way to Chicago. These musicians were a veritable revelation for him, and from that moment on he began to adapt his trombone style to the trumpet style of these two great players. Out of their inspiration he developed a new trombone style based on the New Orleans idiom. This new form was more melodic than the earlier style, and was perfect in every way for solo improvisation. Without any doubt, Jimmy Harrison is the greatest of all jazz trombonists, and only his premature death in 1931 prevented him from attaining the fame he deserved. His musical temperament strongly recalls Tommy Ladnier, with whom he played in 1927 in Fletcher Henderson's orchestra. Ladnier's style, based on King Oliver's, closely resembled his. Jimmie Harrison and Tommy Ladnier had in common a gift for creating beautiful and concise melodic curves. Both had a powerful attack and execution, as a result of which they swung phenomenally.

Numerous trombone players were influenced by Jimmie Harrison and also Miff Mole, a white trombonist. The latter was gifted with a remarkable suppleness of execution but the spirit of his music had little in common with that of the Negroes. At the beginning the white trombonists took their inspiration from Miff Mole alone. As a result they began to play in a loose manner in order to make their instrument as flexible a solo instrument as the trumpet and the other melodic instruments. But toward 1927 one of them, Jack Teagarden, began studying Jimmie Harrison's style and succeeded in mastering the Negro style. Consequently he drew the other white trombonists back to that style little by little.

Jack Teagarden has a good tone, though a little nasal, and he has imagination as well as brilliant instrumental technique. He is one of the few white musicians who has had an influence on the Negroes. But he does not swing as much as the best colored players, and on slow tempos his phrasing is not exempt from a certain sentimentalism which does not belong to the jazz idiom.

Another white trombone player of considerable reputation was Tommy Dorsey (who died in 1956). He first took his inspiration from Miff Mole but soon turned to Jimmie Harrison and assimilated the latter's style quite well. However, a few years later he began specializing in "sweet" executions—in which he excelled—and his playing no longer swung as it did in his younger days.

From a strict jazz angle, the best white trombone player is a little-known musician, Floyd O'Brien, who was very much influenced by Kid Ory and succeeded in playing in the style of the New Orleans trombonists. His sense of ensemble playing is excellent and his solos fully belong to the Negro idiom.

The best colored trombonists among those who followed more or less the Jimmie Harrison style are Dicky Wells, J. C. Higginbotham, Benny Morton, Sandy Williams, Jimmy Archey, Vic Dickenson, and Trummy Young.

In his early years, Dicky Wells sounded quite similar to Jimmie Harrison, although his playing was more exuberant and was scattered with grandiose explosions whose spirited execution produced a striking impression. Later his playing became smoother, more legato, and more humorous too. On slow numbers Dicky Wells has a majestic, sometimes dramatic accent owing to the amazing expressive power he puts into each note.

Higginbotham is very different from all other trombonists. He frequently employs long phrases and fills his solos with an abundance of notes which one is surprised to hear on so heavy an instrument. (Of course, modernists have since been using speed on trombone, but as they do not play their runs with a big tone and full power, like Higginbotham, their solos cannot make the same amazing impression.) Higginbotham's playing is violent, almost savage; hardly any trombone ever gave such an impression of force and vehemence. During his first years, Jimmie Harrison's influence was obvious; later on, Louis Armstrong's phrases often crept into his solos, wonderfully adapted to the trombone technique (one of the best examples is Higginbotham's chorus on Lil Armstrong's *Confessin'*). Sandy Williams and especially Benny Morton are the ones who played the most like Jimmie Harrison (although they also used some Teagarden-ish devices). Morton's concise phrases and solidly structured choruses are, at times, very close to Harrison; however he does not have Harrison's terrific punch and drive. Sandy Williams is more powerful. He is uneven but in his good days he can compete with the best trombones.

Jimmy Archey, although he does not come from Louisiana, expresses himself in the New Orleans idiom. He is a solid, robust trombone player, with a full, round, beautiful tone, swinging all the time, and there are very few trombones who can play the blues as he does.

Vic Dickenson is one of the greatest trombones in the history of jazz—an accomplished musician who is gifted with almost everything: a pretty tone, a startling instrumental virtuosity, a vast imagination, a great range of melodic ideas and a musical humor which is sheer delight. His style has been influenced more by Louis Armstrong than by anybody else, as is obvious in most of his solos on slow tempo (*Tenderly*, recorded for Blue Note, is one of his masterpieces). But Vic Dickenson's personality is so strong that it would be easy to recognize him among a hundred trombones.

Trummy Young, who became famous in 1938 when he played with Jimmie Lunceford's band, was soon to be the greatest influence on other trombones since Jimmie Harrison. Trummy himself got his inspiration from Harrison, and was also deeply influenced by Louis Armstrong. His formidable attack and power would be sufficient to rank him among the greatest trombones. But he also created a new style, playing in a rather high register with astonishing facility, in such a way that one would sometimes think that he was playing a trumpet. In the high register, Trummy's tone is both soft and biting, giving his playing a peculiar accent which almost all trombones who followed him have been trying to emulate. During the past eight years, since 1952, Trummy Young has been playing in Louis Armstrong's "All Stars" group, and quite naturally the Armstrong touch in his playing has been augmented. Also, it has given his playing a marked New Orleans flavor which it did not have before. Trummy is even greater now than he used to be.

A place apart must be reserved for two trombone players who for years worked in Duke Ellington's orchestra—Joseph Nanton, nicknamed "Tricky Sam," and Lawrence Brown.

Tricky Sam (who died in 1946) is to the trombone what Bubber Miley is to the trumpet. With the "growl" and the "wa-wa" mute he achieves deeply moving effects which often recall the sound of the human voice. On slow tempo his solos are full of a poignant accent; as Duke Ellington said, "He sounds so forlorn." Tricky Sam is one of the greatest blues players jazz has ever known. He needs only to play two or three notes with his inimitable expression and repeat them during the whole chorus to move the listener deeply. He tells more with a couple of notes than most trombones do with many and complex phrases. Tricky Sam's sound is unique in jazz.

Whereas Tricky Sam is altogether primitive, one might almost say "savage," Lawrence Brown could be said to be too refined. His tone is polished and his instrumental technique dazzling. He has a fine melodic invention and makes good use of Louis Armstrong's style of phrasing; but at times his playing tends to be grandiloquent, or overly sentimental.

Other very good trombones are Tyree Glenn, who has a pretty yet round and full tone, whose playing is smooth, humorous, and well balanced; Henderson Chambers, a vigorous musician full of drive; Quentin Jackson, whose style is close to the New Orleans idiom and who excels in the Tricky Sam "wa-wa" style; Charlie Green, a powerful trombone player who was at his best on the blues, as shown in his numerous recordings with the famous blues singer Bessie Smith.

In the younger generation, those born around 1920 and the mid-twenties, the best trombone players were more or less inspired by Trummy Young's style. The greatest, maybe, is Benny Green, remarkable for his smooth playing, his beautiful tone, his inventiveness and drive. He often has been associated with boppers on records but he really is a jazzman. Al Grey is equally gifted. He is especially great on the blues and when he uses the plunger mute. His speed is amazing, although at times he has a tendency to overuse it. Britt Woodman is another virtuoso of the trombone, with a wide range; but he also plays solos full of simplicity, which he knows how to swing in an easy and fluent manner. John Ewing is perhaps the closest to Trummy Young. Henry Coker has an amazing wealth of ideas, is very versatile, and plays all kinds of styles. Al Hayse is a pure swingman who is great on the blues and who should be much better known than he is. Dick Harris and Matthew Gee are uneven but they both are capable of very exciting solos. One of the best trombones of this generation was Fred Beckett, who played beautifully in something of an Armstrong-Trummy Young style; unfortunately he died very young.

There are many other good trombone players: "Big Chief" Russell Moore, who has a beautiful tone; Snub Mosely, an amazing virtuoso, who has a style all his own; Albert Wynn and Preston Jackson, two New Orleans men; Fred Robinson, John Thomas, Charlie Irvis, Cuffee Davidson, who also belong to the old school; Harry White, a powerful trombone, at times reminiscent of Higginbotham (and a good arranger, too); Keg Johnson, of the Jimmie Harrison school; Claude Jones, an excellent instrumentalist; Michel Wood, George Stevenson, Ted Donelly, Herb Flemming, Dan Minor, Elmer

Crumbley, Russell Boles, George Washington, Wilbur De Paris, Bill Hughes, Slim Moore, Phatz Morris; and, among the whites, Jack Jenny, Bill Harris, Urbie Green; but the last two often concentrate too much on technique to the prejudice of swing.

7 the clarinets

Here again I can but list the names of the first great clarinetists of New Orleans. For such clarinet players as the brothers Lorenzo and Louis Tio, "Big Eye" Louis Nelson Delile, Alphonso Picou, and George Baquet made no recordings, or so few that it would be difficult to describe their style.

Following them, New Orleans produced a group of marvelous clarinetists who are well known to us: Jimmie Noone, Johnny Dodds, Sidney Bechet, Barney Bigard, Omer Simeon, and Albert Nicholas.

The first three cited are the oldest. Jimmie Noone and Johnny Dodds are the two greatest jazz clarinetists who have ever lived. But Sidney Bechet must be considered separately for he devoted himself primarily to the soprano saxophone, though he is a great clarinetist.

Jimmie Noone (who died in 1944) is so marvelous a musician that one is often tempted to think that he is not only the greatest clarinetist but also the finest jazz musician next to Louis Armstrong.

He seems to possess all qualities. First, his clarinet technique is without equal. The story is told that the composer, Maurice Ravel, heard him in a Chicago night club and was stunned by his virtuosity. The next day Ravel returned with a solo clarinetist from the Chicago symphony orchestra to find

out if it was really possible to play such difficult runs on a
clarinet. The classic clarinetist had to admit that he himself
was incapable of playing certain of Jimmie Noone's phrases.
However authentic this anecdote may be, it is certain that
Jimmie Noone's instrumental technique surpasses all other
jazz clarinetists.

But that is not the only point in which he excels. His style
can be considered the perfect style for the clarinet, for he uti-
lizes to the maximum all the resources of this splendid instrument. His style is essentially supple and loose. His long rapid
phrases flow from the high register, descend progressively to
the lower registers, rise again, then fall with a total ease which
gives the instrument a perfect freedom. Likewise his playing is
filled with intelligence and can be adapted to all circumstances.
When Jimmie Noone plays a solo he creates a melodic line
which is sufficient in itself. But, being a true New Orleans
clarinetist, he prefers the contrapuntal style—that is, playing
against a trumpet or a saxophone. In this case he creates
phrases which complement and give value to the other melodic parts, and that with rare success, for he has a prodigious
sense of ensemble work. His part flows with an unequalled
generosity as it harmonizes with the others. It effaces itself;
becomes silent; then weds the phrases of the other instruments; then opposes them; all in splendid fashion. Jimmie
Noone has an astonishing sense of tonal graduations. In the
opening phrases of the ensemble, he plays with discretion long
phrases of definite and regular cadence which lead and set the
balance of the orchestra. However towards the end, when the
tension augments, he rises into the very high registers and
there plays, with an extraordinary power, a few notes resting on
the beat—as would a New Orleans trumpet—which sharply
stimulate the other sections and swing the entire orchestra.

Likewise Jimmie Noone possesses a warm and voluminous tone of an incomparable purity—the most beautiful clarinet tone I have ever heard. His tonal quality is like his playing, both very powerful and very delicate. It admirably suits his phrases which are always marked with a most delectable and graceful melody. Here is certainly the secret of Jimmie Noone's greatness. Whereas a trumpet by its very nature is "heavy" and imposing, Jimmie Noone's clarinet, though robust and poignant, always retains the grace and fluidity appropriate to his more delicate instrument, for the clarinet should never fight with the trumpet but should round and soften its angles.

Though Jimmie Noone's phrases are frequently very long and filled with notes, they have a great melodic simplicity. He does not search for melodic effects and peculiar harmonies but is, on the contrary, content to return frequently to the same three or four notes, for he knows that melodic beauty depends not upon the number of different notes but upon the intelligent relationship of a few notes. This style is particularly sublime when Jimmie Noone plays the blues. Here, more than anywhere else, one senses in his magnificent flights the breath of a musician of genius.

Johnny Dodds (who died in 1940) is not, like Jimmie Noone, a rapid and flowing clarinetist. His playing is, on the contrary, brutal, abrupt, and almost breathless; he is in fact in almost perfect opposition to Jimmie Noone.

Johnny Dodds has a hard, cutting tone and a violent attack which are due in part to the fact that he uses a very hard reed. His extremely pronounced vibrato—more so than that of any other clarinetist—has none of Jimmie Noone's tenderness, though it has a savage beauty which is profoundly moving. His phrases are always executed with force; he swings as well as Jimmie Noone but in a more "heavy" way.

As a result when one hears Johnny Dodds in an ensemble improvisation one has none of that impression of grace and lightness which Jimmie Noone produces, but one has instead the impression of a musician who plays with a passionate ferocity. Where Jimmie Noone passes without a pause from the high to the low register, Johnny Dodds plays lengthily in the same register, particularly the high range. In this register he produces rending plaints with short breathless phrases which are violently accented. Where Jimmie Noone slides agilely and impalpably, Johnny Dodds forces and insists with violence. Jimmie Noone is by turns gentle and powerful, abundant and concise; Johnny Dodds introduces from the beginning a passionate strain which he holds unrelentingly until the end.

Nonetheless Johnny Dodds' is a true clarinet style. In spite of his violence and harshness, his phrases sing and frequently he creates melodic lines full of charm. He plays the blues as very few jazzmen have, irrespective of instruments. His fire and strident power, and what one might call the "mean" quality of his playing, make his pure "blue" phrases magnificent—phrases so pure that Johnny Dodds should be cited as a perfect model for any clarinetist who wishes to play the blues well.

Sidney Bechet's style is much closer to Johnny Dodds' than to Jimmie Noone's, because of the harshness of his playing, the structure of his phrases, and his very pronounced vibrato—which is not as harsh as Johnny Dodds'.

Though Bechet's favorite instrument is the soprano saxophone, I prefer to discuss him with the clarinetists—first, because his style was formed on the clarinet, and second, because the soprano saxophone, owing to its high pitch, frequently plays a role more like that of the clarinet than that of the other saxophones. It is to Bechet's credit that he revealed the splendid resources of this instrument. For Bechet succeeded in drawing from it an ample tone which is both hot and mellow and which makes the tone of practically all other soprano saxophone players seem poor and restricted.

Though his melodic style is more flowing than Johnny Dodds', Bechet frequently employs short phrases, well founded on the beat, whose structure is analogous to the phrases of the New Orleans trumpets. He swings with definition and brilliance. However since Bechet executes the choppiest phrases with great smoothness and makes his instrument "sing," his improvisations maintain a lightness which differs greatly from the harsh expression of Johnny Dodds. But like Jimmie Noone and Johnny Dodds, Sidney Bechet is a marvelous blues player.

Most striking in Bechet are his prodigious vehemence, and his sudden flights executed with an incomparable fire, which give his choruses a vast and triumphant expression. (Bechet died in 1959.)

The preceding clarinetists have more or less inspired three younger musicians, Omer Simeon, Albert Nicholas, and Barney Bigard. Though these younger men have a somewhat less intense breath, they are nonetheless very great clarinetists.

At certain times Omer Simeon's playing recalls that of Jimmie Noone (in his agile phrases running from the high to the lower registers); at other times, that of Johnny Dodds (in the short abrupt phrases in the high register, and his rending notes). Simeon's style is rather capricious, sometimes containing short dry phrases with a sober melodic line, sometimes long phrases of ravishing contours. That Simeon handles the lower registers far better than the majority of clarinetists is well shown in certain of his solos played entirely in the lower ranges.

In one of these, *Georgia Swing* recorded with Jelly Roll Morton,[1] he plays two prodigious choruses.

Albert Nicholas, on the contrary, holds closely to Jimmie Noone's style. His long elegant phrases flow with a delicious lightness. His tone, though less rounded than that of Jimmie Noone, is fluid and almost liquid. Likewise his playing is more legato.

An altogether different musical personality is to be found in Barney Bigard. Here is a musician among a thousand. His solos are scattered with full and unlimited inflections. His phrases reach dizzy heights, are full of elasticity, and sparkle like fireworks. There is an immense grace throughout his music. His tone is fine and limpid like Jimmie Noone's, though it is not so voluminous. Though Barney's work sometimes recalls Jimmie Noone and Albert Nicholas, his ideas are frequently more personal. Many people think that Barney does not play in a true New Orleans style. But in spite of his imaginative and fantastic playing, Barney certainly plays in the characteristic New Orleans idiom. To be convinced of this, it is only necessary to listen to his interpretation of the blues which he plays with the nostalgic expression and languor typical of the Southern musicians. Without exaggeration one can say that Barney's inspiration is one of the most original and most constant that jazz has ever produced.

During the first period of jazz—that is until about 1930—practically all the clarinetists were directly or indirectly inspired by the Negro clarinetists of New Orleans, principally by Jimmie Noone, but also to a great extent by Johnny Dodds and Sidney Bechet. One among them, a white musician from Chicago named Milton "Mezz" Mezzrow assimilated the style of

[1] RCA Victor LPM 1649.

these clarinetists so perfectly that one would think he had originated in New Orleans.

Mezzrow was especially inspired by Jimmie Noone. He adopted Noone's phrasing, his constantly flowing passage from one register to the other, and his poignant intonations. But one feels Johnny Dodds' influence principally when Mezz plays the blues with that same fire and "mean" quality. In fact Mezzrow's greatest claim to fame is the fact that he plays the blues better than any other white musician, and I am not speaking of clarinetists only—he plays the blues in the same way as the great Negro musicians. Likewise the luminous melodic intelligence of his solos, his fine sense of collective improvisation, and his intuition which equals that of Jimmie Noone, certainly reveal why Mezzrow is by far the greatest jazz clarinetist that the white race has produced.

Nevertheless there are several white clarinetists from Chicago—or at least who play in the Chicago style—who are contemporaries of Mezzrow but who have gained a much greater reputation than his, and that quite unjustly. Among them, Frank Teschemacher (who died in 1932) did have the stuff of a remarkable clarinetist. He proved his good taste when he turned to Omer Simeon and particularly Johnny Dodds for inspiration. But the influence which Bix and several other white musicians had on him harmed his work considerably. Though his solos do occasionally contain some beautiful flights and though his vibrato is moving, he does not have, as Mezzrow has, that flowing ease characteristic of the great New Orleans clarinet players. There are too many choppy, rough phrases in his music. These are all the more regrettable because they frequently appear after phrases played in an excellent style. Nevertheless Teschemacher had a mordant style in his ensemble improvisations.

These faults are exaggerated in Pee Wee Russell. Pee Wee's inspiration, particularly his breathless phrasing, came more from Teschemacher himself than from the New Orleans clarinetists. Nevertheless Pee Wee's clarinet was often agreeable during the first years of his career. But, as time went on, his use of the "growl" often replaced melodic inspiration and rendered his work tiresome.

Fud Livingston is another white clarinetist who played in the Chicago style. He greatly resembles Pee Wee Russell, but plays in an even more choppy fashion. Much of his inspiration likewise seems to have come from Teschemacher.

I know that many people praise the Chicago style for its melodic sobriety, but this is more a trumpet than a clarinet style. The brutal repetition of several notes or short phrases, which gives excellent results on a massive instrument like the trumpet, hardly suits a frail instrument like the clarinet, for the clarinet should be played in a more mobile and flowing fashion. For this reason I much prefer the older white clarinetists of New Orleans such as Leon Rappolo and Larry Shields, to Pee Wee Russell, Fud Livingston, and even Teschemacher himself. For though these older white clarinet players swing far less than the Negro clarinet players from the same area, they at least have an excellent conception of the role of the clarinet in jazz music.

To come back to the colored clarinetists, there is another one who plays beautifully in the New Orleans style: it is Darnell Howard (also a fiddle player). He sometimes comes closer to Jimmie Noone than anybody else does by his warm and moving tone, his fluent phrases going up and down all over the instrument.

Buster Bailey is close to the New Orleans style because he got his inspiration from Jimmie Noone and Johnny Dodds. He is one of the most amazing technicians—jazz or classical—that could ever be heard on clarinet. He can play at an unbelievable speed (his *Man with a Horn Goes Berserk*, originally recorded for Vocalion in 1938, is one of the most stupendous records ever made). Buster Bailey likes long, fluent phrases of an elegant melodic cut, and he executes them with an unequalled suppleness and lightness. His rather thin tone is nonetheless very lovely. He often uses a very legato style, and executes sinuous, legato phrases so smoothly in the high register that, at times, one would think he is listening to a violin.

Other excellent clarinetists are Russell Procope, who got his inspiration from the New Orleans men, has a beautiful low register and a powerful, sparkling high register, and sometimes recalls Barney Bigard; Cecil Scott, who got some of his basic phrases from Jimmie Noone; Edward Inge, a moving and fluent clarinet player; Gene Sedric (better known as a tenor saxist), who is especially good on the slow blues; Jimmy O'Bryant, a typical New Orleans-style clarinetist who sounds very much like Johnny Dodds; Arnet Nelson, who likes to use humorous effects but is a great blues player; and Benny Carter, who could easily be one of the best on the instrument if he had not, after the first part of his career, specialized more on alto sax and trumpet.

After the New Orleans period, the clarinet style changed a lot during the mid-thirties, for two main reasons: one was that the clarinet was no longer a permanent instrument in jazz orchestras and was only incidentally played by saxophone players, who used on it their saxophone style, not too well adapted to the instrument; the other reason was the rise to fame of the celebrated white clarinetist Benny Goodman. His commercial success was so great that it decided most of the younger musicians to imitate him. Goodman, of course, had an instrumental technique superior to the majority of jazz clarinetists (though much less outstanding than that of men like Buster Bailey, Barney Bigard, and Jimmie Noone) and, at the debut of his musical career, he did have a certain musical richness in his improvisations, which nonetheless lacked the feeling, the soul of the great colored clarinetists. However, his melodic vein dried up soon and his playing became mechanical and tiresome. Besides the lack of feeling in his playing, his tone, quite poor, is not to be compared with that of such men as Jimmie Noone, Barney Bigard, Mezz Mezzrow.

Artie Shaw is another brilliant technician who also shines more by instrumental virtuosity than by soul and swing.

There have been numerous white clarinet players of the Goodman-Shaw type, the best ones being Johnny Mince, Sol Yaged, and Peanuts Hucko.

Among colored clarinetists who adopted Benny Goodman's style, the best known is Jimmy Hamilton. He is a first-rate technician, but his fashion of playing the instrument is closer to symphony music than to jazz.

Other good clarinet players are Heywood Henry, who sometimes recalls Barney Bigard; Scoville Browne, a musician full of warmth and finesse (also good on alto sax); Jerry Blake, who is the only clarinetist to have used the "growl" to perfection; Frank "Big Boy" Goodie, a good New Orleans man; Willie Smith, who used to play Barney-like clarinet in the Jimmie Lunceford days; Edmund Hall, an overrated musician, whose forceful style would be more suited to a trumpet or a tenor sax than to the graceful possibilities of the clarinet; Herb Hall, Marshall Royal, Joe Darensbourg, Pete Clark, Eddie Barefield, Prince Robinson, Ben Richardson, Chauncey Haughton, Caughey Roberts, Clarence Grimes, Clifford King, George Lewis. The latter has been hailed by some critics as one of the best New Orleans clarinetists, as a man comparable to Johnny Dodds. This is vastly exaggerating George Lewis' value, but he has a real feeling for the blues and is a good ensemble player in collective improvisations.

Among the white clarinetists, the following should be cited: Jimmy Dorsey (who died in 1957), a Jimmie Noone disciple; Irving Fazola, Joe Marsala, Rod Cless, Sidney Arodin, Don Murray, and Matty Matlock. Among the younger men, the following tried to revive the New Orleans spirit and succeeded to a certain extent: Bob Wilber, a Sidney Bechet disciple; Wally Fawkes, an Englishman who also was inspired by Bechet; and two Frenchmen: Claude Luter, who was first influenced by Johnny Dodds and then by Bechet; and Maxim Saury, a Barney Bigard follower.

8 the saxophones

The only saxophones which are used a great deal are the alto and tenor saxophones. The soprano saxophone has been disdained by most musicians, and both the baritone and especially the bass saxophones are too heavy for any frequent use.

As was said in a previous chapter, the saxophone was employed only relatively late in jazz history. Therefore there are no early New Orleans musicians to mention here. Moreover there is no early saxophone style which contrasts with a modern style, as is the case of the instruments like the clarinet and the trumpet.

On the alto saxophone the first name to be signalled is that of a great New Orleans musician, Joe "Doc" Poston, who has played since about 1920. He rests his music solidly on the beat and hardly leaves the melody. The entire value of his playing lies in his precise tempo, which is like that of the best drummers, and in his manner of phrasing. He scans and articulates each phrase with an authoritative clarity, seldom holding a note, and on the contrary cutting the sound brusquely.

But from the point of view of solo work and imagination the best alto saxophone players are Johnny Hodges, Benny Carter, Willie Smith, and Earl Bostic.

Johnny Hodges, who plays soprano as well as alto, has taken much of his inspiration from Sidney Bechet. He is probably the best soprano saxophonist, outside of Bechet whom he closely resembles, especially in the blues. However his playing is less brilliant, less carried away, nor does he have that perpetual expression of triumph which is so striking in Bechet's music.

Hodges' work on the alto saxophone is even further removed from Bechet. He truly has a style which is admirably adapted to the resources of the instrument. His rich phrases are full of the unforeseen and yet stripped of all attempts at the unusual and peculiar. By that I mean to say that Johnny Hodges is one of the most "natural" musicians there are. Likewise he is a musician who expresses himself with great purity in the typical jazz idiom. Another characteristic is his abundant use of held notes and of hot, ample inflections. These give his playing an inner tension deeply moving by its impartiality. At the same time his playing has an airy and almost impalpable lightness about it. Johnny Hodges' indefinably beautiful tone, with its transparency both ample and delicate, is in perfect harmony with his style.

Benny Carter, on the other hand, plays in the opposite manner. His solos are not impregnated with that suppressed tension which so strongly works upon the listener in Johnny Hodges' improvisations. Carter's is a sumptuous style. His full and lovely phrases have an unheard-of melodic richness. In improvising he uses the slightest chord with an intelligence and musical instinct of genius. It should be noted here that Benny Carter is also one of the greatest arrangers jazz has known. And one can say without fear that Benny's purely musical gifts are so great that he would undoubtedly have been an exceptional musician in any domain as well as in jazz music.

Likewise Benny is different from Johnny Hodges in his clear flamboyant tone which has as big a volume, in his incisive vibrato, and "cleaner" intonations. One of the most striking features of his execution is the incredible way in which he makes his instrument sing with a triumphant expression.

Willie Smith suggests both Johnny Hodges and Benny Carter. Like Hodges he has tense inflections; like Carter, a sparkling tone, a poignant vibrato. He is about the only alto sax player who has as voluminous a tone as that of Benny Carter and who can make his instrument "sing" as much. What is most astonishing in Willie Smith is his powerful execution. He has a lot of imagination, too. But after his years with Jimmie Lunceford (1934–1942), his inspiration became uneven.

During the first part of his career, Earl Bostic often played in a bright, voluble style, often using fast phrases which proved him an accomplished technician. But Bostic was not just a brilliant virtuoso; he had a beautiful, powerful tone and swung as much as (and maybe more than) the best alto sax players. Then, around 1950, he started to specialize in what is known as "rhythm and blues." He played most of the time in a concise style, using short, simple phrases and concentrating on swinging them to the utmost; often he used a "growl." Many critics dismissed him as doing second-rate stuff; and those same critics were praising the unswinging and effeminate style of a Lee Konitz or a Paul Desmond, which shows that jazz appreciation is still at a very poor level. In fact, most of Earl Bostic's so-called "rhythm and blues" records, such as *Flamingo*, *Sleep*, and *Cherokee*, are among the swingiest made during the fifties.

Other excellent alto saxophonists are Hilton Jefferson, Howard Johnson, Booker Pittman, Otto Hardwick, Marshall Royal, Russell Procope, Earl Warren, and Don Stovall.

Hilton Jefferson is a mellow, delicate alto player with an exquisite sensibility. He has great gifts for melody, and his impeccable musicianship often reminds one of Benny Carter.

He is not a very powerful musician but has a nice, easy swing and a clean, warm, very pure tone, and he makes his instrument "sing" beautifully.

I have a special liking for Howard Johnson and Booker Pittman, both of whom have taken their inspiration from Johnny Hodges. Howard Johnson's playing is simple and flowing, and he has a great melodic elegance; Booker Pittman plays in a more capricious, witty, biting manner. Both are good clarinet players as well.

Otto Hardwick, one of the earliest alto players, has a pleasantly alert style, full of grace and melody, full also of the New Orleans musical spirit. His choruses in the early Duke Ellington records (1926–1928) are the best alto sax solos put on wax during that period.

Marshall Royal, an outstanding first alto (with Basie's band throughout the forties), is also a superb soloist, equally at home on ballads (where his playing has a "singing" quality somewhat reminiscent of Benny Carter) and on the blues, which he plays as well as any alto sax one would care to name.

Russell Procope, who was one of the members of John Kirby's band and who has spent the past fifteen years in Duke Ellington's orchestra, has a beautiful tone, strong and firm, yet suave. He is a soloist full of fire and impetuosity who excels at the same time in the slow ballads, which he plays in a melodious, pretty way, without depraved sentimentalism. There he reminds one of Benny Carter, with a slight Otto Hardwick touch.

Earl Warren is known as one of the best first altos, as he led Count Basie's sax section wonderfully for years; but he is a fine soloist as well, one who really swings, full of vigor and bite.

Although Don Stovall is known among the musicians as one of the great alto saxists, he never reached the fame he deserved.

He shines by both his mastery of the instrument and his exceptional "drive."

The celebrated Charlie Parker (who died in 1955) belonged to the jazz idiom during the early years of his career, as one can check through his excellent records with Jay McShann's orchestra. His tone never was either warm or beautiful like that of a Hodges, a Carter, or a Bostic, but he played at an incredible speed. When he developed what was called "bop," he ceased to be a real jazz musician.[1] I would not for one minute contest that Charlie Parker had great creative gifts, but this book is on real jazz.

Parker's early style stems from Buster Smith, a fine altoist from Kansas City whom musicians much admire, but who has not been featured much on records.

There are some alto sax players who are especially good on the blues, such as Louis Jordan and Eddie Vinson, who both happen to be great blues singers as well.

Among the white musicians, Frankie Trumbauer is the most famous alto sax (he sometimes played the C melody sax, which is closer to an alto than to the usual tenor sax, anyway). He worked with Bix Beiderbecke for a long time, which probably explains the similarity of their styles. Some of Bix's solos on cornet, had they been copied and played note for note by Trumbauer on the saxophone, would sound absolutely like Trumbauer's own creation. Trumbauer has a very pure tone and employs abundant inflections but he does not swing much.

Other notable white altoists are Boyce Brown, who played much more like the colored saxists; Toots Mendello, Dave Matthews, and Jimmy Dorsey.

[1] I advise those among my readers who feel that I am making a strange statement here to read—or to reread—what Parker himself said on the matter (see p. 19).

Among the good colored altos, the following should be mentioned: Stomp Evans, one of the best from the old school although his frequent use of heavy slap-tonguing makes his solos less enjoyable than they should be; Edgar Sampson and Ted Buckner, two straightforward and melodious musicians; Scoops Carey, an inventive and expressive musician; Bill Johnson, a Willie Smith disciple; Bobby Smith, a swinging alto in the Hodges tradition; Jimmy Powell, who has some of the Benny Carter touch; Bobby Plater, a fine, all-around musician; Pete Brown, who played a staccato swinging style, with short choppy phrases, but who sounded better in the early part of his career than he did later; Don Redman, greater as an arranger, but who played very fine alto in various circumstances; Charlie Holmes, a Johnny Hodges disciple; Harry Carney, who played Hardwick-like alto solos in some Ellington records of the late twenties; Tab Smith, who is very uneven; Rudy Powell, Lester Boone, Omer Simeon, Glyn Pacque, Joe Eldridge, Wayman Carver, Joe Walker, Arthur Hampton, John Jackson, "Sax" Mallard, Charlie Singleton, Johnny Board, Donald Hill, and Emmett Matthews, who is especially remarkable on the soprano saxophone.

The tenor sax is deeper and heavier than the alto, and consequently does not lend itself so well to the light and "singing" phrases of the alto. Most of the time, the tenor sax is played with a more powerful and passionate swing.

Although it is difficult, as we have seen, to designate one alto saxophone player as frankly superior to the others, there is one tenor who clearly stands out: it is Coleman Hawkins, who is rightly considered one of the greatest soloists that jazz has produced.

Though Coleman Hawkins' style has evolved considerably with the years, four principal periods can be distinguished.

During the first period (1923–1928), his tone is rough, his style has a bite and strength recalling sometimes the powerful simplicity of the New Orleans trumpet players, sometimes the mobility of a clarinet. During the second period (1928–1932), his tone becomes rich and velvety; he begins to use large and poignant inflections; and while his style remains as passionate in the execution, his melodic line, still as mobile (with almost as great a use of the staccato), becomes more varied and full of pathos. The third period (1933–1939) finds Hawkins adopting a more legato style of playing, smoothed down by a still more velvety tone, with a majestic accent and a flow of phrases executed with a total, supreme abandon, especially in the slow numbers. The fourth period (from 1939 on) is characterized on fast tempos by a frequent use of the "growl" and riffs"; on slow tempos, by variations of amazing richness and incredible subtleness in both melody and harmony, with the most accurate and munificent use of altered notes. Hawkins improvises on slow numbers as if the rhythm section were about to double the time behind him, thus creating on his horn a subdued pulsation of extraordinary swinging effect. A typical example of this is *Body and Soul*, which Hawkins recorded for RCA Victor in 1939, one of the greatest jazz records of all time.

Within his successive changes, Hawkins has always remained outstanding, not only for the enormous volume of his tone but also for his amazing invention, the power of his attack and execution, the thrilling way he rocks a band. His creative gifts seem to have no limit. His improvisations, more and more daring, show his supreme mastery in using each and every chord with a perfection and musicality equal to that of a Benny Carter. In fact, Coleman Hawkins is such a genius that despite the heavy competition on this instrument, "Hawk" today is still ahead of them all.

Coleman Hawkins has been the biggest influence in the tenor sax style. Countless musicians of all eras have emulated his phrases, as well as his tone and his vibrato.

The best tenor sax players in the Hawkins style are Leon "Chew" Berry, Herschel Evans, Ben Webster, Joe Thomas, Don Byas, Ike Quebec, Paul Gonsalves, and Lucky Thompson.

Leon "Chew" Berry (who died in 1941) had a big tone and a power comparable to that of Hawkins, although the tone was not as velvety. Chew could play at an incredible speed, and when he did so, it was not for virtuosity's sake; he was really *creating* as well. But he excelled most of all on medium tempos. Here he swung as much as Hawkins at his best, and created the most ravishing melodic lines, developing his melodic ideas in such an intelligent, logical way that he really was telling a story. This aspect of Chew's style is the one that has been most imitated by his disciples, especially the excellent Julian Dash (from Erskine Hawkins' band), who seems to be the best tenor sax in Chew's style.

Herschel Evans (who died in 1939) has been considered by quite a number of musicians as the greatest tenor sax after Hawkins. Evans raved over Hawk's music, and it may be that his playing most reflects Hawkins' poignant accent, especially as his vibrato is the closest to Hawkins' vehement, dramatic vibrato. Herschel resembled the Hawkins of the second period. His phrases were more concise, less sinuous and complex than Hawkins'. Herschel was not interested in flashy and technical effects. He was a soul man, and a pure swingman, remarkable for his impetuosity, his indomitable ardor.

Ben Webster was most influenced by Hawkins' third and fourth manners. Much more than either Chew or Herschel, Ben Webster could be mistaken for Hawkins at first hearing. Ben is the closest to Hawk in tone (which has the same "velvet" quality) and musical breathing. His vibrato also resembles Hawkins', and he sometimes builds his solos with the same kind of phrases. But he also has been influenced by Benny Carter and has a very recognizable tender, suave accent in some of his solos on slow tempos. Ben Webster is a little uneven, but when he is right he is one of the greatest tenor players.

Joe Thomas (not to be confused with the trumpet player of the same name) gained his fame during his many years in Jimmie Lunceford's orchestra. He does not use subtle, complex phrases like most of the abovementioned musicians, but his straightforward style is very effective because he tells a story with sober, concise phrases, and he swings them. Besides, he plays the blues as few tenor saxists do, and he has a beautiful, moving tone which sounds almost like the human voice.

Don Byas, in his early days, sounded very much like Herschel Evans, whom he greatly admired. Later, Hawkins' influence became predominant, and few tenor saxists have sounded so much like Hawkins as the Don Byas of the mid-forties (they were mistaken one for the other in some of the records they made together at that time: Cozy Cole's Continental and the sax quartets made for Keynote-Mercury). Don's tone, round and full, has the "velvety" quality of Hawk's. He is an amazingly fast player and uses chord changes with a wonderful musicianship. He is a master at stating a melody.

Ike Quebec recalls Hawkins by the power and impetuosity of his playing, also by his vehement accent. He is great on slow blues and usually expresses himself with simple phrases which lend themselves to a great swing.

Paul Gonsalves is about the best among the younger Hawkins followers. He has almost everything: a warm, velvet tone, a lot of soul which deeply moves the listener, an exceptional technique, and an invention which surpasses that of most saxophone players. The richest and most unexpected ideas just flow in his solos. He is one of the most creative of the musicians of his generation (those born around 1920).

In Lucky Thompson's playing, the influence of Don Byas and of Ben Webster blends with that of Coleman Hawkins. In his ideas, his style of phrasing, Lucky Thompson leans toward Byas owing to his accuracy in using chord changes in order to build very intriguing solos. But his "feeling," the soul of his playing, is nearer to Hawkins and Ben Webster's musical spirit.

Next to Hawkins, the man who had the biggest influence on tenor is Lester Young (died in 1959). Although in his formative years Lester was influenced by Coleman Hawkins, he soon developed an entirely different and very original style of playing, almost opposite to that of Hawkins. Lester's tone is small and does not give that impression of warmth, color, and richness that one gets from listening to men like Hawkins, Webster, and Byas; yet Lester's tone and way of phrasing combine so well as to give his music a fascinating charm which is difficult to put in words. Lester is not a powerful musician but he is not sweet; he swings not forcefully but intensely, thanks to the touchy rhythmic variations and the subtle, incessant contrasts of his musical setting. There is something dreamy about Lester, a nonchalant accent in the execution which makes his music seem as if it were spoken confidentially to each of his listeners. His melodic invention is so vast that there always is something unforeseen in his improvisations. In fact one might speak of the "Lester mood," unique in jazz music. Lester Young probably stands as the strongest personality among tenor saxists, along with Coleman Hawkins, Herschel Evans, and Chew Berry.

Although he became well known in 1936–1937, as one of the

featured soloists with Count Basie's orchestra, it was only in the early forties that Lester Young's influence became important and that he started to have many followers.

However, none of Lester's disciples has become a first-class tenor sax comparable to Ben Webster, Chew Berry, Paul Gonsalves, or other Hawkins disciples. The best are Paul Quinichette, the closest to Lester, who is excellent when inspired but is rather uneven; Gene Ammons, who imitated Lester more freely and plays more vigorously; Dexter Gordon, uneven but capable; Wardell Gray, Stan Getz, and Allen Eager.

In fact, the best of Lester's influence is not to be found in his direct disciples but in other musicians who combined elements of his style with that of other great tenor players. We will meet them later.

Next to Hawkins and Lester Young, the most influential tenor man has been Herschel Evans, despite his premature death.

Buddy Tate is the greatest tenor sax in the Herschel Evans tradition (whom he followed in Count Basie's band). He uses simple, straightforward melodic lines as Herschel used to do, he has a strong, full tone, and probably he is the greatest of all tenor saxists when it comes to playing the blues—the pure, unadulterated blues. He is not interested in technical skill and dazzling effects but concentrates on swinging all the time as very few sax players can do. Because he does not strive for effects and does not try to show off, he has been disdained by so-called jazz critics who, in fact, know very little about this music or judge it by other musical standards; otherwise they would feel and admire Buddy Tate's terrific swing. The truth is that Tate is a pure jazzman, and of the best kind.

Another great tenor sax player who got his inspiration from Herschel Evans is Illinois Jacquet. In too many minds Jacquet is but a screaming, honking tenor sax. He did this sort of thing only for commercial purposes. Most of the time he did not play at all like that, and I think he has not been doing it for years now. The real Illinois Jacquet is a musician full of ideas and sensitiveness, one of the most creative tenor players that ever was. There is a lot of Herschel Evans' accent in Jacquet's playing, even more than there is in Buddy Tate's, but Illinois Jacquet often uses more complex melodic lines and chord changes than Evans or Tate. Moreover, he has taken some phrases from Lester Young's style, and some from Coleman Hawkins' too, and has integrated beautifully the three styles within his own strong personality.

Arnett Cobb, one of the most powerful men who ever blew a tenor saxophone, expresses himself in a style which at times recalls Jacquet but has a little more of Hawkins in it, a little less of Evans. He has a terrific "punch" and drive but, contrary to what some people think, he also has a great musicianship and invention. He really makes his horn "talk" in a sort of "preaching" style full of expressiveness.

Jesse Powell is another fine swingman who has some of the Herschel Evans feeling. He never plays unnecessary notes but gets the most out of his sober, well-built phrases.

Red Prysock, a musician full of bite and vigor, roughly resembles Arnett Cobb and Jacquet, although he inclines a little more toward Lester Young.

There are some other first-class tenor sax players whom I have not yet mentioned because they are not as easy to classify. Such is the case of Gene Sedric, who started to play at about the same time as Hawkins and who is one of very rare tenor saxists not to have been influenced by Hawk. Sedric is a very genuine musician. He does not seek for fast or "pretty" phrases but has a style of his own and plays phrases that one is not likely to hear from other saxophonists. Since he joins to his inventive spirit an extremely vigorous attack and execution, the minute he starts blowing he swings irresistibly.

Budd Johnson should be much better known than he is. In the early thirties, he played somewhat like the Hawkins of 1930. Later, he put several of Lester Young's ideas and riffs into his playing. But most of all he was influenced by Louis Armstrong, this being easily noticeable when he plays on slow tempos with a wonderful lyricism. However, Budd Johnson always kept a marked personality. He is a powerful player, capable of swinging a whole band by his dynamic outbursts; he can play simple and telling solos; he can play fast phrases and nice changes without losing his natural drive; and he can play the blues, too. It should be mentioned that Budd Johnson is also a first-class alto soloist.

A younger musician, Eddie "Lockjaw" Davis, also must be numbered among the greatest tenor players. Eddie Davis, by reason of his beautiful, velvet tone, his warm and vibrant accent, belongs to the Hawkins-Webster school of blowing. His solos often include phrases that recall these two musicians, and Don Byas as well. Eddie Davis also uses some of Lester Young's riffs. But he has a way all his own of setting the phrases and then cutting them abruptly that gives his playing a protrusive dynamism and makes it swing to the utmost. This is so highly personal that it would make Eddie Davis recognizable among dozens of tenors. And he has a vast imagination, which seems never to let him down.

Unlike Eddie Davis, Jay Peters is not known as he should be. He has combined the Herschel Evans style with Lester Young's, which makes him sound at times like the tenor saxists of the Cobb-Jacquet type. His solos are full of soul and invention and he is swinging all the time. Unfortunately, he has not yet been given a real chance on records.

Hal Singer is another fine swingman, a powerful musician who happily combined the styles of Hawkins, Byas, and Lester.

Jimmy Forrest is a versatile man, capable of playing hard, biting tenor and also of playing with a lot of speed without losing any swing. He has an exceptional command of his instrument, and he has a lot of ideas, including very humorous ones.

George Kelly, another tenor sax who is not half as well known as he should be (and a good arranger too), has few peers when it comes to stating a melody; he does it with some of that Louis Armstrong taste and feeling which makes any tune click. His playing is full of flame and impetuosity, and he belongs to that category of musicians for whom swinging is the main thing.

John Hardee is a powerful and vehement tenor sax, who especially shines in the exuberant performances and in the blues; unfortunately, it seems that he quit playing owing to lack of recognition—which, if true, would be a shame.

Al Sears is a very individual player with a strong, firm tone, owing nothing to the Hawkins or to the Young school. He is a versatile musician who sometimes expresses himself through sinuous, legato phrases, sometimes through short, staccato sequences powerfully performed. He makes an excellent use of contrasts.

Another tenor sax to use staccato effects to good advantage is Eddie Chamblee, who gets out of them and other devices plenty of swing. He plays the blues remarkably.

A musician who, chronologically, should have been mentioned earlier, as he was one of the first great tenor players, is Cecil Scott (already mentioned among the clarinetists), who started playing like the Coleman Hawkins of the first period and with almost as much drive! He later used on tenor a style more like his clarinet style, including a few riffs that he got from Jimmie Noone. He is a powerful, enthusiastic player who, nowadays, sounds just as young and incisive as in his early years. And it is refreshing to listen to a tenor sax who plays so differently from all the others.

Another excellent old-timer is Frank "Big Boy" Goodie (who also plays the clarinet). He is not much known in the States because he spent most of his life in Europe and South America. He uses long, mobile phrases full of melody and is a first-class blues player.

Owing to the vogue of the instrument since the mid-thirties, there have been so many good tenor sax players that there still remain quite a few musicians worth mentioning: Bob "Little Sax" Crowder, who creates phrases in the Chew Berry vein; Prince Robinson, from the old school, who sounds at times as Hawkins used to; Happy Cauldwell, another good old-timer; Bob Carroll, who knew how to play simply and effectively; Paul Bascomb, a Chew disciple; George Clarke, who plays in an easy, sober way; Dick Wilson, who had a beautiful tone and could have become one of the best if he had not died young; Bob Dorsey, Ernie Powell, Morris Lane, Clifford Scott, Percy France, Stafford Simon, Frank Wess, Frank Foster, Bumps Myers, Sam "The Man" Taylor, Candy Johnson, Gene Morris, Freddie Williams, Lem Johnson, John Sparrow, Vernon Story, Johnny Board, Count Hastings, Buddy Floyd, Eric Dixon, Billy Mitchell, Sheldon Powell, Elwyn Fraser, Dave Young, Teddy McRae, Joe Garland, Castor McCord,

Albert Washington, Antonio Cosey, Benny Waters, Davey Jones, Greely Walton, Fletcher Allen, Johnny Russell; and a very gifted newcomer called Harold Ashby.

There is some fine new talent among the youngest colored tenor saxists, some vigorous and straightforward musicians such as Noble Watts, King Curtis, Plas Johnson, whose virile, rocking playing is a welcome reaction against the emasculate, lugubrious sounds of "cool" and "progressive" saxists who have lost almost all contact with jazz. David Newman (from Ray Charles' band) is another youngster who can play very well in the right surroundings. Another gifted young tenor is Benny Golson, possessor of a warm tone, who unfortunately wastes most of his time playing with progressive musicians whose unswinging music does not fit his style.

Among the white tenor saxists are to be cited Bud Freeman, Eddie Miller, Babe Rusin, Herbie Haymer, Vido Musso, Charlie Barnet, and Sam Margolis. But the best white tenor saxist is a Frenchman, Alix Combelle, who got his inspiration from Coleman Hawkins and Chew Berry. Combelle has a big, round tone and a tremendous power of expression. He assimilated the idiom of jazz so perfectly that he sounds exactly like the great colored sax players and swings as much as they do.

France has produced another first-class tenor sax, Guy Lafitte, who excels on slow tempos, where he sounds somewhere between Herschel Evans and Don Byas.

The baritone saxophone is much less used than the alto and tenor, especially for solos. There has been only one great soloist on the baritone sax: Harry Carney, from Duke Ellington's band, who gets an impressive, big, yet mellow sound out of that difficult instrument. He plays it with an amazing suppleness, swings it as easily as if it were a tenor or an alto. Some people were foolish enough to rate Gerry Mulligan above Harry Carney: it is laughable. Next to Harry Carney, the best baritone player undoubtedly is Heywood Henry (also a clarinetist), a long time standout of Erskine Hawkins' band. Another good one is Charlie Fowlkes.

9 the violinists

There are few great jazz violinists, for the violin is an instrument which is rarely employed in jazz.

The best of the older ones is Eddie South, a musician of extraordinary gifts. His incredible melodic invention and a superb technique allow him to execute the most subtle and intricate phrases with a total abandon and perfect ease. His tone is of a beauty and purity comparable to that of the best classic violinists. And more than any other jazz violinist he makes his instrument sing.

Another great Negro violinist of the same era is Juice Wilson. Not much of his work can be heard on records because after having been quite active in the jazz world until 1930 he left the States and went to live in Malta and other countries, where he recorded no more. His playing has a somber accent, yet is very melodious, and he swings a great deal.

One of the most famous Negro violinists now active is Stuff Smith. His style is quite in opposition to that of Eddie South. Stuff uses an electric amplifier and treats his violin with an extraordinary forcefulness, thus drawing from a fiddle sounds which often recall the effects of wind instruments. His melodic invention leads him to embroider his music with exuberant phrases, full of unexpected notes, daring discoveries, and terrific glissandos. He can play a melody note for note and make it sing beautifully, with an attractive subdued swing, then get into a sort of "fury" at most unexpected moments and swing the number with a fire and passion that led Mezzrow rightly to call Stuff Smith "the mad genius of the jazz violin."

Ray Nance, the trumpet player, when he plays the violin resembles Stuff Smith—with less fury. He has created a technique of the fiddle all his own, unorthodox but very effective. He makes a generous and excellent use of inflections and glissandos, puts into his variations humor as well as emotion, and always pleases by his spontaneity and unexpected ideas.

Another violinist who should be mentioned is Darnell Howard, who is the oldest of all. It is said that he influenced Eddie South. Though he has many indisputable qualities, he has divided his time for many years between the violin, the alto saxophone, and the clarinet—which can only mean that he has not given all that he might to the violin. The same may be said for Edgar Sampson, who has proven himself to have real gifts as a violinist; and also for Ray Perry, who died too young.

The principal white violinists are Joe Venuti and a Frenchman, Stéphane Grappelly.

Venuti's style reminds one of Eddie South, but he has less melody, less ease and imagination. His tone has none of Eddie South's tenderness, and his execution and vibrato have much less sensitiveness. Moreover, Venuti is very uneven. Though he is capable of improvising good choruses, his solos are frequently filled with tiresome clichés and acrobatic tricks, such as the inevitable high notes which appear here and there in almost all his choruses.

I greatly prefer Stéphane Grappelly—his style is purer, his melodic invention and sensitiveness are greater. Grappelly has been abundantly and very happily inspired by Louis Armstrong. His style is a model of equilibrium and intelligence. He swings with directness and intensity, frequently recalling the New Orleans musicians period. His sense of ensemble work is very fine.

Another white French violinist should be mentioned: Michel Warlop (who died in 1947), who had incontestable gifts, notably in his charming melodic ideas.

10 the pianists

Since the piano was not used in the first jazz orchestras, there is only one famous New Orleans pianist, Jelly Roll Morton (who died in 1941). He can be considered chronologically as the first great jazz pianist, and many were influenced by him.

Jelly Roll's style is typically New Orleans. His splendidly constructed phrases strikingly recall the phrases of the great New Orleans trumpets. The passion in Jelly Roll's music is tempered by an airy touch, and his beautiful feeling for melodic curves and flourishing lines gives his playing a delicious freshness revealing an ingenuous and most moving sensitivity. Few jazz pianists are as melodious as Jelly Roll, but owing to certain traces of ragtime in his playing, his music was dismissed by some as "dated." The truth is that the beauty of his discoveries is amazing and that he swings with a typical New Orleans beat.

There was also in New Orleans a pianist older than Jelly Roll Morton, who was reputed excellent, Tony Jackson, but he died without having been recorded so his music is lost forever.

The jazz pianists can be divided into two principal categories. The first treats the piano in a very orchestral manner. By playing with very full harmonies the pianist makes the piano a miniature orchestra. The second group, on the other hand, treats the piano as a solo instrument. In the right hand the pianist embroiders amply in a fashion more melodic than harmonic, using phrases similar to those of the trumpets and saxophones. Such musicians as James P. Johnson, Fats Waller, and Willie "The Lion" Smith belong to the first category; Earl Hines and Teddy Wilson belong to the second.

An odd thing to note is the fact that musicians of corpulence seem as a rule to belong to the first category, while the skinny musicians generally belong to the second. If it isn't done too systematically, one can divide jazz pianists into "fat" and "thin." The first play with a comfortable and placid power, making the piano roar with its orchestral possibilities. This is the muscle style. The second, on the contrary, play with their nerves. Their solos, instead of rolling out in a single sweep, are filled with unexpected and uneven passages. Their style is less robust and more incisive.

James P. Johnson and Willie "The Lion" Smith are the earliest pianists of importance belonging to the first category— and two of the greatest pianists jazz has ever known.

James P. Johnson (who died in 1955) had some of his inspiration from Lucky Roberts, perhaps the best of the early ragtime pianists. Although passionate and powerful, James P. Johnson's playing is stamped with a profound sensibility and an extreme melodic grace. He is the perfect example of the "stride" pianist. With the left hand, he masterfully pounds his basses on the strong beat. This method of stressing the strong beat with a powerful bass is common to the "fat" pianists; they enjoy getting a dynamic, "round" sound out of that bass. James P. Johnson was the composer of many good numbers, and this inventiveness also shows in his improvisations at the piano. He also was a perfect accompanist and a wonderful sender for many blues singers.

James P. Johnson had a tremendous influence on the other pianists of the orchestral type. One of his disciples was the famous Thomas Waller (nicknamed "Fats" for 285 pounds of obvious reasons) who died in 1943. Fats' playing so recalls that of his master that occasionally it seems almost identical. Nevertheless there are great differences between these two marvelous musicians. Though Fats is not superior to James P. as a soloist, he surpasses Johnson as a pianist in orchestra work. Fats' tempo seems immutable. His force, suppleness, and solidity stand up against everything. He is one of the rare musicians who never hurry and never slow down. His harmonic and rhythmic foundation is so sure and comfortable, his playing is so simple and clear, that all musicians who play with him feel completely at ease in improvising. For this incomparable pianist seems, in some way, to carry them along. Moreover Fats swings an entire orchestra. In fact I believe that he is the most perfect orchestral pianist jazz has ever known.

Fats is also a great soloist, quite the equal of any other. He plays the blues magnificently, and in this even surpasses James P. Johnson who is withal a fine blues player. Moreover—and this shows what a complete pianist Fats is—he can accommodate himself to the most banal themes and vulgar melodies better than any other pianist. By a few light touches he so transfigures such music that the listener is led to believe that he is hearing the most delightful melodies. Fats has a great love and understanding of melody which permit him to sense instantly what has to be done to give life to a mediocre number. And at the same time he has a sense of humor, a constant good spirit and insouciance which give his music a savory lightness and a spiritual tone and make it different from that of all other jazz musicians. Throughout every one of his choruses one feels his irresistible *joie de vivre*. He seems to love to play the piano, and needs only to be seated before his instrument to feel happy and want to play. There, he seeems to talk to his listeners. Unlike most musicians, he is not subject to heights and depths. One feels that he is constantly overflowing with good health and life; his joyous and lively music is a veritable tonic for the listener.

Many people, for whom musical grandeur is synonymous with tearful pathos, have not grasped Fats' genius and assume that his music lacks profundity. As if sad music were the only profound music! Actually people who criticize Fats only prove that their reaction to music is much too sentimental. They have no liking for Fats because his music does not evoke defined sentiments for them. In fact, Fats' music is *white*; it is without pretension. And because of that it is beautiful and pure. Fats is the perfect antidote to the musician or composer who pretends through his music to carry to the listener I hardly know what metaphysical revelation. Fats does not pretend to reveal anything. But no other musician has been able to reveal as he has, that music is not a complicated and methodical art, as those who are smothered under their blanket of culture would have it, but is on the contrary a simple cry of love and of relaxation coming from the heart of man—a cry one gives because one cannot do otherwise, a feeling that must come out.

But this ease and good humor do not prevent Fats from being profoundly moving. In his blues, for example, he moves you, not with the impetuosity of Louis Armstrong, but with his calm and ease which never fail to transport the listener.

Moreover Fats' playing is so well based and *weighted*, yet completely easy, that one never tires of it. His left hand always finds the proper notes and functions with an absolute precision. He gives an impression of a total *security* which is indeed one of his greatest qualities. Even when he breaks loose in the fast tempos and plays with a power, which is persuasive rather than aggressive, he never loses his calm or assurance. His basses are of a terrific strength; he doesn't merely touch the keys but seems to *bear down* on them with such force that they are pressed into the piano. Truly it is impossible to swing more than he.

Likewise Fats plays the organ superbly. He never was equalled on this instrument, as far as playing jazz is concerned. Here his style is like his piano style; we find again all the same qualities of ease and precision, and his same formidable bass part. Fats is a power. Outside of Louis Armstrong I think that his personality is the most dynamic in all jazz.

Another great pianist of the same school which produced James P. Johnson, and Fats, is Willie Smith who was nicknamed "The Lion" because of the courage he showed in France during the war of 1914–1918. Though he reminds one of Fats and James P. in his manner of playing basses and in certain phrases in his right hand, Willie Smith cannot for an instant be confused with them or with any other pianist. His extraordinarily original style gives him a unique place among jazz musicians.

His melodic ideas are often reminiscent of certain celebrated classic musicians, especially the harpsichord composers of the eighteenth century such as Daquin. He prefers motifs and phrases of charming contours, with much more graceful lines than are customary in jazz. What is striking in his music is his fresh and tender accent which reminds one at times of Schumann. The titles of some of his compositions, *Echoes of Spring, Morning Air,* and *Rippling Waters* suggest in themselves the atmosphere of his music. The harmonies used by Willie Smith are frequently different from the usual jazz harmonies; they are richer and more unusual. Here again his work recalls certain classic composers. Because of this Willie Smith's music is generally appreciated by many who do not understand jazz. However it would be a mistake to assume from this that "The Lion's" style is not an authentic jazz music. His most original creations always have the typical jazz flavor. He swings just as much as Fats Waller and James P. Johnson, with the same terrific power and drive. "The Lion" can take a simple riff, repeat it several times, and swing it more and more. He also is one of the best orchestral pianists jazz has known. It is a joy for the ear to follow the intelligent progression of his sensitive and powerful bass behind the solos and the orchestral ensembles.

Another great pianist of the same brand is Teddy Weatherford (died in 1945), who originated in the South. He is little known because he left the United States in 1926 and never returned, preferring to live in Asia, and in China especially. Though his playing is less polished and more brutal than that of Fats Waller or Willie Smith, it is powerful and impetuous. Here again the solid left hand must be admired. And in his blues, Teddy Weatherford has that same expansive nostalgia which is in general typical only of the musicians from the South.

Other good pianists of the same school are Eubie Blake (born in 1883), who might well have been the first "stride" pianist of a high standard[1]; Cliff Jackson, who employs mobile basses of a rare power; Joe Turner, whose style strikingly resembles both Fats Waller's and James P. Johnson's; Hank Duncan, who sounds at times somewhat like Willie "The Lion" Smith; Don Frye, simple and melodious; Freddie John-

[1] It is ironical to note that Eubie Blake had to wait until the age of 75 years to make his first solo record, *The Wizard of the Ragtime Piano* (Fox LP 3003), but it was worth recording him even at that age: his music sounds as fresh and swinging as that of a young man.

son, mostly a good band pianist; Pat Flowers, a close imitator of Fats Waller; and Claude Hopkins, the best of them, who is not only an excellent "stride" pianist but has developed a pretty melodic style, full of the most varied ideas.

Duke Ellington is more famous as a band leader, composer, and arranger than as a pianist. However, his musical genius is as much in evidence when he plays piano as in the other spheres of his activity. Duke started playing the typical "stride" piano of Fats Waller-James P. Johnson, and was even more influenced by Willie "The Lion" (to whom he even dedicated one of his orchestral works: *Portrait of The Lion*), whose melodic grace and musical pulsation are often recalled in Duke's piano choruses. As years went by, Duke developed a highly original piano style, a very percussive and "orchestral" style, so full of unforeseen, unexpected harmonic and rhythmic ideas that it completely sweeps out the so-called "modern" or "progressive" pianists—the more so since Duke is really telling a story when playing his complex variations, while the others are telling no story at all. Besides, Duke's touch on the keyboard, the beautiful way he makes the instrument *sound* is unique, and anyone familiar with Duke Ellington's playing can recognize him from among all other pianists just by the way he hits a couple of chords.

Earl Hines is by far the best of the "thin" pianists, and one of the most creative musicians in the history of jazz.

Earl Hines practices what is called the "trumpet-piano" style. With his right hand, and by octaves, he creates melodic variations of a style like that usually employed by the trumpet; while his left hand provides the role of the rhythm section. He took his inspiration from Louis Armstrong—so much so that he has often created melodic lines which one would swear had come from the brain of Louis Armstrong, as for instance in his piano solo 57 *Varieties*. In this record it would be easy to imagine Louis Armstrong's trumpet playing the phrases which are executed by Earl Hines with his right hand.

But this does not prevent Earl Hines from standing as a great personality. His playing in the left hand is really astonishing. Sometimes he merely furnishes an even tempo, but at other times he throws himself into indescribable rhythmic fantasies. For example, while the right hand is playing some vertiginous phrase, his left will stop for a moment, then unexpectedly begin to play with violence one or several chords on the counterbeat. Earl Hines employs amazing rhythmic combinations which demand an extraordinary independence of the two hands. These rhythmic interruptions and confusions of parts are sometimes so prolonged that one wonders if Hines will be able to escape. But suddenly he will fall back on the regular rhythm and start off again with power. This produces a most amazing contrast.

During the course of the last few years the style of this great pianist has evolved immensely. Now his phrases only recall those of Louis rather incidentally. His playing has become more harmonious and fuller. His rhythmic jumps and vertiginous phrasing have become even more fantastic. At the same time I am persuaded that he now has a greater freedom and an even stronger personality than earlier. His inspiration has remained as fresh and his flights as magnificent as in the past. Listening to him today, one has more than ever the impression of a roaring torrent and an indomitable force which beats its way through the most incredible difficulties. It would be impossible to measure the vastness of his imagination, for his ideas seem inexhaustible and continually surprising by their originality. Without any doubt Earl Hines is one of the greatest creative geniuses jazz has produced.

His imitators are numberless. The musician who has achieved the closest resemblance is probably Zinky Cohn. Though Cohn's harmonic play is generally fuller, he has none of the supreme ease and sparkling genius characteristic of Earl Hines.

Other good followers of Earl Hines are Buck Washington (from the "Buck and Bubbles" dance team—Buck died in 1955), William Barbee, Casino Simpson, Burroughs Lovingood, Horace Henderson (Fletcher's brother), Alex Hill (who was an excellent arranger, too), and Garnet Clark (who died in 1938), who was to become one of the best. Those musicians were inspired by the Earl Hines style of the late twenties. Billy Kyle and Eddie Heywood, Jr., were influenced by the Hines of the thirties. Billy Kyle has a nice, percussive touch and—when at his best—flowing melodic ideas. Eddie Heywood is very gifted too, but he spent much of his time playing a rather commercialized kind of jazz.

The celebrated Nat "King" Cole is the greatest of the piano players who took their inspiration from Earl Hines. He does not have Earl's leonine touch but sometimes uses whipping punctuations with the left hand which recall, if not literally, the spirit of Earl's music. There are fewer contrasts in King Cole's playing than in Earl's, and the pulse is quite different. While Earl's swing comes from a bewildering contrast between his total ease and indomitable energy, King Cole's swing remains constantly obsessive, apparently tense and yet relaxed. He is most inventive, using more altered notes than Earl does, and there is a lot of wit in his music. King Cole's playing also shows at times the influence of another pianist: Art Tatum.

Art Tatum's case is unique among jazz pianists. He is the most amazing virtuoso of them all, and his instrumental technique even matches that of the greatest "classical" pianists.

But far from being a mere virtuoso, Tatum is a creative artist of the highest class. When improvising, his mind works so fast, he has so many ideas at a time that it seems that his fingers, unbelievably fast as they are, will not be able to move fast enough! Even good musicians had a hard time keeping up with him. Everett Barksdale, a guitarist who often played with Tatum, once said: "If you start on a solo idea, Tatum won't go across you. His reflexes are so fast that he'll feel what you're going to do and—if you're not careful—you'll find by the time you get there he's there ahead of you."[2] Art Tatum could play a tune without altering the melody and yet make an entirely new piece out of it by the harmonies—all his own and always beautiful—that he would build the melody on.

Rhythmically, too, Tatum had fantastic ideas. His hands would be working in entirely contrary motions, or he would play half a chorus off tempo—at least it would sound so, but if you really followed what he was doing, you would discover that the tempo was there all right, only subdued, and that Tatum had not missed a beat. Then, all of a sudden, he would start "striding" for eight or sixteen bars, with a power and swing equal to anyone!

Stylistically, Art Tatum was influenced by James P. Johnson and Fats Waller, and he also incorporated in his playing some of Earl Hines' trumpet-style phrases at the right hand, using the biting and incisive Hines attack. The deepest influence, though, is that of Fats Waller—the spirit of it more than something literal. The way Art Tatum makes a melody "sing" has something in common with Fats. But Tatum is so original that most of the time his solos have a sound, an accent that is to be found nowhere else in jazz music. To sum up, Art Tatum is one of the few geniuses jazz has produced.

[2] *Melody Maker*, August 11, 1956, p. 3.

Teddy Wilson, another pianist influenced by Earl Hines, has a wonderful musicianship and a remarkable instrumental technique. His solos are full of ideas; few jazz pianists are as inventive. Yet his sallies are smothered to some degree by a perhaps too "refined" touch which has much in common with that of the "classical" pianists; and his playing, lacking in contrasts, has not the power, the dynamic quality of Earl Hines'. However, his left-hand chords, well placed and intriguing, give his solos an attractive touch. Also influenced by Art Tatum, Teddy Wilson has a rich, pretty, harmonic idiom which he uses to best advantage on slow and moderate tempos.

During the late thirties and early forties Teddy Wilson had considerable influence on younger pianists—for instance Clyde Hart, Sonny White, Ram Ramirez, James Sherman, Dave Rivera, Ellis Larkins, and Sammy Benskin. The influence was not always a good one, as most of Teddy Wilson's followers tried to get his "refined" touch, but several have proved to be very talented musicians, especially Sonny White, who finally came back to a more biting touch and more vigorous playing.

One of the greatest pianists to have come up during the thirties is William "Count" Basie. In his early years, Count Basie was a powerful stride pianist whose style was formed under the influence of Fats Waller more than anybody else. Soon Basie added a touch of Earl Hines' "trumpet-piano" style to his playing, sounding alternately in the course of one chorus like Earl and like Fats. It was during the late thirties that Basie developed fully such an original style that he can be easily distinguished from thousands of other pianists. With the right hand he plays brief phrases, built on a few notes and well detached from one another. As for the left hand, either it remains silent (with the guitar and string bass supplying the harmonic and rhythmic part), or it plays several chords made of a few

notes and drily introduced here and there at the most unexpected intervals. Basie has a way of hitting the keys that gives
an effect at the same time muffled and clear-cut—and that
makes his solos jump lively. His way of swinging rests on a
rhythmic vividness constantly on the alert, full of unexpected
bounces: he introduces a riff, repeats it, but by the time the listener gets accustomed and waits for a new repetition, Basie
stirs him with the most unforeseen chord, suddenly interrupt-
ing the normal flow and bringing up a perfectly well-intro-
duced new development. All this makes Basie a very great
soloist as well as one of the best orchestral pianists; and he plays
the blues better than almost any other jazz pianist. Count
Basie is also a wonderful organist, probably the next best to
Fats Waller.

Basie has been widely imitated. But instead of having a lot
of direct disciples like a Hines or a Wilson, he gave some of
his most typical effects to pianists practicing other styles. In
other words, some Basie-isms became an integral part of the
jazz idiom, just as had been the case with Louis Armstrong's
familiar turns a few years before.

Nonetheless, Basie's style was taken as a basis by some
younger pianists, the two best being Sir Charles Thompson, a
very gifted musician with a rare sense of melody and swing; and
Nat Pierce, a white pianist who plays the blues as few white
musicians have succeeded in doing.

Shortly after 1940 a new piano style was originated by Milton Buckner in Lionel Hampton's band. It soon was to be
called "block-chords" or "locked-hands" style: it consisted of
playing packs of chords with both hands simultaneously, instead of the left hand playing its part separately, as it had always done; thus, the piano sounded as if it were a melodic section in the band. Milton Buckner being a wonderfully swing-

ing musician, he made the best out of that new way of expression, which he invented mostly because the small size of his hands did not allow him to play easily in the usual way. Later he became also a wonderful organist and succeeded in making the one instrument sound like a whole band.

Milton Buckner has been widely imitated, but nobody has ever swung in the "locked-hands" style as he did. In fact, most pianists used it as one of their ways of expression, not all the time. Such is the case with men like Oscar Peterson and Jimmy Jones, who, in fact, are heard to better advantage when they use the "locked-hands" style than when they express themselves otherwise.

After Buckner, the next great piano stylist to appear was Erroll Garner. Around the mid-forties, Garner reintroduced a vigorous, two-handed piano style into jazz, but a newly invented one. Garner is an innovator and he cannot be connected directly to any pianist before him. His playing is full and orchestral, like that of Fats Waller. Most of the time Garner plays the four beats with the left hand, hitting full chords like a guitar player. With the right hand he often delays notes or chords, thus giving an impression of intense swing. He has introduced harmonic ideas of his own, often audacious but always musical and beautiful. His formidable attack, his power of expression, his terrific drive, his vast imagination, and the beautiful way in which he states a melody—all these make him the greatest pianist of his generation (born around 1920).

The fifties saw the rise of two first-class young piano players: Ray Bryant, who got his inspiration from Art Tatum and Teddy Wilson, who has bite, invention, and taste, and who is a superb accompanist as well as soloist; and Ray Charles, whose percussive, soulful playing is solidly rooted in the blues as well as in church music, and who has great creative gifts for melody.

There are many other good piano players whom I have not yet had opportunity to mention. One of the best is Hank Jones, an accomplished musician with a real flair for pretty harmonies —and the only pianist who ever succeeded in soloing beautifully in the Tatum style. Ahmad Jamal is amazingly gifted. He can play complex and rich variations; and he can also create exciting choruses by playing just a few notes and using understatements. Other good pianists are Marlowe Morris, who also is one of the best jazz organists; the band leader Buddy Johnson, an accomplished piano player; Kenny Kersey, a swinging pianist with a Hines-like touch; Avery Parrish, whose *After Hours* with Erskine Hawkins' band is one of the greatest blues piano performances ever waxed; Bobby Henderson, who is rather on the Fats Waller side but has his own personality; Al Waslohn, a very swinging band pianist as well as a good soloist; Red Richards, a complete musician with a fine sense of melody; Garland Wilson, excellent blues pianist; Mary Lou Williams, one of the best female pianists, who gave her best during the first part of her career, before being influenced by "progressive" musicians; Fletcher Henderson, a solid band pianist and a good accompanist to singers; Jay McShann, especially good on the blues and when he uses the boogie-woogie style; Milton Sealey, a young Canadian pianist who can play splendidly in a sort of Waller-Garner style; Don Abney, a first-class accompanist; Sam Allen, who plays the blues very well; Herman Chittison, fast and brilliant; Sonny Thompson, Billy Taylor, Bill Doggett, Roy Johnson, Ace Harris, Arnold Jarvis, Fletcher Smith, George Rhodes, Cedric Haywood, Tommy Fulford, Don Kirkpatrick, Buster Wilson, Charles "Dizzy" Lewis, Clarence Profit, Eddie Wilcox, Cecil Gant,

Clarence Williams, Pearl Wright (a fine accompanist for singers), Lil Armstrong, Charlie Alexander, and Jimmy Blythe (one of the best of the old-time pianists).

Bud Powell started as a very good jazz pianist, when he was in Cootie Williams' band, but he soon switched to bop.

Among the white pianists, the good early ones are Joe Sullivan and Jess Stacy, but the best, now, are John Guarnieri, who integrated very well in his playing elements of Hines, Waller, and Basie; Ralph Sutton, a good stride pianist from the Fats Waller-Willie "The Lion" Smith school; Lennie Felix, an Englishman who took his inspiration from Earl Hines; Claude Bolling, a Frenchman who plays alternately like Earl Hines and Duke Ellington; André Persiany, another Frenchman, who expresses himself very well in the Milton Buckner "block-chords" style. Others to be mentioned are Don Ewell, who plays like Jelly Roll Morton; Joe Bushkin, and Bob Lane.

Boogie-woogie pianists are too much apart to be compared with other pianists, as some musicians are great boogie pianists but can play nothing else. The main characteristic of that style lies in a permanent bass figure of a rolling nature (eight to the bar, most of the time). The boogie style is usually played on the twelve-bar blues, although it can be used on any kind of tune. It is an adaptation to the piano of some figures that the old blues guitarists played.

The greatest of all boogie-woogie pianists, Pine Top Smith, died very young (1929). The exquisite delicacy of his touch and the perfect suppleness of his execution give his playing a lightness seldom reached by other boogie pianists. Pine Top seems to skim over the keyboard and yet he swings in a powerful way. One of his compositions, *Pine Top's Boogie Woogie*, a well-known number, gave boogie style its name.

Jimmy Yancey (who died in 1951), one of the earliest

boogie pianists and strictly a blues man, was especially wonderful on the slow blues (which he did not always play in the boogie style). He had an unmistakable accent, deeply moving and nostalgic, peaceful and serene, and when caught by his special mood, one feels like listening to him for hours.

Sammy Price is another pianist of whom one never tires when he plays the blues. He also is a powerful boogie pianist, one of the best there ever was.

Pete Johnson, another of the greatest boogie-woogie men, is not by any means confined to the boogie. He can play powerful "stride piano" as well, in the best Fats Waller tradition, and is a first-class band pianist; in fact, Pete Johnson ranks among the best jazz pianists of all time, and it is a shame that he is regarded as such by connoisseurs only and not by the public.

Albert Ammons (who died in 1949) also was more than just a blues and boogie pianist, although he excelled in those specialties.

Other good exponents of the boogie style are Speckled Red, Ellsworth Liggett, Cow Cow Davenport, and Meade Lux Lewis. Among the younger players, Fats Domino is a terrific boogie pianist; and Camille Howard plays more boogie and blues than any other woman I have heard.

Little Brother Montgomery, from New Orleans, is also a first-class blues and boogie pianist, but he plays in a different way.

There remain some blues (and boogie) pianists of still another kind: the most primitive, who were accompanists of primitive blues singers or are blues singers themselves. They play crude, "in the alley" blues with a flavor similar to that of the blues-singing guitarists. The greatest of them is Joshua Altheimer (who died in 1940) who never made a record under his name but can be heard in many vocal records by Big Bill

Broonzy, Sonny Boy Williamson, Washboard Sam, Jazz Gillum, the Yas Yas Girl, and some others.

The greatest living blues pianist of the same type is Memphis Slim, and other first-class ones are Roosevelt Sykes, Otis Spann, Sunnyland Slim, Curtis Jones, Champion Jack Dupree.

A little less "primitive" but still in the pure old blues tradition, Big Maceo (who died in 1953) is one of the most powerful and swinging boogie pianists ever; his recording of *Chicago Breakdown* (RCA Victor) is a masterpiece in the boogie style. He has a fine disciple in Little Johnny Jones.

Bob Call and Eddie Boyd, next to Memphis Slim and Otis Spann, are about the greatest living "in the alley" blues pianists known to us through records. Bob Call has recorded the best slow blues piano solo I have ever had a chance to hear (*House Party Groove* by "Nature Boy" Brown, made around 1950 for the United label).

Although their playing has not as "low down" a flavor, Horace Malcolm, Simeon Henry, and "Black Bob" also are fine blues pianists; and so were Leroy Carr (who, although he died very young—1935—influenced many), Charlie Spand, and Blind John Davis.

Before this chapter closes, the best organ players should be mentioned. The organ, it must be observed, had not been used in jazz, with very few exceptions (Fats Waller and Count Basie being the only important ones), until the fifties. Despite the recent vogue of the instrument, there have been as yet but a few first-class organists. The greatest one is Wild Bill Davis, who swings the organ with unbelievable power and drive, and has wide imagination as well. The other top organists, besides Milton Buckner and Marlowe Morris who have already been mentioned, seem to be Doc Bagby, who swings plenty; the well-known Bill Doggett, who expresses himself in a concise, powerful style; Shirley Scott, who though uneven can do pretty things on the organ; and Jimmy Smith, when he wants to play in the jazz idiom.

11 the guitarists

Two very distinct factors must be considered in a guitarist, his accompaniment as a member of the rhythm section, and his work as a soloist. In fact a guitarist who is a remarkable soloist may not always be a satisfactory accompanist, and vice versa.

As a general rule the first Southern guitar players seemed to furnish a harmonic base that was more complete than the modern guitarists. Probably the absence of the piano in the New Orleans orchestras was the reason for this, obliging the guitars to provide a fuller and more accurate chording. The guitarists of today, on the other hand, can count on the piano for a solid base harmony.

From the viewpoint of orchestral support, the greatest guitarist of the first period of jazz seems to have been John St. Cyr, a New Orleans musician. As a matter of fact St. Cyr plays the banjo in most recordings, but since he plays it quite as well as the guitar, and since his banjo style is the same as his guitar style, there is no need to make a distinction.

St. Cyr almost continually marks the four beats with almost equal force, though he lightly accents the weak beats. This light accent causes his playing to swing enormously. He far surpasses all the other guitarists by the perfection of his supple and solid tempo. Likewise his harmonic play is full and sure, denoting his extraordinary ear.

The following anecdote is told about St. Cyr. One night he was playing in an orchestra in which Earl Hines was pianist. St. Cyr was very tired and was half asleep while he was playing. However this did not prevent him from striking the right chords without a false note. Earl Hines soon saw that St. Cyr was going to sleep. Therefore when Hines' turn came for a piano solo, he brusquely changed keys, and watched St. Cyr to see what would happen. Hardly had the first notes in the new key sounded, when St. Cyr jerked his head suddenly as though he had been slapped and began to play violently in the new key, while looking at Earl Hines with an air of defiance. Lucky indeed are the musicians who are supported in their improvising by such a guitarist. As a soloist St. Cyr has a sober and intelligent style, but it is not as unusual as his orchestral work.

Lonnie Johnson, on the contrary, is a marvelous soloist. He uses a single string rather than chords. Because of his brilliant instrumental technique, he plays with exceptional fluency. He is a fine blues player; at every instant his solos contain the expression and feeling so characteristic of the Southern musician. This expression is very sensitive not only in his phrases, which are typical of the New Orleans style, but even more in his powerful and sustained inflections which move the listener profoundly. But as an orchestral guitarist Lonnie Johnson is far from equalling St. Cyr, principally because he is not so strong from the harmonic point of view.

Next to these two musicians, must be mentioned Buddy Christian, whose playing strongly recalls St. Cyr; and Bud Scott, whose solos on one string are typical of the Southern guitarists and have a beautiful feeling of raciness. By using a single string in the lower registers of the guitar, he sometimes produces an unusual accompaniment which recalls the string bass. Most often of course he accompanies with chords in a way which is perhaps more robust than St. Cyr, but also drier and less supple.

The guitarists of the next generation play in a rather different style. In an orchestra they make their guitar ring on the strong beats, and allow their chords to resound for a long time on the first and third beat. One of the best of these musicians is probably Teddy Bunn. Particularly as a soloist he is one of the greatest guitar players of this period. His solos are played with one string, and have a suppleness and fine sensitivity. His ideas are many. When Teddy Bunn interprets the blues in a slow tempo, he plays with a purity and a feeling reminiscent of the New Orleans guitars.

Leonard Ware can be placed along with Teddy Bunn. These two musicians have played together frequently and seem to have influenced one another. Leonard Ware has been one of the first guitarists to use an electric amplifier. He is a very inventive musician.

Another remarkable musician is Albert Casey. He has probably achieved the best results from the system of making the guitar ring on the strong beats. His resonance and the singing quality of his chords are a joy to the ear. In solo work, when he does not use the single string style, he proceeds with chords in such a way that the succession of chords reveals a very lovely melody. His improvisation is always sober and intelligent, and the structure of his phrases recalls the great days when jazz was in its purest form.

Although Bernard Addison retains the system of playing chords on the strong beat and allowing a prolonged resonance, he uses one string abundantly in his solos, and even sometimes in orchestral ensembles. He has a fine technique and has proven to have much imagination.

A guitarist who surpasses, from many points of view, all

those just discussed, is Django Reinhardt, a gypsy born in a
wagon on the France-Belgium border and who died in Fon-
tainebleau in 1953.

Django is an unusual personality in the world of jazz. Because of his gypsy origins his musical temperament is very
different from that of other musicians; yet he expresses himself
in the true jazz idiom, which he assimilated perfectly. If his
playing may at times have little in common with the Negro
guitarists, it is because he had a very different guitar technique,
and his many original ideas prevent his phrases from ever recalling those of other guitarists.

As an orchestral guitarist, Django plays with a solid and
steady tempo. In fact one would search in vain among the
Negroes for a guitarist who could surpass him. He often accents the counterbeat in a strong and cutting manner, and
from time to time he doubles his strokes and swings in a fashion which galvanizes the other musicians. At other times he
accents the strong beats, and allows his chords to resound. His
playing is, as we can see, astonishingly varied. He is not content, like most guitarists, to furnish a mere rhythmic support
and regular harmony. Instead, during the breaks, or sometimes
at the most unforeseen moment, he will start off on an audacious improvisation, using a succession of chords in a broken
rhythm suggesting the breaks of the great drummers. His accompaniment is so fascinating that one is sometimes tempted
to follow it with more interest than the solo part itself! But it
should not be assumed from this that Django plays for himself
alone, without concern for the musicians he is accompanying.
On the contrary, he furnishes a marvelous support and inspires
the musicians by his harmonic and rhythmic discoveries. With
this tremolo or that chord, brusquely accented, he provides a
whip to the musician who is improvising. As a matter of fact

the greatest Negro musicians were avid to play with him. To fully appreciate his genius one must listen to his accompaniment of the Negro violinist, Eddie South, in records such as *Eddie's Blues, Sweet Georgia Brown, Somebody Loves Me,* and *I Can't Believe that You're in Love with Me.*

If Django is extraordinary as an orchestral guitarist, what can one say of him as a soloist! First of all his instrumental technique, vastly superior to that of all other jazz guitarists (although he practically never played with more than three fingers of his left hand since the other two were burned in an accident which obliged him to invent a technique all of his own), permitted him to play with inconceivable velocity and to do anything he wanted on his guitar. Though this virtuosity was stupefying, it was no less so than his creative power. In his solos, which he played almost always on one string, his melodic ideas are sparkling and ravishing, and their abundance scarcely gives the listener time to catch his breath. Django's ability to bend his guitar to the most fantastic audacities combined with his expressive inflections and vibrato was no less wonderful; one feels an extraordinary flame burning through every note.

It is interesting to note that Django, one of the rare white jazz musicians comparable to the Negroes, belonged to a race which has remained very "primitive," for in truth the gypsies' lives and customs are closer to those of the Negroes than those of the whites.

The vogue of the electric guitar, which started in 1939, led the musicians to change their style again and return largely to one-string guitar solos.

A musician rapidly became the champion of this new style, Charlie Christian (who died prematurely in 1942). He was an amazing soloist, creating all the time. His phrases, sometimes sinuous, sometimes plain, never lost an extraordinary singing quality in the melodic line. There was also something very percussive in his improvisations that made his music swing plenty. It is to be noted that Charlie Christian had a beautiful tone, which is hard to get on amplified guitars. He had the most solid tempo ever, and brought back to big-band accompaniment the four beats to a bar struck even, as in the New Orleans music, except that Christian had what might be called a drier strike.

Next to Charlie Christian (and influenced by him), the best electric guitar players are Tiny Grimes and Billy Mackel, both of whom are swingmen of the purest type and play straightforward, well-constructed solos with a tremendous drive. They both play the blues magnificently and, in this respect, they are better than Charlie Christian, who was not as outstanding on the blues as on other numbers. Billy Mackel has been for years the soul of the rhythm section in Lionel Hampton's band. Tiny Grimes was the guitarist of the Art Tatum Trio of the best era and, later, led a fine small orchestra.

Other excellent soloists of the electric guitar are Jimmy Shirley, joyful and voluble; Wes Montgomery, a very inventive musician; Billy Butler, who especially shines on the blues; T-Bone Walker, who is much better as a guitarist than as a singer and who created a style of his own on the blues; Slim Gaillard, who can play brilliant guitar solos in the Charlie Christian vein when he wants to; Mickey Baker, who is great on the blues; Willie Lacey, another fine blues man; Skeeter Best, Everett Barksdale, Chauncey Westbrook, Ike Perkins, Irving Ashby, John Collins, Oscar Moore, and Kenny Burell.

The most recent of great soloists on the guitar is a young musician named Roy Gaines, who might well be the greatest since Charlie Christian. He is at his best—which is not saying little—on the blues, where he displays a vivacity and exuberance most exciting, alternating in his solos swinging runs and solid riffs. His playing, full of invention and subtle contrasts, is at the same time really "low down." His contribution to ensemble work is amazingly efficient. Roy Gaines' example is one among many which proves that there still are first-class youngsters to follow the tradition and play real jazz.

There are guitar players who hardly ever play solo and thus cannot be compared to the foregoing but who nonetheless are first-class "rhythm guitarists," who give a wonderful "body" and drive to the rhythm section of which they are part. Such is the case of Freddie Green (one of the very few who never switched to the electric guitar), whose work in Count Basie's band has been invaluable—the perfect rhythm man on guitar. Such is also the case of Danny Barker, a solid guitarist from New Orleans; of Bobby Johnson, and John Trueheart, who both played in Chick Webb's band; of John Smith, Al Norris, and John Mitchell.

Other good guitarists are Eddie Durham, who was one of the first to use electric guitar (in 1935 with Jimmie Lunceford's band); Floyd Smith, especially good on the blues; Lawrence Lucie, Ulysses Livingston, James Smith, Douglas Daniel, and Herman Mitchell.

Some musicians have mostly been known as banjo players, although many of them also played guitar from time to time. The best of these banjo players are Elmer Snowden, excellent both as a rhythm man and soloist; Lee Blair, Charlie Dixon, Mancy Carr, Papa Charlie Jackson, Eddie Gibbs, and John Smith.

Among the white guitarists, one must mention among the older ones Eddie Lang, who had a brilliant instrumental technique but did not swing much; Eddie Condon, Dick McDonough, and George Van Epps; and among the younger ones,

George Barnes, who plays the blues better than white guitarists usually do; Les Paul, more outstanding as a technician than
as a jazzman; Barney Kessel, one of the most gifted, who can
play the blues very well; Mike Bryan, and Herb Ellis.

There remains to be mentioned certain colored guitarists
who form a group of their own because they are great only as
blues players—guitarists who never played in jazz orchestras
but who are blues singers accompanying themselves on the
guitar in a wonderful way. Their technique of the instrument,
the way they express themselves on it, sets them entirely apart
from the band guitarists. Most of the strictly blues guitarists
play without a pick and use all—or almost all—the fingers of
the right hand; often the thumb plays on the low string a sort
of bass accompaniment to what they are doing with the other
fingers of the same hand. The effect is that the guitar sounds as
full and complete as a piano. These blues men make full use of
the possibilities of the guitar; they do not need any backing
other than themselves when they sing and they can even play
solos with any extra accompaniment. They possess the art of
making their guitar "talk" and give a sort of answer to their
vocals. Some of them play with a bottle neck around the little
finger of the left hand, to make the instrument "ring" in a
special way.

The greatest of these guitarists are Blind Lemon Jefferson,
Sleepy John Estes, Big Bill Broonzy, Kokomo Arnold, Barbe-
cue Bob, Willie Bee, Tommy McLennan, Scrapper Blackwell,
Casey Bill, Blind Boy Fuller, Robert Johnson, Son House,
Memphis Minnie (the best female guitarist), Charlie and Joe
McCoy, Joe Williams, Brownie McGhee, Lightnin' Hopkins,
John Lee Hooker, Muddy Waters, and Elmore James (each of
the latter four has often used the electric guitar during the
second part of his career). Blind Blake is also to be mentioned,

but his playing tends to be more like that of the jazz guitarists. He has a wonderful technique and feeling, and he had a tremendous influence on both blues and jazz guitarists.

Almost all blues singers of the younger generation have been using the electric guitar to conform to the trend, although it does not fit the blues as well as the traditional guitar. The amplified guitar popularized the one-string style at the expense of the "full" playing of the previous era, although most of the newcomers know how to use chord-style in the real blues vein and still do at times. The best blues players on the amplified guitar are B. B. King, Clarence "Gatemouth" Brown, Larry Dale, Chuck Berry, Jimmy Reed, Otis Rush, and a very talented youngster, Matthew "Guitar" Murphy, who seems about to become one of the greatest. The style of all these guitarists derives more or less from T-Bone Walker's. They really make their guitar talk, wail and shout, creating a new style out of the peculiarities of the electrical amplified sound.

12 the string bassists

As was the case with the other instruments, the New Orleans musicians who played bass had a distinctly different style from the later string bassists. Theirs was a simple and extremely conscientious style, which limited itself to furnishing impeccable and fundamental bass notes. This is the main role of the bass player, before indulging in harmonic fantasies. These musicians, then, were content to play fundamental notes, a part which corresponds to the part furnished by the pianist with his left hand.

The best New Orleans bass players are George "Pops" Foster, Wellman Braud, Al Morgan, John Lindsay, and Bill Johnson. These men have many points in common. First, when they play pizzicato—as most string basses do in jazz—they "slap" their instruments. In other words, by cracking the strings against the wood they obtain a dry tone. Secondly, they clearly accentuate the strong beats. Finally, they swing in much the same way, for the extreme power of their tone causes their rhythmic accents to be sober and intelligent. By a break in the rhythm, and a strong syncopation during the breaks, they swing intensely. The syncopation is primed little by little by doubling the third beat, then every beat, and as the chorus goes on by a series of pointed notes and ⅛ notes. Their rhythm is thus accelerated to a point where they use only ¼ notes fol-

lowed by ⅛ notes toward the end of the chorus. They also like
to draw out the reprises, or repetitive phrases, by a series of
descending notes, played against the flights into the high
registers by the melodic instruments such as the trumpet or
clarinet.

The greatest of these bass players is probably Pops Foster,
for the extraordinary power of his playing, and his attack, are
a precious stimulant to the musicians with whom he is playing. He scarcely ever seeks harmonic subtleties but is content
to underline the general lines of the theme with an admirable
simplicity. He almost always marks the four beats of the bar
regularly; sometimes however, he only marks two beats (the
strong beats naturally) for several bars, then returns to four
beats. This gives an intense vitality to the rhythm section. At
one time he used the bow frequently at the beginning of a
number; then played pizzicato, in such a way that he contributed in large measure to the increasing tension which rises
during an execution. But this method, long in favor with the
New Orleans basses, has fallen more and more into disuse.
Foster—like the majority of the New Orleans bassists—has
partly abandoned the "slapping" method during the years,
though he has not modified the character of his playing notably.

Wellman Braud cedes nothing to Foster in the way he
swings, and he is gifted with the most sensitive ear. His way of
playing has a "dancing" touch about it as if the notes would
jump joyfully out of his instrument—notes most intelligently
chosen harmonically and executed with a mastery that gives
to what he does a tremendous sense of security. Braud is a
"classic" on the string bass in that one feels nothing else could
ever be better and more effective than what he does, which
always is full of taste and simplicity. He has a wonderful use

of the bow, and the vibrations he gets out of a bass are a real treat to the ear. One can feel, when Braud is on bass, that he is only preoccupied in giving the musicians with whom he plays a solid support.

Foster and Braud made such an impression on their fellow musicians that they moved most tuba players, around 1930, to put down their instrument and take the string bass instead. And at around the same time, because of Foster and Braud, many band leaders began including a string bass in their groups.

Al Morgan has a very imaginative style. He rarely holds to the simple complementary notes, but follows the melodic contours of the theme rather than its harmonic base. This is what is called the "walking bass," a definition which suggests very well the counterbass who is in perpetual motion instead of remaining on fundamental notes. The mobile power he displays causes his playing to swing a great deal.

One of the oldest of the New Orleans bass players is Bill Johnson, who seems to have a style somewhat more primitive than the others. He is closer to Foster than to Al Morgan; he furnishes a support of exemplary solidity using double notes abundantly, in a way which many modern musicians find "out of date."

John Lindsay also resembles Foster. His simple, harmonic base, is however less rudimentary than Bill Johnson's. His playing is also lighter and more mobile. Another good bass player is Ed Garland.

After the New Orleans era, let us say roughly after 1930, there emerged other fine bassists who no longer used "slapping," and concentrated on producing a more singing tone and enriching the harmonic trimming of the numbers. Their tone is generally smoother, more mellow, with a mobile melodic line acting as a kind of countermelody to the soloist or the orchestral ensemble.

John Kirby (who died in 1952) is probably the finest bass player using this style. His notes have a full and modeled volume, and run from the upper to the lower ranges of his instrument with the mobility and audacity which only a practiced ear could achieve. To listen to his part in an orchestra is a pleasure. Though his daring discoveries never actually break out of the harmonic frame, they often go so far that one fears he will lose his equilibrium, but this never happens. His violent musical temperament is dammed up against error by the exceptional acuteness of his ear. Sometimes he marks two beats in each measure. At other times, especially at the end of an execution, he marks all four beats with a deafening power which is very characteristic of his style.

Billy Taylor can be ranged alongside of Kirby. He too possesses a fine ear and great harmonic richness. Like Kirby, Billy Taylor's playing is very light, and he seems to be skimming over the bass. His notes sound like balls of tone tossed out with astonishing precision. Billy Taylor ordinarily employs a much smaller range than Kirby.

Walter Page (who died in 1957), rightly considered by many musicians as one of the greatest bass players, took his inspiration from Wellman Braud. He has an amazing power and drive. He often plays the four beats even, and the notes run from high to low with an admirable precision and suppleness. His part is always steady, complementing the left hand of the piano with an astonishing abundance. In fact, his playing seems to ease the entire rhythm section, for his tempo is steady as a rock.

Hayes Alvis' playing stems from the New Orleans style, of which it has the pulse and dynamism. Dick Fullbright and

Elmer James are two others whose playing recalls the New Orleans bassists, especially Pops Foster.

Milton Hinton, although he was already active in 1930 and has the qualities of the old-timers, sounds like a musician of the next generation—for he has taken ideas and effects from younger musicians and added them to his style. But the remarkable thing is that Hinton always rejected the weak points and rightly assimilated the best ones. By doing so, he constantly improved his playing. He has a beautiful tone, a wonderful instrumental technique. His execution is clean, smooth, relaxed, and incisive. He is one of the rare bass players who are equally at home with any kind of band, light or heavy, big or small, with trios, quartets, old-timers, middle-of-the-roaders, or newcomers. Besides, he is one of the few bassists who can play good solos. String bass is really not a solo instrument; in fact, most bass solos are quite boring, for even if the musician has interesting ideas, they do not come out in an attractive way on a bass fiddle. Only a handful, among bass players, have been able to play appealing solos. Milton Hinton is about the best of them, thanks to his sense of humor, his imagination, and the way he makes his bass "talk" with a suppleness of expression comparable to the human voice.

Jimmy Blanton, who was revealed by Duke Ellington in 1940 and who died prematurely in 1942, was so amazing that he gained the admiration of all musicians. He probably played more string bass than any other man. He was incredibly fast and supple in his phrasing. But he was more than a virtuoso. He had a beautiful tone and an innate sense of harmony, and he swung to the utmost. Duke Ellington liked his playing so much that he had him make several bass solo records where he accompanied him on his piano. Jimmy Blanton probably was the greatest string bass soloist ever—and in the orchestra he would at least equal the greatest.

Jimmy Blanton had such an influence on bassists that it may be said he really changed the style of the instrument. His influence can be felt in the playing of such celebrated bassists as Oscar Pettiford, George Duvivier, Charlie Mingus, Al McKibbon, Wendell Marshall, Ray Brown, and countless others.

Oscar Pettiford has come nearer to Blanton's genius than any other bassist I know. He has a great deal of invention and swing, his playing is varied, and he is one of the best string bass soloists. He also is the only musician to have used the cello to good effect in jazz music.

George Duvivier, with his good tone, his perfect musicianship, and his Blanton-like solo style, is always nice to listen to.

Charlie Mingus has "crazy" ideas and a tremendous drive, and he knows how to make his bass "talk" and express a lot of things that one would not expect to hear on this instrument.

Al McKibbon and Wendell Marshall are accomplished bassists, too, and so is Ray Brown. But the latter has been overrated. Too often he has been hailed as one of the two or three greatest bassists of all time, which is an exaggeration. He has a fine technique, a nice musicianship, but does not swing as much as a Milton Hinton or an Oscar Pettiford.

A special case is that of Slam Stewart. He found a very attractive way of playing solos on the string bass: he uses the bow (which some others did too) but at the same time he sings (or rather "hums") an octave higher the phrases he is playing with the bow. As Slam is inventive, full of humor, and all the time swinging, he undoubtedly stands as one of the few bassists that one would want to hear play solos. And he is wonderful in a rhythm section, too.

Wilson Myers is one of the few bassists to use the bow often —and very well—to perform solos.

Other excellent bassists are Israel Crosby, who has a wonderful command of his instrument, an exceptionally good tone, and who swings plenty; Eddie Jones, who spent most of the fifties in Count Basie's band with whom he made one of the best recordings a bass player could wish to wax: *Meet B. B.* (in the *Basie—One More Time* LP), where he shows his art of varying his playing; Beverley Peer, whose style recalls John Kirby's and who knows how to make an efficient use of the two-beats-to-the-bar playing; Ernest "Bass" Hill, a powerful bassist who reminds one of the New Orleans bass players; "Truck" Parham, a solid bassist in the Walter Page style; Al Hall, Lloyd Trottman, Aaron Bell, John Levy, Red Callender, John Simmons, Gene Ramey, Alvin Raglin, Jr., Charlie "Fat Man" Turner, Cedric Wallace, Lee Stanfield, Eddie Calhoun, Arvell Shaw, Bam Brown, Billy Hadnott, Rodney Richardson, John Browne, Jimmy Lewis, Buddy Banks, Joe Benjamin, Major Holley, Johnny Williams, Graham Monchur, Bob Ysaguire, Eddie Cole, Moses Allen, Quinn Wilson, Peter Badie, Al Lucas, Jimmy Butts, Benny Moten, Monk Montgomery, Curley Russell, Percy Heath, Leroy Vinegar, Paul Chambers, and Addison Farmer.

Among the younger men we should note Jimmy Woode, whose playing is very lively, thanks to the variety of his accentuations; and Tom Bryant, brother of pianist Ray Bryant, who plays a sober and straightforward but very effective bass.

Two bass players deserve separate mention: Ransom Knowling, from New Orleans, and Big Crawford. Both have made numerous recordings with blues singers and are perfect accompanists on the blues. In the same category is Willie Dixon, whom I do not know as well.

Among the white bassists, let us mention Chubby Jackson, gifted with an amazing virtuosity; Sid Weiss, Artie Shapiro, Bob Haggart, and Eddie Safranski.

Until the year 1930 and even later, the wind bass, that is to say the tuba, was much more in favor in jazz than the string bass. The tuba gave the orchestra a more weighty support, and from the point of view of sound volume and background it was far more imposing and carried much further than the string bass. But in time it no longer brought the desired suppleness and sensitive rhythm, and it could not be swung as easily as the string bass—and the latter took over.

However, the tuba has produced some great musicians. Peter Biggs has a mellow tone, a steady tempo, and a keen musical sense; he is one of the surest tubas one can hear. Bill Benford has somewhat the same qualities except that his playing is a little lighter, rounder, and possibly more mobile. Usually both are content to mark the strong beats, but from time to time they add grace notes which are rhythmically very effective. Cyrus St. Clair had a big yet smooth tone, and at times he would play beautiful counterlines to back the soloists. June Cole is remarkable for his beautiful tone, the delicacy of his attack—an astonishing thing for an instrument like the tuba—and the very melodious quality of his playing. Some string bass players also handled the tuba very well, notably Billy Taylor, John Kirby, and especially Elmer James. The names of Quinn Wilson, "Bass" Moore, Bert Cobb, and Escudero should also be mentioned.

13 the drummers

Perhaps the drums are the most important of all the instruments in the jazz orchestra. For if the drummer does not have a good tempo, it is very difficult for the other musicians of the orchestra to play well. The essential requirement of a drummer then is to furnish a solid and regular support. That he give color to the orchestral parts with his sonorous effects is of secondary importance. As for the role of soloist, the drummer fills it only exceptionally, since his instrument is purely rhythmic. Nevertheless there is no reason to condemn drum solos, as there is a tendency to do. When a drum solo is beautiful it is quite as effective as the tap dancing of great artists like Bubbles or Bill Robinson, whose dance figures are a wonderful rhythmic treat for the ear as well as an exciting sight.

New Orleans has produced a number of magnificent drummers. The oldest are known to us by reputation alone—"Old Man" Cottrell, considered by many as the best of all, who had a style which it seems was a model of sobriety; Happy Henry Zeno, Black Benny, Robichaux and Mack. The next generation also gave the world four of the greatest drummers—Arthur "Zutty" Singleton, Warren "Baby" Dodds, Fred "Tubby" Hall, and Minor Hall.

Zutty and Baby Dodds have many points in common. Both have an extraordinarily solid tempo, at the same time supple and firm, smooth and powerful. By their strong accentuation of the afterbeat on the snare drum or with the cymbal, they underline music based on the strong beat—that is, music in the New Orleans style. They play in a fashion which admirably cuts the various parts of the measure, rendering the execution clear and easy to follow. Nonetheless they never hesitate to go into breaks, using a number of small instruments like the wood block, the hand cymbal, or even a rattle. But they do not play these breaks merely to sparkle, or draw attention to themselves, but only to emphasize the discoveries of the soloists, and to create rhythmic patterns destined to urge the musicians on their improvisation. Far from being complicated, these breaks are, on the contrary, very clear. Most of them end with a beat which is more violent than the others, which is generally played on the bass drum, the cymbal, or the rim of the snare drums, and falls on the fourth beat of the measure—that is the beat which immediately precedes the reprise of the melody. This variety of break is typical of the New Orleans drummers.

Various shadings distinguish Zutty's playing from Baby Dodds'. For example, Baby Dodds' roll on the snare drums is more crackling than Zutty's, and more prolonged on the strong beats. In fact one can say without exaggeration that Baby Dodds' roll is one of the best. Likewise his tempo is easier though more brutal, whereas Zutty's has a greater suppleness. Zutty seems to follow the melodic lines of the improvisation more closely and in this reveals veritable genius. He seems to accompany rather than support; he jumps from one break to another, from one instrument to another, and always returns to his tempo with the precision of a juggler.

Tubby Hall and his brother Minor never use this sort of jugglery, which so often characterizes the playing of Zutty and Baby Dodds. They mark few breaks, but from one end of an execution to the other they maintain an unvarying tempo, generally on the snare drums. They play with sobriety and force; their rolling is muffled, solid, and condensed.

We might best characterize the pulse of great New Orleans drummers like Zutty, Baby Dodds, and the Hall brothers by saying it is the very same pulse as in Louis Armstrong's music—especially Zutty's.

The other New Orleans drummers—at least the drummers playing in that style—include Paul Barbarin, who plays in a style very similar to Zutty's, Johnny Wells, whose sober style reminds one of the Hall brothers, Morris Morand, and the late Andre Hilaire.

After the New Orleans era, that is to say around 1930, there emerged another style of drumming. The afterbeat was less emphasized and the tempo on the high-hat cymbal came into prominence until, in the mid-forties, drummers preferred to use the top cymbal. The only trouble was that the snare drum, which together with the bass drum comprises the most important part of a drum set, was neglected. Drummers would still beat or rub the snare drum with wire brushes but they never would play a steady tempo on it with the sticks, except for breaks and punctuations. Some would even go so far as to assert that rolling on the snare was "corny"—which is one of the most stupid statements I have ever heard, for what may make jazz sound "corny" is an unswinging, jerky way of playing an instrument, not the instrument in itself.

The truth, I am afraid, is that many young drummers would be unable to execute a steady press-roll on the snare the way a Zutty or a Baby Dodds can do it. The same can be said about the regular four beats marked by the foot in the bass drums. Continuous press-roll and four-beat in the bass drums—"It's uncomfortably heavy," they say. It *is* uncomfortably heavy when played heavy, by people who are unable to play it lightly and smoothly.[1]

Now, the above criticisms do not apply to the drummers who immediately followed the New Orleans men and were raised on them. Most of the greatest drummers jazz has known came into the limelight in the early thirties: Chick Webb, Sidney Catlett, Cozy Cole, Jo Jones, Lionel Hampton.

Chick Webb (who died in 1939) may well be called *the* genius of jazz drumming. His way of swinging defies description. It seems to come from a masterful precision in the percussion, an unexcelled sense of tempo, and an overwhelming power of execution. Chick Webb was an abnormally small and puny man, yet he would hit those drums with a greater power than the veriest athlete.

Chick Webb's drumming, like that of the New Orleans men, was neat, clear, direct; yet Chick brought into vogue various novelties, especially the high-hat cymbal, which he used in the most magnificent way. But the innumerable drummers who imitated him abused this cymbal and never were able to play it as well as he. And when Chick Webb would hit the large cymbal to mark the afterbeat, he was still more terrific.

Whether long and copious or consisting of only one or two explosive strokes, Chick Webb's breaks were always conceived with rare intelligence and executed with a bewildering power and mastery. There was in his attack something *conclusive* which ranks him above all other drummers—just as a

[1] Of course, not all young "progressive" musicians prove to be so stubborn. Here is what Philly Joe Jones, the celebrated young drummer, said about Baby Dodds: "I went to the Onyx, and Baby Dodds was playing in there with a bass drum, and a snare drum, and one cymbal. He was swingin' SO MUCH I was late an entire set" (in getting back to his work). *Down Beat*, March 3, 1960.

single note played by Louis Armstrong makes one forget all other trumpets.

The way Chick worked his foot in the bass drum was also unique, for he would thus obtain so full and mellow a volume that it would distinguish him from a thousand other drummers.

Another of his greatest qualities was his taste for underlining every nuance of an arrangement. His dynamism when he was breathing loose is impossible to describe, especially when he would build a climax by strongly marking the afterbeat on the snare or the rim of the snare at the end of a chorus or of a number.

Sidney Catlett (who died in 1951), nicknamed "Big Sid" for his broad stature, was first influenced by Zutty and other New Orleans drummers, and some of the flavor of the New Orleans drumming always stayed in his playing. But he soon developed a strong personality. His tempo was extremely supple and bouncing. His instrumental technique was outstanding, and when he played a drum solo he had few equals. As I have said, drum solos are not to be condemned. A good drummer can make rhythms talk, tell a musical story—and a very expressive one. It is easier to create an attractive solo on drums than on string bass. The latter has a full range of notes, of course, but comparatively little can be got out of them; while a drum is such a powerful instrument that a first-class musician can get an infinite quantity of extremely expressive sounds out of it. Sidney Catlett was a consummate artist at that, and his long solo on *Steak Face* (in the *Satchmo at Symphony Hall* LP), although not perfectly recorded, is one of the best that has been preserved.

Cozy Cole also is one of the greatest drum soloists. His style is quite different from Catlett's. Cozy likes to set a good riff and stay on it, swinging it more and more and altering it slightly until he goes into another one which is the logical continuance. Then, Cozy might superpose two riffs, sometimes in entirely different rhythms, and he might even play three different riffs at a time. His instrumental technique is nothing short of fantastic. At times it sounds as if he had three hands, or even as if two drummers were playing simultaneously. But it is never technique for technique's sake: Cozy Cole swings all the time, and by staying on a few rhythmic figures and getting the most out of them, he produces the most fascinating, haunting effects; then all the listener would wish to say is, "Play it all night long," as musicians do when they enjoy the music they are listening to.

When he accompanies a soloist or underlines an arrangement, Cozy gets the same fascinating, hypnotic effect. He "pushes" the other musicians so well that he injects an infectious drive into the performance.

Jo Jones, again, drums in an entirely different way. Originally a dancer, he puts the dance feeling into his drumming in an almost unbelievable way. If he solos, what he plays (and the way he plays it) may well lead the listener to visualize the steps of a great dancer. Behind a soloist, Jo Jones sets the most supple and driving tempo, and at the same time creates all kinds of little rhythmic figures and accents that make the music jump like mad. He gets beautiful tone and contrasts out of all the instruments that are part of the drumming material. He is one of the few who have succeeded in getting a perfect, beautiful sound out of the high-hat cymbal, and he is equally at home with the top cymbal. He has so much invention, so many ideas that even when familiar with his style, one may be unable to anticipate what Jo Jones is going to play next.

Lionel Hampton is mostly known as a vibraphonist. But he originally was a drummer, and is every bit as great on drums (which he still plays from time to time) as on the vibes. He has a dazzling instrumental technique which he uses with intelligence and taste. The exuberance, youth, and vigor of his playing hold the listener absorbed. In solo choruses he displays an uncanny dexterity, and his rhythmic discoveries have a cumulative impact. The dry force of his percussion is extraordinary, almost matching Chick Webb's. He also is a stupendous band drummer, favoring a strong, "lazy" afterbeat which has something in common with that of the New Orleans drummers.

The amazingly percussive quality of Lionel Hampton's drumming also finds its way through his vibraphone playing. At times he swings the vibes by the use of a good, simple riff; at other times, the most dizzy phrases fuse and succeed one another at an amazing speed. Lionel's dexterity is as stupendous at the vibes as on the drums. And he has just as broad a melodic invention as a rhythmic one. In fact, Lionel is about the only musician who succeeded in drawing that much out of the vibraphone. Of course, a few musicians like Tyree Glenn and Clarence Redd can be very pleasing on the vibes—and Milton Jackson also. But they are not on a level with Hamp. Milt Jackson, for instance, has invention and pretty musical ideas, but he lacks Hamp's drive, power, and strongly contrasted accents; the latter, especially, contribute more than anything else to make Lionel's vibes solos sound so lively and biting, while other vibraphonists, after a few bars, tend to be monotonous.

Lionel also plays the piano in a very original fashion. He generally uses only two fingers and percusses the keys with hammerlike violence in a technique like that of the vibes. In this fashion, he plays phrases of incredible speed in the upper registers of the piano. While many people see in this nothing but a display of virtuosity, I feel that Lionel reveals here a great creative force, and by this method swings in a most enthusiastic manner. However, Lionel also plays the piano in the usual way very well, as he has proved in his superb recording of *Denison Swing* (on the RCA Victor label). Lionel Hampton is in fact what is called a "natural"—unquestionably one of the most creative jazz musicians.

Other first-class drummers who came along about the same time as the foregoing, or a little later, are Jimmy Crawford, Alvin Burroughs, Slick Jones, Manzie Johnson, O'Neil Spencer, J. C. Heard, Kansas Fields, and Denzil Best.

Jimmy Crawford, who was Jimmie Lunceford's drummer in the band's best days, contributed much to what came to be known as the "Lunceford beat" by his strong and lazy afterbeat. Less flashy than other drummers, Crawford is to be numbered among the most "solid" ones.

Alvin Burroughs (who died in 1950) probably was the nearest to Chick Webb by his powerful bass drum playing and the percussive strength of his breaks, but he had a way of his own of "whipping" the cymbal and swinging a whole band, as he did when he was in Earl Hines' big band in its heyday (1939–1940).

Slick Jones, a longtime drummer with Fats Waller, has a very original way of playing the high-hat cymbal: instead of allowing it to continue resounding as other drummers do, he cuts the vibration almost immediately after the attack and gets a very effective swinging effect out of it.

Manzie Johnson took some of his original inspiration from the New Orleans drummers. He has an incisive roll on the snare, and he makes the cymbals vibrate with a beautiful lightness.

O'Neil Spencer (who died in 1944), a longtime drummer in John Kirby's orchestra, was an accomplished musician with a brilliant technique and a flowing swing.

J. C. Heard, when at his best, is the equal of the greatest drummers. When he starts swinging behind a soloist, he has a way of "pushing" him in an impetuous, urgent manner that is as impressive and effective as Cozy Cole's, although in a different style. And J. C. Heard also is one of the most attractive drum soloists thanks to his imagination and wonderful instrumental technique.

Denzil Best and Kansas Fields both show a Sidney Catlett influence in their playing, Denzil Best mostly in the way he beats a steady tempo (he is the closest to Big Sid at that), Kansas Fields in the style of some of his breaks as well as in his pulse-beat.

Other excellent drummers are Kaiser Marshall (who died in 1948), one of the best of the old school, who was a master on the cymbals and created very inventive solo breaks; Walter Johnson, who also made an extensive and nice-sounding use of cymbals; Keg Purnell, a powerful, swinging drummer somewhat in Chick Webb's style; Wilbert Kirk, a solid man rather of the Sidney Catlett type; Specs Powell, whose light yet strong drumming swings intensely; Les Erskine, never flashy but sober and solid; Joe Marshall, one of the most constantly swinging drummers in jazz since he came to the limelight around the mid-forties, one of those who get the most out of a strongly accented afterbeat; Panama Francis, a driving man, who got closer to Chick Webb's pulse-beat than anybody else, I believe; Fred Moore, a solid man from the old school; George Jenkins, a fast, clever, and biting drummer; Sonny Greer, a first-class technician, somewhat uneven but capable of swinging a lot when at his best; Wallace Bishop, robust and incisive; Alton Reed, who never tries to show off but can make any band swing; Shadow Wilson (who died in 1959), who could play with a magnificently supple and "lazy" swing but who, at times, fell into the be-bop style of drumming; Osie Johnson, who also can be a first-class swingman when he stays away from the intolerable bop licks.

Other good drummers who deserve to be mentioned are Chris Columbus (a solid man!), "Big Jack" Morrisson, Jack "The Bear" Parker, Roy Milton, Eddie Dougherty, George Stafford (who died in 1936), Lee Young (Lester's brother), Eddie Bourne, Kelly Martin, Butch Ballard, Mousie Alexander, Fred Radcliffe, Berisford Sheperd, Jessie Sailes, Curley Hamner, Fats Donaldson, Rufus Jones, Harold Austin, June Gardner, Gus Johnson, Rudy Traylor, Tommy Benford, Harry Dial, Pete Jacobs, Jesse Price, William Diemer, Baby Lewis, Jimmy Hoskins, Ted Fields, Arnold Bolden, Yank Porter, Cuba Austin, Bill Beason, Bobby Donaldson, and Dany Barcelona.

Men like Kenny Clark, Art Blakey, and Max Roach were excellent drummers at the outset, but they switched to the bop style of drumming, which is absolutely incompatible with the music of the real jazzmen.

Among the drummers who spent most of their time accompanying blues singers with small groups, we should cite Judge Riley, Tyrell Dixon ("Little T"), Fred Williams, Alfred Wallace, and Fred Below.

Some excellent young drummers appeared during the fifties: Sam Woodyard, who has as terrific a drive as that of his elders and who makes a wonderful use of the accented afterbeat; Oliver Jackson and Eddie Locke, who both got their main inspiration from Jo Jones; Sonny Payne (son of Chris Columbus), a very gifted musician who has been with Count Basie's band since the mid-fifties; and James Johnson.

Very few are the white drummers who swing as much as the colored ones. The best of all is Buddy Rich, gifted with a fantastic virtuosity and a real swingman as well, full suppleness and power; Dave Tough (who died in 1948), one of the most gifted; Gene Krupa, who is a very brilliant technician; George Wettling and Ray Beauduc, who both drum in the New Orleans style; Ray McKinley, Kenny John, and Louie Bellson—the latter being more remarkable for an exceptional virtuosity than for soul.

There are also "washboard" specialists (the washboard is held upright and played by rhythmically drawing thimbled fingers or a pair of spoons across it): Jimmy Bertrand (who is a fine drummer, too, and had a considerable influence in Chicago during the twenties); Floyd Casey, Jasper Taylor, Bruce Johnson, and Willie Williams.

14 the singers

Singers, in jazz, are mostly blues singers. There have been few great jazz singers other than blues singers.

The old-time blues singers were among the originators of jazz. They were singing the blues in the country and in small towns before there was any orchestral music; and it was only when people from the cities heard that music and converted it into orchestral language that what was to be called jazz came into being.

Way back in the eighties and nineties, blues singers in Mississippi, Arkansas, Texas, and several other Southern states would sing the blues, each in his own way. They sang about their own troubles, woes, and joys, accompanying themselves mostly on guitar—the guitar being sometimes made out of a box or some other handy material.

Some of them would go from town to town and sing the blues for their people—and the words they put to the blues would be understood, felt, laughed at, cried at, danced to by their own people.

They had a gift for music, they invented a melodic setting that fitted their way of expressing what they had on their mind —and they had rhythm, too. They invented the most appropriate accompaniment to their lyrics, which they would render with little care for the diction, but the feeling was there, tense and very moving. What they came out with was seldom the strict twelve-bar blues (they took it easy with the "meter")— but it was the blues all right! It was rough and crude, but it was genuine; it had melody and swing. They had something to say that was bound to come out. And it did. The form improved little by little, acquired a definite setting, and gave way to definite musical rules. The first blues singers did not know about rules, they were beyond and before them, and it would be up to those who came afterward to polish and work on what they had done, and establish from the music of these ancestors —the blues singers—a tradition in which jazz music is rooted.

The two oldest blues singers whom we know through records are Blind Lemon Jefferson (born in Texas towards the end of the nineteenth century, died around 1930), and Sleepy John Estes (born around 1880 in Georgia, died in 1953).

Blind Lemon's way of singing is rough, biting, and poignant, with a decidedly primitive flavor. It is the typical country blues of a man who originally had no contact whatsoever with the city's polish. All the angles are there all right—and there is a beauty of all times that can be felt as if Blind Lemon were singing right after the creation of the world. It is roar, yet beautiful.

Sleepy John Estes is easily recognizable from among all the others. "When he sings, you'd think he's crying," Big Bill Broonzy used to say. Sleepy John takes it particularly easy with pronunciation. He sings in a sort of chewed-up, nonchalant way, and usually has very good lyrics. The inflections in his voice are very keen despite their lazy accent.

The best of the old-time blues singers is Big Bill Broonzy (born in 1893, died in Chicago in 1958). Big Bill was gifted with a beautiful voice, perfectly fitted to sing the blues, which he used masterfully to express with the greatest accuracy and precision each and every nuance of what he wanted and had to say, through the words and between the words. His voice had a beautiful timbre, not at all rough and yet not suave—like a bell. He could be tender, strong, powerful, majestic in his singing—he was never vulgar and never sought the easy way or easy effects. There was in his singing something of the nobleness of a peasant, more subtle than refined.

Big Bill was born in Mississippi, where it seems that the blues were born—at least that was where they were most sung at first. An impressive proportion of great blues singers come from Mississippi: Kokomo Arnold, Robert Johnson, Muddy Waters, Johnny Temple, Tommy McLennan, Jazz Gillum (who also plays the blues splendidly on harmonica). Of these blues singers, who are slightly younger than Big Bill, the first three, especially Kokomo Arnold and Muddy Waters, stand out. They both have a roar style, hardly pronouncing the words, with something harsh about the voice which might remind one of a diamond still in its gangue.

One of the most famous among blues singers was Leroy Carr, who was born in Tennessee in 1905 and died in 1935. Unlike those we have considered so far, Leroy Carr accompanied himself on piano instead of guitar, in the same polished and pleasant way as he sang: full of "nuances," smooth, moving. His diction was neat, his voice had a very welcome touch of melancholy. Thus, Leroy Carr does not belong to the primitive, "in the alley" type as the above-mentioned blues singers do.

Strangely enough, there are two blues singers and mouth-organ players with the same name, Sonny Boy Williamson, who both have the same trick in common. Both play harmonica between the vocal parts, the instrumental and vocal parts alternating so quickly that when one hears the performance on records, it is hard to believe that the two parts are executed by only one man.

The real name of one of these men is John Lee Williams. He was born in Tennessee and was killed in 1948; his records are on the RCA Victor and Bluebird labels. His style is vehement and tense, and there is a light and bantering sense of humor in his voice, with a tongue-tied way of rendering the lyrics.

The real name of the other Sonny Boy Williamson is Rice Miller; he was born in Glendora, Mississippi, in 1901, and his records are mostly on the Checker and Trumpet labels. He has a beautiful voice, ideal for the blues, a deeply moving accent, and sarcastic and yet tender inflections. He handles his voice with a mastery recalling that of Big Bill.

Other good blues singers in the old style are Casey Bill and Champion Jack Dupree (two of the best), Curtis Jones, Blind Blake, Texas Alexander, Leadbelly, Washboard Sam, Blind Boy Fuller, Barbecue Bob, Tampa Red, Big Maceo Merryweather, Roosevelt Sykes (nicknamed "The Honeydripper"), Memphis Slim, John Lee Hooker, Lightnin' Hopkins, and Elmore James. The four last named, although younger, still play and sing in the "non-dressed-up" blues tradition and can be numbered among the greatest.

As for Josh White, although he is a very fine blues guitarist, he has a "dressed-up" way of rendering the blues that makes him somewhat tiresome to listen to, and real blues connoisseurs will prefer the genuine old-timers or their like.

Lonnie Johnson, with his melodious voice and more elaborate technique of the guitar, renders the blues in a more kindly way than the foregoing. He is, in fact, a jazz musician singing the blues.

Such is also the case with the "blues shouters." Their style no longer has the earthy flavor and forlorn accent of primitive blues singers. Their singing is louder, very percussive; it corresponds to the instrumental style of the soloists in jazz orchestras. But they were very much inspired by the old-time blues singers, and the best of them always succeeded in creating, each in his own way, a very moving blues climate, especially Joe Turner, Jimmy Rushing, Cousin Joe, Wynonie Harris, Sonnie Parker, Eddie Vinson, Lips Page, and Louis Jordan.

Joe Turner stands as the prototype of blues shouters. The Southern forlornness has disappeared to give way to the Kansas City blues, which bloomed in the Middle West during the late twenties and was to take jazz music by storm when Count Basie and others came East in the thirties. Gifted with a powerful voice, richly timbred, Joe Turner constantly shouts the blues. His power of expression is especially moving on slow blues.

Jimmy Rushing also sang in Kansas City during the early part of his career. He was influenced by the greatest of all female blues singers, Bessie Smith (whom we will meet later). His rather high-pitched voice is full, vibrating with a biting sensibility and rich inflections. His tempo is solid as a rock; he stimulates and sends a whole band as nobody else can. Jimmy Rushing is not only a great blues singer, he sings wonderfully any kind of tune, as is also the case with Joe Turner and most of the singers we are dealing with now.

Lips Page's way of singing was quite in the Kansas City blues style also, but his veiled voice was very reminiscent of Louis Armstrong, and Lips had something like Louis' accent. And when Lips was singing numbers other than the blues, he resembled Louis very much.

Cousin Joe has a strong sense of humor and his lyrics are full of the most comical and witty sallies. The jeering touch in his voice recalls that of the Tennessee-born Sonny Boy Williamson, but is less nonchalant, more tense.

Wynonie Harris was inspired by Joe Turner. His voice is far from matching Turner's in power, and his mastery is not as great, but he swings plenty, with a fire that recalls Lionel Hampton's band—a manner that could be referred to as the "swing of the forties."

Louis Jordan is a most colorful singer, very fast and picturesque; he delivers the lyrics with an amazing volubility, a real mastery in the fluency of the speech.

Sonnie Parker (who died in 1957) had a style which was halfway between Joe Turner's and Louis Jordan's. He had a very attractive way of clear-cutting his phrases which is typical of the most recent authentic style for singing the blues.

Other good blues singers are Jimmy Witherspoon, who has a beautiful voice and a perfect command of his great vocal technique; L. C. Williams, who in many ways resembles Joe Turner; Roy Milton (the band leader and drummer); and T-Bone Walker, although the latter tends nowadays to sing in a manner that is too refined and "sweet" for the blues; he is better as a guitar player. Joe Williams, if he is to be judged by the way he sings since he joined Basie's band, is not a blues singer in the real sense of the word.

Among the best younger ones are B. B. King, the most influential one since Joe Turner; Little Walter (who also is the greatest "blues" harmonica player of today), Clarance "Gate Mouth" Brown, Larry Dale, Bobby Blue Bland, Chuck Berry, Jimmy Reed, Fats Domino, and Otis Rush.

The most original and talented of the young ones is Ray Charles. He is not only a blues singer, he excels in other types of numbers as well. His way of singing the blues, unlike that of his predecessors, is very much like the style of the great church singers (such as Mahalia Jackson and Rosetta Tharpe), with broad inflections, biting calls in the high registers, accents coming right down from heart and soul. His impressive use of the "growl" reminds one of the way Bessie Smith used it, and of the instrumental "growl" of trumpet players like Cootie Williams. On ballads, Ray Charles is every bit as outstanding as on the blues. Unlike so many singers who interpret ballads in either a way that is sugary and emasculate or with a pompous display, Ray Charles renders them with perfect taste, swinging them in a light, easy way, giving them a moving yet virile accent. In fact, he is such an accomplished vocalist that one is tempted to rank him next to Louis Armstrong as the greatest all-around singer.

To deal with all the good church singers would put me too far astray from the matter of the present book. Still, I want to mention the two best and most typical church singers I have heard through records: Blind Gary Davis and Blind Willie Johnson, who both accompany themselves beautifully on guitar, in a style quite similar to that of the old-time blues singers.

Not many of the jazz singers are of real worth. The greatest —by far surpassing the lot—is Louis Armstrong (see the chapter on "Trumpets"), who created a style that altogether changed jazz singing and influenced all the other jazz singers, notably Lips Page, Clarence Palmer, George Morton, Steve Washington, Stuff Smith, Walter Fuller, Freddie Taylor, Taft Jordan, and Ray Nance.

There also are instrumentalists who sing occasionally—and very well: Jelly Roll Morton, Jimmie Harrison (who was particularly good), Fats Waller (to whom I will return in another chapter); King Cole, who is a good jazz singer but who has specialized in a sugary style of ballads; Cecil Gant, whose singing recalls that of King Cole, though he has a less caressing voice and is more a jazz singer than King Cole.

There was a very promising jazz singer who could have made a successful career had he not died very young (1930): George Thomas. He had an exceptionally beautiful voice, with an unexpected timbre, a mellow and smooth volume, and shadings in his intonations that were extraordinarily vibrant.

Other good singers are Tiny Bradshaw, Sy Oliver, and Trummy Young.

Among the women, the two greatest blues singers are unquestionably Bessie Smith (who died in 1937) and Gertrude "Ma" Rainey (who died in 1939). Since Ma Rainey is the older, her singing has a more primitive note. She sings the blues with complete simplicity and without affectation. The beauty of her low, strong voice rests in its harsh somber accent which completely lacks any calculated effects. But unlike Bessie Smith and the younger blues singers, Ma Rainey does not put much emphasis on the vibrato and scarcely varies her inflection. She seems instead to force her voice. Only at the close of a phrase does her voice vibrate gently with a scarcely perceptible feeling. Her intonations are abrupt, and she does not phrase like Bessie Smith. While Bessie's voice swells and seems almost to burst, rises and falls with suppleness, Ma Rainey sings without detours, with a brusqueness which gives a poignant tone to her singing. Hers is a folk song. Though this quality is to be found in some of the other older singers, none, to my knowledge, has the majesty and grandeur of Ma Rainey.

Though still harsh and sharp, Bessie Smith's singing sounds almost sweet after Ma Rainey's. The timbre of her voice is warmer; her inflections are more nuanced and better project the qualities she seeks to express, lending greater variety to her interpretations. She injects a joyous note into her singing that is not found in Ma Rainey's, for Ma Rainey's song is one of desolation which closely hugs the earth. "I think she was a little lower than Bessie—more bluer," said Kid Ory, when speaking of Ma Rainey.[1] However Bessie Smith has that same endless subterranean nostalgia, and an added luminescence which springs from the warm strength and mellow volume of her voice. She takes more initiative than Ma Rainey, employs more unexpected notes, and is—in a word—more creative. One of her most remarkable qualities, in fact, is the variety of her interpretations. While most blues singers interpret each song in the same manner, Bessie changes astonishingly from one number to another. Sometimes her song is full of a weighty and crushing sadness; sometimes it is calm; sometimes tender and imploring. Her voice is very strong, and assumes a truly imposing volume in the crescendos. But instead of remaining on one level, as Ma Rainey's does, Bessie's voice is now vehement, now low, now brilliant, without any affectation.

Not only has Bessie Smith had a tremendous influence on the majority of blues singers, but she has greatly inspired any number of trumpeters, trombonists, and other instrumentalists who considered her the "Queen of the Blues." As a result they have tried to reproduce on their instruments her moans and inflections, in fact her entire dynamic, powerful, and moving way of singing blues.

Next to Ma Rainey and Bessie Smith, the best blues singer was probably Clara Smith (who died in 1935), whose way of expression had the moving touch of feminine despair through a rich voice quite catching.

Other singers more or less in the same school are Ida Cox, Trixie Smith, Lizzie Miles, Cleo Gibson, Bessie Tucker,

[1] *Jazz Information*, November 22, 1940.

Bessie Jackson, Maggie Jones, Mae Alix, Rosetta Crawford, Ada Brown, Coot Grant; and Susie, from the famous team, "Butterbeans and Susie," who is reputed to be one of the best but whom I never had a chance to hear. Juanita Hall, who came a little later, has a beautiful voice and revived amazingly the Bessie Smith spirit of singing.

While both Ma Rainey and Bessie Smith sharply differ from the old-time male blues singers, Merline Jackson, better known as "The Yas Yas Girl," expresses herself in a style recalling that of Big Bill—or, more generally, that of the Mississippi blues singers.

Such is also the case of Memphis Minnie, who is the only woman blues singer among those known to us through records who accompanies her singing with wonderful blues guitar comparable to, say, Big Bill or Kokomo Arnold.

Georgia White is also a fine blues singer, falling somewhere between the Bessie Smith style and the country blues style of the old male singers. Her rather high-pitched voice has a moving sound and vibrato.

I must also mention Blue Lu Barker, who has a very personal and enjoyable way of singing the blues, with a cynical sense of humor; and Lil Green.

The gospel singers, although their vocal technique is reminiscent of that of the blues singers, stand in a category quite apart. Yet the great Mahalia Jackson once said that she was inspired at least to some degree by Bessie Smith, whom she recalls by her power of expression—and the way she swings. But there is a majesty, a deepness, a mastery in Mahalia's style that is to be found in no other gospel singer. The gravity in rendering slow songs reaches such a beauty, she has such a mastery in the inflections, that the listener could easily be moved to the point of tears. But there is no sticky sadness in

Mahalia's ways; there is nothing morbid about her singing. On the contrary, one always feels in Mahalia's music the deeply rooted and serene joy of the believer. Mahalia Jackson's exalted way of singing is one of the most beautiful things to be heard, not only as one of the aspects of the colored musical tradition, but among all the singing of the world.

Quite opposite to Mahalia Jackson's style, Sister Rosetta Tharpe's is as remarkable. Her voice is high, her singing is light, joyful, voluble, intensely swinging and expressive, and she accompanies herself on guitar in the most exciting and splendid way. She has the fastness of rippling waters; and the rare melancholy touches are soon swept off by a youthful confidence in the resources that every day brings.

Other good gospel singers are Marie Knight and Katie Bell Nubin (Rosetta Tharpe's mother). And there are many more, of course, but it would be beyond the scope of this book to enter the subject in more detail.

Among the jazz singers, the greatest is Ethel Waters. Her voice, although a miracle of smoothness, is nonetheless firm and penetrating, clear and supple, swinging, caressing, cynical, with myriads of little touches and inflections going from mockery to profundity with an amazing mastery. Her diction is perfect. She sings with incomparable ease; every note is so exactly tuned and her range is so extensive that she gives the impression of being immensely relaxed in any pitch, from the highest to the lowest. Since 1930, she has been influenced to some degree by Louis Armstrong. As a matter of fact, Ethel Waters' influence on female jazz singers is almost as great as that of Louis Armstrong.

After Ethel Waters, the best jazz singer is Ella Fitzgerald. Her voice has a vigorous, clear, extremely warm timbre. She probably does not have Ethel Waters' mastery, but there is in

Ella a most inspiring youthfulness and enthusiasm, and she has developed an artistry which has enabled her to express herself in vaster domains without losing an unelaborate simplicity where moving bursts of tenderness show as if her heart were singing through her voice.

I have a particular liking for Helen Humes, whose high and sweet voice is full of fire, joy, and a melancholy touch of self-mockery that gives a lot of pep to her singing. She is one of the greatest.

Billie Holiday (who died in 1959) was one of the most celebrated singers. To my mind she has been overrated, especially during the last years of her career, as she had then lost her voice. But in her earlier days she was a swinging and creative singer, although I never liked her style as much as that of an Ethel Waters or a Helen Humes.

Other good jazz singers are Adelaide Hall, Ivie Anderson (who died in 1949), June Richmond, Dinah Washington, Valaida Snow, Pearl Bailey, Una Mae Carlisle, Velma Middleton, Ella Johnson, Bertice Reading, Rosetta Howard, and Ruth Brown.

The most recent great female singer is La Vern Baker, who is in a class with the best singers of the previous era, and who is probably the best since Ella Fitzgerald. True to the musical tradition of her race, La Vern Baker deliberately ignores sophistication or effects of the sort that spoiled the style of such singers as Sarah Vaughan. La Vern Baker took her inspiration and style from the great artists of her race, not in Hollywood schools. She is gifted with a beautiful, clear, ample voice, especially limpid in the high registers. She is great on the blues as well as on ballads and, just like Ray Charles among the men, she shows the influence of the great church singers of the order of Mahalia Jackson and Sister Rosetta Tharpe.

15 big bands and arrangers

To mention the numerous big bands which have followed one after the other since the birth of jazz would be not merely tedious but of little value. Therefore I will consider only those rare groups who sought out orchestral originality and who thereby have created something new in the realm of jazz.

The earliest of these orchestras was Fletcher Henderson's, which was also one of the best in the entire history of jazz. Of course this orchestra frequently made commercial concessions, particularly at its debut when it attempted to be the "Paul Whiteman of the race." But after 1925–1926, it was clearly oriented toward true jazz. And naturally this orchestra must be judged by those interpretations which are free of commercialism.

Fletcher Henderson's orchestra changed a great deal during the years. There are two principal reasons for this. There were constant changes in personnel (many musicians would remain with Fletcher Henderson no longer than a few months), and the orchestra followed without resistance the general evolution of jazz, adapting its style to the formulas of the moment.

Nevertheless two main periods can be distinguished. The first began in 1924, the second in 1928. During the earlier period, Fletcher created an original orchestral style, and his group was really the first large orchestra of value to swing its interpretations. During the second period, however, he followed rather than led the fashion and consequently his orchestra lost much of its character.

During the first period, insofar as possible, Fletcher realized with a large orchestra about the same sort of music as that of the small orchestras of the New Orleans type. His soloists played in the New Orleans style, or were inspired by it. On trumpet he had Louis Armstrong, Tommy Ladnier, Joe Smith, Rex Stewart, and Bobby Stark; on trombone, Jimmy Harrison, Charlie Green; on tenor sax, Coleman Hawkins; on clarinet, Buster Bailey. In ensemble work Fletcher did not use complicated arrangements but sober and direct ones which were similar to his soloists' style. Moreover many of the arrangements were not written; they were "head" arrangements which the musicians themselves worked out during rehearsals, and which had, as a result, a spontaneous character. In fact sometimes during the last bars of the final ensembles, there was collective improvisation by a part of the orchestra.

What made the orchestra so great was the community of feeling among its members. Ardent and imposing solos followed one another. The musicans understood each other and played in similar styles. Such records as *Sensation, Fidgety Feet, Wabash Blues, Stockholm Stomp, St. Louis Shuffle, The Stampede*,[1] are marvelous proof of this. The orchestra played a lot of blues in the most appropriate spirit. *Snag It, Jackass Blues, St. Louis Blues*, and *Livery Stable Blues* should be cited as among the best. In many of these blues, such as *Snag It*, the abundant use of three clarinets instead of three

[1] Most of them have been unavailable for a long time, but some might be reissued by the time this book comes out, as Columbia plans to release on LP many Fletcher Henderson recordings.

saxophones contributes greatly to the tonal surrounding. Fletcher favored this use of ensemble clarinets in all sorts of numbers; in fact this was one of the distinctive features of his orchestra. Certainly three clarinets playing in both upper and lower registers achieve beautiful tonal effects, and it is regrettable that modern orchestras do not make more use of this combination. Fletcher obtained marvelous results from such ensembles. Listen for example to *The Meanest Kind of Blues*. Here, from one end of the record to the other, the three clarinets alternate and flow together with Armstrong's trumpet in a magnificent fashion. *Henderson Stomp* creates similar effects.

During this period (1926–27) the orchestra sometimes used written arrangements by one of its members, Don Redman, who later became well known in jazz as an orchestra leader and arranger. Fletcher recorded several of Redman's arrangements, e.g., *The Whiteman Stomp, Hot Mustard, I'm Coming Virginia*. This last arrangement maintains a perfect balance between solos and ensembles and includes a marvelously imaginative chorus for three saxophones.

At that time the exact make-up of Fletcher Henderson's orchestra was: Russell Smith, Joe Smith, and Tommy Ladnier on trumpet; Jimmy Harrison and Charlie Green—later replaced by Benny Morton—on trombone; Buster Bailey, Coleman Hawkins, and Don Redman—later replaced by Jerome Pasquall—on saxophone and clarinet; Fletcher Henderson on piano; Charlie Dixon on banjo; June Cole on tuba; Kaiser Marshall on drums. All the records mentioned above were recorded by this group, with the exception of *The Meanest Kind of Blues, Jackass Blues*, and *The Stampede* which were recorded earlier. The first was recorded with Louis Armstrong on third trumpet; the other two were recorded with Rex Stewart in the same chair.

But little by little, as Fletcher changed musicians, the New Orleans style ceased to prevail in the orchestra and the arrangements became more labored. However, Benny Carter, who entered the orchestra in 1928 as alto saxophone, often wrote arrangements which sparkled with verve and great musical richness such as *Keep a Song in Your Soul* and *Somebody Loves Me.* Without doubt Bennie is one of the greatest arrangers jazz produced and it is regrettable that persistent bad luck prevented him from having an orchestra of his own most of the time. Among other things, Bennie could write magnificent choruses for three or four saxophones better than any other arranger. In style these choruses are identical with his alto saxophone solos; they are as mobile and as spontaneous. This can be seen not only in the two records made with Fletcher, which were mentioned above, but also in such records as *Heebie Jeebies* by Chick Webb's band; *Symphony in Riffs, Lonesome Nights, I Can't Escape from You,* all three by Benny Carter's own band; *I'm in the Mood for Swing* by Lionel Hampton. Benny also has a gift for writing ingenious and supple modulations. Although there is little attempt at harmonic originalities in his arrangements, there is always a great melodic richness which gives a light and extremely singing accent.

That Fletcher Henderson's group remained among the best until 1935 was especially due to the fact that Henderson always surrounded himself with great soloists and employed a remarkable rhythm section. But his orchestra had lost that characteristic accent of earlier days. Perhaps the high point of this period was in 1934 and 1935, when Fletcher himself began writing excellent arrangements, such as *Down South*

Camp Meeting, Shanghai Shuffle, Wrappin' It Up, Can You Take It. Here the ensembles are admirably balanced so that the orchestra can swing to the maximum.

Unfortunately, a little after this, Fletcher was forced to break up his band. When he formed his new orchestra, in 1936, it was quite good but Fletcher never again ranked among the best bands.

I shall turn now to the orchestra which is unquestionably the most marvelous jazz has known—Duke Ellington's orchestra. At first, Duke Ellington had a small group of six musicians. Then in 1926 his orchestra, which had grown to ten men, began to create attention.

Duke's band rather resembled Fletcher Henderson's at the beginning. As a matter of fact Duke took inspiration from Henderson, notably in the use of a clarinet trio in the blues and other numbers. Likewise the soloists were used in the same way, and played in a style closely allied to New Orleans.

But Duke was not, like Fletcher, merely a good orchestra leader of taste and discrimination, he was also an arranger and composer of genius, ranking with Louis Armstrong as the greatest personality of jazz. Though Duke is a wonderful pianist, he never did feature himself much as a soloist, preferring to express the music in him through the medium of an entire orchestra, and, in fact, he led his orchestra down very original paths which made it radically different from all other jazz groups.

Consequently Duke's orchestra is truly an exceptional creation in the history of jazz. In contrast to other orchestras, it depends entirely upon the leader; this orchestra is a body of which Duke is the head and nerve center. However brilliant the various musicians, the orchestra is before all else the instrument through which Duke expresses his ideas.

And Duke's musicians are extremely brilliant. Outside of Fletcher Henderson, no other orchestra leader has succeeded in gathering together so great a number of stars. In 1927, the group included the following musicians: "Bubber" Miley and Louis Metcalf on trumpet, Joe "Tricky Sam" Nanton on trombone, Otto Hardwick on alto sax, Harry Carney on baritone sax, Barney Bigard on tenor sax and clarinet, Fred Guy on guitar and banjo, Wellman Braud on bass, Sonny Greer on drums, and Duke at the piano. While from 1929 to 1932, the orchestra was composed of Arthur Wetsel, "Cootie" Williams, and Freddy Jenkins on trumpet, "Tricky Sam" and Juan Tizol on trombone, Johnny Hodges, Harry Carney, and Barney Bigard on saxophone and clarinet, and the same rhythm section. Then in 1932, Duke added a third trombone, Lawrence Brown, and Otto Hardwick returned to the orchestra as fourth saxophone.

Later, Duke had Rex Stewart on cornet; Hayes Alvis and Billy Taylor on bass, followed by the famous Jimmy Blanton; and Ben Webster was the first important tenor sax soloist in Duke's band.

During the forties, besides the addition of Billy Strayhorn as second arranger (Strayhorn wrote fine scores for Duke's band, for instance Take the "A" Train and Clementine), there were too many changes to follow them name by name; anyway, the second half of the forties was not Duke's happiest period (although he kept being the best big band). Then, in the fifties, Duke had more terrific bands than ever, for instance the one which changed but slightly during the years 1955–1958 and included most of the time Harold Baker, Ray Nance, Cat Anderson, Clark Terry on trumpet; Quentin Jackson, Britt Woodman, John Sanders on trombone; Johnny Hodges, Russell Procope, Paul Gonsalves, Jimmy Hamilton, Harry

Carney on saxes (and clarinet); Jimmy Woode on bass; Sam Woodyard on drums.

Not only was Duke able to choose musicians who were remarkable in themselves, but he picked men who fit in so well with his own musical temperament that he has been able to keep them with him for years. This, added to the fact that Duke has been able to make these musicians faithful translators of his thought, explains the astonishingly homogeneous quality of the orchestra.

But do not suppose that Duke Ellington, like the classic composers and conductors, merely presents his musicians with orchestra parts prepared in advance and directs the execution, baton in hand. On the contrary, Duke works in close collaboration with his musicians. He comes to rehearsal with a melody in mind; he plays it or hums it to his musicians; then with the piano demonstrates his principal ideas for the ensemble arrangement and designates several soloists to improvise a chorus or a half-chorus at this or that point. But perhaps it would be best to let Duke describe it in his own words:

> If you're what people usually call a "serious" composer, what you have done is a theme and variations, and you publish it as a part of an opus—a big piece of work. But if you're a swing musician, you may not publish it at all; just play it, making it a little different each time according to the way you feel, letting it grow as you work on it. . . . I can score with a lead pencil while riding on a train. But usually I gather the boys around me after a concert, say about three in the morning, when most of the world is quiet. I have a central idea which I bring out on the piano. At one stage, Cootie Williams, the trumpeter, will suggest an interpolation, perhaps a riff or obbligato for that spot. We try it and, probably, incorporate it. A little later on, Juan Tizol, the trombonist, will interrupt with another

idea. . . . Thus, after three or four sessions, I will evolve an
entirely new composition. But it will not be written out,
put on a score, until we have been playing it in public quite
a while. And, this is important to remember—no good
swing orchestra ever plays any composition with the same
effect twice.[2]

Sometimes one of the musicians of the orchestra will sub-
mit a composition to Duke and the other musicians. Together
they work out the arrangement. This is truly a fine example
of a collective musical creation. But whatever the musicians
may contribute to the arrangements, Duke's ideas and inspiration dominate everything and even seem to orient the soloists
in their improvisations—though they may not suspect it—
which accord perfectly with the arranged parts. Though Duke
will occasionally tell a musician what phrases to play in his
solo, that is very rare.

While the arrangements used by other orchestras sound as
though the orchestration of a melody had been done quite
separately, and moreover that it could have been done very
differently, with Duke one feels that theme and arrangement
are so closely united that they cannot be disassociated. For
actually Duke is not, like the others, a simple arranger; he is a
creative musician working through the intermediary of an
entire orchestra, a musician who thinks in orchestral terms.
Even his piano solos sound more like orchestral ensembles
than specifically pianistic music.

Duke's musical personality distinguishes his orchestrations
from those of all others and his ideas seem inexhaustible.
Though he has evolved a great deal during the years and has
never ceased to make astonishing discoveries, which is only
normal for a great musician, his oldest recordings still re-

[2] *Tops*—Diamond Jubilee Number.

semble his more recent ones, for one senses the same musical conception in both.

One of the characteristics of Duke's music is the use of what was labelled the "jungle style." It refers to the abundant use of the brasses with the "wa-wa" mute and the "growl"—supposed to suggest the noises of the jungle. Duke has had the finest "wa-wa" mute specialists. In the whole realm of jazz it would be difficult to find better men than "Tricky Sam" on trombone, or Bubber Miley, Cootie, and Ray Nance who followed one another as trumpets in Duke's orchestra. With the mutes they achieve effects of intense lamentation which profoundly move the listener. But Duke does not use these effects in the solos alone, he often has the entire brass section play in this style. Thereby, he creates ensembles of a mournful and imposing sonority. Two particularly magnificent examples are Duke's recordings of *Black and Tan Fantasy* and *Echoes of the Jungle*.

Aside from the strictly "jungle" interpretations Duke often draws a superb part from his brass section by powerfully swinging the "riffs" with the "wa-wa" mutes, behind a solo. Sonorous color and marvelous dynamic qualities are thus obtained. I will only cite one of innumerable examples—Barney Bigard's clarinet solo in *Lightnin'*. Here the brass supports Barney Bigard's solo in this fashion. In *The Gal from Joe's* beautiful sonorous relationships are obtained by the muted "wa-wa" brass section which alternates with a soloist who is improvising (in this case, Johnny Hodges on the saxophone).

But it is not only in this "jungle" type of interpretation that Duke achieves the most unforeseen and varied tonal proportions. Naturally he seeks first of all to create authentic jazz music and to swing his orchestra, but he is no less interested in giving rich tonal color to his orchestrations, unlike most

other arrangers who are invariably content with the same effects. A number like *Lazy Rhapsody*, in which the brass plays
"piano" with the mutes, is a particularly striking example of
Duke's ability to create original tonal combinations.

As a composer, Duke has a gift for conceiving charming
and melancholy melodies which in no way resemble the usual
jazz melodies. *Black Beauty, The Mooche, The Dicty Glide,
Shout 'Em Aunt Tillie, Lazy Rhapsody,* and *Blue Ramble* are
characteristic examples. From time to time Duke has also
borrowed the framework of the blues to inscribe a simple
fresh melody on the traditional harmonies. He often has it
played by three harmonizing clarinets or by the brasses. Following this he has the soloists "sing" the blues in their own
way, then as a finale, he returns to the theme first introduced.
The following numbers are more or less constructed in this
fashion: *Lazy Duke, No Papa No, Jungle Blues, Creole Love
Call, Beggars Blues, Blues With a Feeling.* In the last number,
however, a different and very beautiful theme, 32 bars in
length, is introduced in the middle of the interpretation (as a
matter of fact Duke often uses two or even three different
themes within the body of the same number). The influence
of the New Orleans style and of the kind of blues played by
King Oliver's orchestra can be felt in his blues themes. At
other times, in the blues, Duke allows his musicians to play a
series of solos resting on a sober but effective background, such
as *Bundle of Blues, Sweet Chariot, Country Gal.*

Naturally Duke's gift for melody is translated in his arrangements, in his trios and four-part arrangements for saxophones, and his trombone trios—as for example the beautiful
Slippery Horn. In fact no one has succeeded in making a big
band sing the way he does. His great ability is again reflected
in the way he combines the saxophones with the brass part to

produce an extraordinarily blended ensemble. Here one can see that Duke is essentially an "orchestra man" who expresses himself in an orchestral language with the same ease and spontaneity as Louis Armstrong on his trumpet.

From the point of view of harmony, Duke was the first to break through the limitations of elementary harmony in which most other arrangers had remained enmeshed. Over the years he has become increasingly daring and consequently his interpretations became full of harmonies which had never before been used in jazz. Duke has even gone so far as to use the traditional twelve-bar blues to create ensembles with un- expected harmonies but curiously enough he always succeeded in staying in the harmonic "climate" of the blues. Such is the case of his amazing *Diminuendo in Blue* and *Crescendo in Blue*.

Although Duke was not the first to write ensembles serving as harmonic background for improvised solos, his abundant and intelligent use of them has largely contributed to the spread of their use. The harmonies he creates are not only in themselves a treat for the ear but make the solo part sing even more. The rhythmic figures played by the brass or saxophones, as an accompaniment for the solos, swing his interpretations intensely. Moreover, unlike what generally happens in most large orchestras, Duke gives an important place to the clarinet part. He not only lets it play solo, but allows it to improvise around the ensembles, especially in the final choruses. In fact Duke is one of the rare orchestra leaders who has retained the clarinet in its true jazz role.

But all this creative richness would more or less be wasted if Duke's orchestra were not able to project its value. Luckily, Duke's musicians are such faithful translators of his thought that it is impossible to imagine better ones. The brass section has a tone, a volume, and a punch which probably rank it above all other brass sections I have heard up to now. The saxophones, too, are extraordinarily warm and singing. And what is amazing about Duke is that even though there are today but a couple of musicians left of the old group, the band still has the very same kind of unique *sound* and tone color as thirty years ago. Duke really seems to possess a magic power in getting from his new men the very same kind of tone and phrasing as from the previous ones—and yet without hampering in the least their own musical personality.

It must be observed that Duke's wonderful piano accompaniment and punctuations have, of course, a direct and considerable influence on the playing of his musicians. By just hitting one chord at a certain spot, Duke can inspire a soloist or make the whole band swing.

Duke's band has been the greatest for at least thirty years now. His musical genius has been recognized by many, and he has been hailed by some as the best American composer up till now. This is fine. But so much praise has been given to Duke Ellington's symphony-like works that too many people have not fully realized how genial Duke is in the pure jazz idiom. Some of his comparatively simple but most wonderful numbers such as *Ducky Wucky, Ridin' on a Blue Note, Just A-Settin' and A-Rockin'* were overlooked by the critics (not by the *musicians*, though!). Even today, the same phenomenon can be observed. One of the greatest ever of Duke's recorded performance, *Just Scratchin' the Surface*,[3] has hardly been given any notice by the "critics." Why? Because instead of posing as an ambitious work, it is straightforward and simple and has nothing that appears particularly original or "picturesque" to offer. But the truth is that it would be impossible

[3] From the *Newport 1958* LP, on Columbia CL-1245.

to find, in 40 years of recorded jazz music, another performance like this one. It has all the superiority of a "live" performance over those made in recording studios.[4] The band swings
so much and plays with such fire that it almost scares you.
Duke's wonderful piano part and Paul Gonsalves' beautiful
tenor sax solo are perfectly integrated in a concise, effective
orchestral arrangement. Here you have the very substance of
good jazz: the music is great, not by reason of elaborate, complicated researches but thanks mainly to the overwhelming
way a band swings a well-conceived arrangement. This is the
quality that completely passes above the heads of would-be
intellectuals who cannot help but judge jazz music according
to the classical music standards.

Numerous other things could be said in appraisal of Duke's
musical genius but it would take more space than can be given
in the present book.

The two most important big bands in the history of jazz,
along with Duke Ellington's and Fletcher Henderson's, are
probably the orchestras of Jimmie Lunceford and Count
Basie.

Although Jimmie Lunceford's orchestra was organized only
a few years after Duke's, it only began playing in New York in
1934, at which time it began to get recognition. It came to an
end in 1947 with Jimmie Lunceford's death.

Lunceford's group had several points in common with
Duke's. Like Duke's, it was a stable group whose composition
was hardly modified over the years. In 1934 the members
were: Eddie Tompkins, Sy Oliver, Tommy Stevenson on
trumpet; Henry Wells and Russell Boles on trombone; Willie

---

[4] I must point out that *Just Scratchin' the Surface* is (with *Prima Bara*)
the only number in the album that was actually recorded at the Newport Festival.

Smith, Joe Thomas, Earl Carruthers, and Laforet Dent on saxophone; Edwin Wilcox on piano, Al Norris on guitar, Moses Allen on bass, James Crawford on drums, and Lunceford himself, who played either saxophone or flute but more frequently only led the orchestra. In 1935, Paul Webster replaced Stevenson in the trumpet section; Eddie Durham was added as third trombone; Edward Brown replaced Laforet Dent on saxophone, and Dan Grisson was added as 5th saxophonist and "sweet" singer. Then in 1938, Trummy Young replaced Eddie Durham, and Ted Buckner replaced Edward Brown. In 1939 and 1940, two new trumpeters, Garry Wilson and "Snookie" Young, replaced Sy Oliver and Tompkins. After 1942, the band began to decline.

Another point of similarity with Duke is Lunceford's profoundly original style which distinguishes his orchestra from all others. A great part of this is due to Sy Oliver's style of orchestration, for Sy was the principal arranger for the orchestra until the end of 1939.

Sy Oliver is perhaps, with the exception of Duke, the most original arranger jazz has produced. His originality is manifested in many ways. He chooses altogether unforeseen tempos. For example, he worked out numbers like *Margie* and *Ain't She Sweet* for a slow tempo, though they are customarily played in a fast tempo. Inversely, he sets a very fast tempo for a number like *Lonesome Road* which seems designed for a slow tempo. And every time the result is marvelous. Moreover Sy writes very full arrangements which are sometimes as complex as Duke's. He writes vertiginous passages which are very difficult to play and fantastic interplays between the saxophones, trumpets, and trombones.

Many people have used this as a pretext to claim that Lunceford's orchestra plays "sophisticated" music which departs from the true spirit of jazz. As though complex and brilliant arrangements could not, at the same time, have a very direct style permitting an execution to swing a great deal! Actually, in Sy Oliver's arrangements, everything is so organized that the interpretation swings with a maximum intensity. Likewise his style is very clear. Though Sy frequently orchestrates for three trumpets in a very high register, he almost always writes an accompaniment or countermelody in a low register to be played by either the trombone or the baritone sax. As a result the orchestra is well rooted and marvelously balanced. In fact the tonal balance created by this bass part, which is generally absent in the interpretations of large orchestras, recalls that of the primitive jazz groups of New Orleans, where, as I mentioned earlier, the trombone furnished the bass part. Like Duke, Sy Oliver takes care to create beautiful and sonorous combinations and has, in fact, pushed the art of contrasts further than any other jazz arranger. This can be seen in many of his arrangements, but it is especially noticeable in *Organ Grinder's Swing*, which is one of his masterpieces. Here "piano" and "fortissimo" parts alternate; the passages are played either lightly or with force.

The following are among Sy's most beautiful arrangements: *Organ Grinder's Swing* and *Stomp It Off* seem to overflow with melodic and orchestral ideas and are written in a style which is exemplary for swinging. *Margie* is treated in a very simple fashion; seemingly unimportant light and subtle touches are written underneath the solo improvisation and give the interpretation a great deal of grace, and permit it to swing in a unique fashion (the beautiful saxophone parts accompanying the vocal chorus should be particularly noted). *Swanee River* and *My Blue Heaven* are both arrangements with full shadings and contrasts. In *For Dancers Only* Sy has refrained from all melodic novelty and has worked with the single aim of creating an interpretation which swings as much as possible. The prodigious *Annie Laurie* is a veritable orgy of sounds which is an apotheosis.

Finally I want to mention Sy's gift for arranging the most vulgar and insipid themes in such a way that Lunceford's orchestra is able to make first-class jazz out of them, as for example *On the Beach at Bali-Bali*.

Several other musicians of the orchestra have an arranging style rather similar to Sy Oliver's. The pianist, Wilcox, was directly inspired by Sy; Willie Smith, who has a greater imagination, wrote arrangements of dazzling verve such as *Runnin' Wild* and *Mood Indigo*; Eddie Durham, who had developed an excellent style before joining Lunceford, has furnished the orchestra with more brutal and less finished arrangements than Sy Oliver's, but works which swing magnificently, such as *Harlem Shout* and *Avalon*. Durham's temperament is rather different from Sy Oliver's, consequently his arrangements only suit the orchestra because he voluntarily bends himself to write in the Lunceford style—notably with the use of a strong bass part. Otherwise for an entire ensemble chorus he frequently uses a very simple "riff" which is repeated indefinitely. This can be heard in some of the arrangements he wrote since he left Lunceford, like *Wham*. However this style of arrangement is better suited to an orchestra like Count Basie's, whom we will discuss shortly, than to Lunceford's.

After Sy Oliver's departure, Lunceford's principal arranger was Billy Moore, a musician who was not a member of the orchestra. He is a very fine arranger and works in a spirit altogether similar to Sy Oliver's. As a matter of fact I believe that Sy himself advised Lunceford to use him. Among others,

Moore has arranged *Monotony in Your Flat, I Got It, What's Your Story Morning Glory*. Moore's arrangements swing like Sy Oliver's, and have the same sonorous and orchestral subtleties, the same fertility of ideas which are now conservative and concise, now vivid.

As is the case with Duke, one hardly knows which to admire most—the actual music played by the orchestra, or the way in which that music is played. Lunceford's group possessed such cohesion and was so admirably disciplined that the most difficult ensembles were executed with a technical perfection which leaves the listener gasping. Moreover the orchestra had a fire and a great enthusiastic power; it used to swing, not in a massive or heavy way, but in an alert, incisive, delicate, and well-knit fashion which was sometimes supple and restrained as in *Margie* and *Organ Grinder's Swing* and sometimes violent and tempestuous like *Runnin' Wild, Annie Laurie*, and *For Dancers Only*. In moderate tempos, the orchestra played with an ease and indescribable nonchalance, in so unusual a fashion that the expression "Lunceford tempo" was used. Likewise this orchestra was one of the most consistent, never knowing any "off nights" which are the bane of most orchestras.

Lunceford's orchestra has also been richly provided with great soloists—three of the saxophone players, Willie Smith, Ted Buckner, and Joe Thomas, and the trombonist Trummy Young.

As a section, the saxophones strike one by their exceptionally rich and voluminous tone and by the perfection with which they execute the most difficult passages, such as the beautiful quartets in *Sleepy Time Gal, I'm Alone With You*. Willie Smith, one of the most powerful altos, carries the entire section when he swings. In fact Sy Oliver once said, "We brass men have to blow hard not to be outdone by those saxes." Actually I think this section even matches Duke's; only a Bennie Carter could have organized and led such a magnificent saxophone section.

However the brasses, though first class, are not as exceptional as Duke's. But the rhythm section is very solid, particularly because of the great drummer, James Crawford.

In sum, Lunceford's group is a complete and extremely original orchestra, and practically the only one which could in some way bear comparison with Duke Ellington's orchestra.

Count Basie's orchestra was formed more recently than the preceding two. Basie played for several years in Kansas City before coming to New York in 1936, the year which marked the beginning of his fame.

At that time the orchestra was composed of Joe Keyes, Carl Smith, and Buck Clayton on trumpet, George Hunt and Dan Minor on trombone, Jack Washington and Caughey Roberts on alto saxophone, Herschel Evans and Lester Young on tenor saxophone, Count Basie at the piano, Claude Williams on guitar, Walter Page on bass, and Jo Jones on drums. Jimmy Rushing was singing in the band.

After various changes the orchestra was stabilized in 1938, in the following way: Edward Lewis, Buck Clayton, and Harry Edison on trumpet, Bennie Morton, Dan Minor, and Eddie Durham (who was quickly replaced by Dickie Wells) on trombone, Earl Warren and Jack Washington on alto saxophone, Herschel Evans and Lester Young on tenor saxophone, with the same rhythm group except for Claude Williams (guitar) who was replaced by Freddie Green.

Then in 1939 the physiognomy of the orchestra was again changed by the addition of a fourth trumpet, "Shad" Collins, and the death of Herschel Evans who was replaced by Buddy

Tate. Later, Lester Young's chair was successively taken by Don Byas, Illinois Jacquet, Lucky Thompson, and Paul Gonsalves, and there were several other changes. In the early fifties the band became firmly established, and since 1955 it has included most of the time Joe Newman, Wendell Culley, Thad Jones, and Snooky Young on trumpet; Henry Coker, Benny Powell, Bill Hughes (replaced in 1957 by Al Grey) on trombone; Marshall Royal, Frank Wess, Frank Foster, Charlie Fowlkes, Billy Mitchell (the latter was preceded for a short while by the great Eddie Davis) on saxes; Freddie Green on guitar, Eddie Jones on bass, Sonny Payne on drums.

What is known as the Basie style is to be looked for in the records of the thirties and forties rather than those of the fifties. Just as Fletcher Henderson had his own style during the twenties and more or less conformed, later, to the style of the others, Count Basie really created a new big band style, which was widely imitated by other bands, but he started, towards the late forties, to mix other orchestral styles with his own. So, when I describe the Basie style, I have mostly in mind the band as it can be heard in the records made during the years 1937–1947.

In general, Count Basie does not use subtle and complex arrangements like those of Duke Ellington or Jimmy Lunceford; his orchestra is entirely different. It can be characterized by its use of excellent "riffs" which are repeated by the entire orchestra in the opening or final choruses, or played by one of the sections as a support for the solo improvisations. Many of the arrangements used by this group are "head" arrangements. In fact during an interpretation a new riff is sometimes inaugurated by Basie or some other musician, and as a consequence there is a great deal of exciting improvisation in the orchestra. When the musicians are feeling good, choruses are added to choruses, and the soloists improvise fully while a series of riffs is played behind their improvisation by the brass or saxophones. The total effect swings in a formidable way. Some of the written arrangements are the work of men who played in the band, such as Eddie Durham (*Topsy, Out the Window*), Buck Clayton (*Love Jumped Out*), Herschel Evans (*Doggin' Around*), and others. Besides, the band has had two of the greatest swing arrangers in Jimmy Mundy, who wrote such masterpieces as *Coming Out Party, Super Chief, Blue Skies*, and Buster Harding, author of such arrangements as *Rockin' the Blues, 9:20 Special, House Rent Boogie*—all this being ideal music for a band like Basie's, much more so than the scores Neal Hefti wrote for the Basie band in the fifties. During the latter period, Ernie Wilkins' and Quincy Jones' arrangements have been much better than Hefti's.

Count Basie succeeds in getting the very maximum out of his orchestra. Instead of having the entire orchestra play the first chorus, as is generally done, Basie himself frequently plays the introduction and the first chorus on the piano—sometimes even the second chorus. Only then will he have the entire orchestra come in. When the pianist is as fine as Basie, this method offers a great advantage. During the first bars, Basie himself hunts for the exact tempo for the interpretation. When the rhythm section joins in, it takes up this perfect tempo, and, by the time the rest of the orchestra comes in, the tempo is already solidly established and it is impossible for anyone to vacillate. On the contrary, when an entire orchestra comes in at the beginning of a number, the perfect tempo is not always found immediately. In fact sometimes the musicians will look for it during the entire number, and play to the very end without finding the right tempo. Parenthetically, I want to note that Lunceford's orchestra is one of the rare groups which used to find the right tempo at once, from the first bars of the number. But to return to Basie—there are numerous examples of his method of playing, notably in *Don't You Miss Your Baby, One O'Clock Jump, John's Idea, Honeysuckle Rose, Baby Don't Tell on Me.* This question of tempo is, in fact, of capital importance, for without a perfect tempo there can be none of that total ease which is absolutely essential if a number is to swing—and swing, let us say it once again, is the very foundation of jazz music.

As a matter of fact, often in spite of a good departure the perfect tempo is not found, and it is only after the execution has gone on for a time that the tempo comes closer and closer to perfection. The *Panassié Stomp* is a typical example. Here, after the opening piano chorus, the band does not really "find" itself until it reaches the splendid saxophone riffs which support the third chorus played by Dickie Wells on trombone, and only achieves its full height during the two last choruses of riffs which are swung by the ensemble in a magnificent fashion.

Another characteristic method is the use of a piano solo played by Basie in the middle of a number. Sometimes the left hand plays only a little or not at all. Meanwhile the right hand plays a chord or several notes from time to time, while the rhythm section furnishes a full background and Walter Page runs up and down his bass with an inconceivable mobility. A succession of tonal and rhythmic effects of great originality is thus obtained. Although many orchestras have sought to imitate it they have had little success, for it is essential to have a Count Basie and a bass of Walter Page's breadth in order to avoid falling into mediocrity and even ridicule.

One of the orchestra's strong points is the splendid fashion in which it plays the blues. A large orchestra rarely plays the blues so well, for it is difficult to achieve the spontaneity and freshness indispensable to this type of interpretation. But thanks to the simplicity of its arrangements and its spirit of improvisation, Basie's orchestra plays the blues in a direct, pure style. Moreover the presence of a great blues singer, like Jimmy Rushing, and Basie's piano are definitely trump cards.

The band frequently plays the blues, and has made many magnificent recordings of it: *Good Morning Blues, Blues in the Dark, The Blues I Like to Hear, Harvard Blues,* which are blues in slow tempo; *One O'Clock Jump, Swingin' the Blues, Sent for You Yesterday, Baby Don't Tell on Me, The World Is Mad,* blues in fast or moderate tempo which are based, mostly, on the use of appropriate riffs.

The band has, or has had, the following remarkable soloists: Buck Clayton, Harry Edison, Emmett Berry, Joe Newman (trumpet); Dickie Wells, Bennie Morton, Vic Dickenson, Henry Coker, Al Grey (trombone); and more great tenor saxists than any other band: Herschel Evans, Lester Young, Buddy Tate, Don Byas, Illinois Jacquet, Lucky Thompson, Paul Gonsalves, Paul Quinichette, Eddie Davis, to name but the most important ones—not to speak of Basie himself on piano.

As an ensemble, the brass section has a sparkling tone, a heavy and compact volume which is a treat to the ear. The saxophone section likewise is remarkable for the warmth of its tone; while the rhythm section, when it had Walter Page's bewitching bass, Jo Jones on drums, Basie on piano, and the one and only Freddie Green on guitar, was one of the best in the history of jazz. Freddie Green is still in the band, at the time of writing, together with that fine bassist Eddie Jones and one of the best young drummers, Sonny Payne, and they make a first-class rhythm section.

The year 1940 saw the rise of a new big band, which was to create and spread a new orchestral style: it was Lionel Hampton's band.

Lionel Hampton succeeded in blending most happily Basie's and Lunceford's styles, and added to these a strongly personal touch. His orchestra recalls Basie by an abundant use of well-chosen and often combined riffs, such as in *Flying Home*, his theme song and most celebrated number. At other times Hampton would use more elaborate arrangements requiring an instrumental virtuosity like that of Lunceford's band, such as *Turkey Hop*; also like Lunceford, Lionel frequently uses high-register effects by the trumpet section; but it is mostly through the use of a certain type of tempo that Lionel Hampton vividly recalls Lunceford. Hamp always wanted from all his drummers a strongly accented afterbeat. Numbers like *Chop Chop* and *Hamp's Got a Duke* are very reminiscent of the typical Lunceford pulse.

Lionel Hampton's band reflects the vitality and dynamism of the leader. Powerful as Basie's may be, Lionel's band is a tornado. When one hears the horns blowing up a storm with biting attack and the rhythm section pounding behind them, there is no way to escape and stand still. Lionel Hampton's is the most impetuous orchestra in the history of jazz.

Lionel always had a special liking for the fast or medium-tempo blues played in boogie-woogie style by the piano and the rhythm section, with Hamp improvising at length on the vibes—or with other soloists—and the horns riffing in the background. Many numbers were recorded in that style, such as *Hamp's Boogie Woogie*, *Tempo's Boogie*, *Beulah's Boogie*, *Beulah's Sister Boogie*.

Besides excelling in explosive numbers, Lionel Hampton can also make successful music on slow numbers, such as the subtle *Eli Eli,* which he dedicated to the State of Israel, or *Midnight Sun,* where there is to be found some of the Ellingtonian finesse of touch.

One of Lionel's main arrangers has been the remarkable pianist Milton Buckner, who has arranged many numbers quite fitted to the band's style. *The Lamplighter, Overtime, Slide Hamp Slide,* and *A Million Dollar Smile* are typical of Buckner's style of arranging. Other musicians in Hamp's band also wrote fitting arrangements, notably Bobby Plater, author of *Hamp's Got a Duke, Giddy Up, Hamp's Gumbo.*

Lionel Hampton has always had a flair for discovering new talents, and since tenor sax solos always were featured in the band, great musicians successively occupied the tenor sax chair: Illinois Jacquet, Lucky Thompson, Arnett Cobb, Morris Lane, Gene Morris, Billy Williams, Clifford Scott, Jay Peters, Eddie Chamblee, to quote but the best. It was in Hampton's group that there was created and developed what was to be known as the "wild tenor sax style," which took over during the mid-forties and was particularly well illustrated by Illinois Jacquet and Arnett Cobb.

Lionel has had other remarkable musicians in his band: Milton Buckner on piano; Ernie Royal, Cat Anderson, Wendell Culley, Walter Williams, Wallace Davenport on trumpet; Al Hayes and Al Grey on trombone; Bobby Plater on alto sax; Billy Mackel and Wes Montgomery on guitar; Charlie Mingus on bass; Shadow Wilson, Fred Radcliffe, George Jenkins, Curley Hamner (who is a great dancer) on drums; and the vocalist Sonnie Parker.

Most other big bands of renown flourished during the thirties and the first half of the forties.

Chick Webb's, one of the oldest, was already active in the late twenties. It was one of the most swinging, thanks mostly to the phenomenal drumming of the leader, but it also had some first-class arrangers, such as Edgar Sampson (author of the famous *Stompin' at the Savoy* and *Don't Be That Way*) and Charlie Dixon, who wrote one of the most original and beautiful arrangements in the whole history of jazz: *That Naughty Waltz*. According to some musicians, it is also Charlie Dixon who wrote the score of the celebrated *Harlem Congo*; but Harry White wrote the tune and he might have arranged it too, as it sounds like his style of writing. Whoever wrote it, *Harlem Congo* is a great record, maybe the best Chick Webb's band ever made. Another of the band's masterpieces is *Liza*, arranged by Benny Carter.

Chick Webb also had some excellent soloists, such as Bobby Stark and Taft Jordan on trumpet, Sandy Williams on trombone, Edgar Sampson, and, later on, Hilton Jefferson on alto sax; and, of course, the celebrated Ella Fitzgerald as main singer.

Cab Calloway's band reached its top during the years 1939–1941, when it had an amazing rhythm section headed by Cozy Cole on drums, with Milton Hinton on bass and Danny Barker on guitar; and wonderful soloists such as Jonah Jones on trumpet (or Irving Randolph before him), Chew Berry on tenor sax, Hilton Jefferson on alto sax. In records like *Ratamacue*, *Crescendo in Drums*, and *Jonah Joins The Cab*, Cab Calloway's band plays with a fire and drive equal to any other orchestra.

Erskine Hawkins' band, which played at the Harlem "Savoy" for many years, was one of the best dance bands from 1937 up until 1952. And I mean a *real* dance band, which is a swinging, rocking one, not one of the "blue-peppy syncopated" schmaltzy orchestras that are considered "dance bands" only by those for whom dancing merely consists in moving languorously with a girl in their arms. By dance band, I mean a band to be enjoyed and danced to by those who live the music they hear and express it through the rhythm, gestures, and impulse given to their whole body.

Erskine Hawkins' band, in its early days, imitated the Lunceford band in both its arrangements and its soloists, although simplifying the Lunceford style; later, the Basie influence mixed with it. Erskine Hawkins, himself a brilliant trumpet virtuoso, had such good men as Julian Dash on tenor sax, Heywood Henry on baritone sax and clarinet, Bill Johnson (later replaced by Bobby Smith) on alto sax, Dud Bascomb on trumpet, and Avery Parrish on piano. Some of these musicians wrote good arrangements, too, but Erskine Hawkins' main arranger was Sammy Lowe (one of his trumpet players). Among the band's best records are *Tuxedo Junction*, *Gin Mill Special*, *Bicycle Bounce*, and the celebrated *After Hours* featuring some of the best blue piano ever waxed (by Avery Parrish).

The famous piano player Earl Hines was the leader of a big band most of the time from 1929 until 1947. Several of his groups were excellent but the best one was that of the years 1939–1940, with Budd Johnson (tenor, alto sax, and arranger), Walter Fuller (trumpet and vocal), "Little Sax" Crowder (tenor) followed by Franz Jackson, the formidable Alvin Burroughs on drums, and other fine musicians. This group recorded such masterpieces as *Boogie Woogie on St. Louis Blues*, *G. T. Stomp*, *Piano Man*, and *Father Steps In*.

Several times in the years around 1940 Benny Carter had such good bands that it is a shame he did not achieve the success and fame of a Duke Ellington or a Count Basie. Among the records made during that period, *Sleep* (arranged by Benny Carter himself) stands out as one of the most exciting big-band records ever.

Other good big bands that should not be forgotten are three orchestras of the late twenties which, next to Fletcher Henderson and Duke Ellington, were the best of their time: McKinney's Cotton Pickers, when they were under the leadership of Don Redman (after Don had left Fletcher); Charlie Johnson, who was playing most of the time at the Harlem "Small's Paradise" and sounded somewhat like Fletcher; and Luis Russell, whose band had a New Orleans flavor because it included some New Orleans men, especially the incomparable Pops Foster on string bass. Other good men in Luis Russell's band were Higginbotham on trombone, Al Nicholas on clarinet, Henry Allen on trumpet, and Paul Barbarin on drums.

In the early thirties Don Redman formed an excellent orchestra; and other good contemporary groups were Elmer Snowden's (which unfortunately was never recorded); Bennie Moten's band, from Kansas City, which included some of the men who were to become the nucleus of Count Basie's band; and the Blue Rhythm Band, which later became Lucky Millinder's orchestra and reached a very high standard around 1940 (*Ride Red Ride*—the Decca version—and *Apollo Jump* are their best records). Other good bands of the thirties were Andy Kirk's, with Mary Lou Williams as a pianist and arranger; Teddy Hill's, and Horace Henderson's. In the early and mid-forties Jay McShann had a good Kansas City band, in the Count Basie line; and Cootie Williams, the ex-Ellington trumpet player, headed a first-class band, which excelled on the blues (with Eddie Vinson on alto sax and singing the blues). In the mid-forties Billy Eckstine, the singer, had a swinging band which did not live long, and soon afterward Dizzy Gillespie got together his first big band, which could and did play at times some good jazz but too often performed some of those exotic would-be progressive arrangements of the Afro-Cuban type. In the fifties, Gillespie had another band which could have been good if it had not featured too much progressive and exotic music.

The most recent of permanent big bands—besides Sy Oliver's which was an excellent but short-lived group—is that of Buddy Johnson, which from the mid-forties up till now has constantly maintained a good standard. Dismissed by a very indiscriminating critic as a "rock 'n' roll" band, Buddy Johnson has kept a nice, swinging beat and instead of wasting his talents in complicated and more or less unfortunate experiments, he has succeeded in remaining one of the favorites among the colored public and dancers, who know far more about jazz than more critics one would care to name. The way this band swings is more related to the Lionel Hampton style than to any other band, with a strong afterbeat predominating most of the time.

There have never been any large white orchestras comparable to the Negro groups. The oldest, like those of Jean Goldkette and Ben Pollack, had several good soloists but turned toward commercial executions rather than real jazz.

However since 1935 and especially 1936, with the arrival of the "swing fad" a number of white orchestras have grown up. These groups have freed themselves to a great extent from commercial concessions. The principal were Benny Goodman's, Tommy Dorsey's, Woody Herman's, and Artie Shaw's. These orchestras have many excellent qualities. They play with a good sense of ensemble work; they are polished and precise, and in fact hold to a minute exactness. But they have never had the *abandon* of the Negro orchestras. Consequently they play with a stiffness which prevents them from swinging much. Moreover the majority of their soloists are not sufficiently fine musicians. Ironically enough practically all their arrangements are written by Negroes. Thus Benny Goodman has successively used Fletcher Henderson, James Mundy, and the excellent Fred Norman as well as several others; while Tommy Dorsey employs Sy Oliver.

In my opinion, Benny Goodman's orchestra was at its best in 1935 and 1936. At that time Gene Krupa and Bunny Berigan were members of the orchestra, while Fletcher Henderson was principal arranger. He wrote some magnificent arrangements of a pure and charming style such as *Sometimes I'm Happy*, *Blue Skies*, and especially the unforgettable *When Buddha Smiles*. Unfortunately Benny Goodman's orchestra plays these arrangements stiffly so that one gets only a rather mixed pleasure from them.

Tommy Dorsey's orchestra, with Dave Tough on the drums, has more warmth than Benny Goodman's. This was especially true during 1937 and 1938, and was probably due to the greater personal merit and enthusiasm of the leader. His repertoire includes a number of excellent orchestrations by Dean Kincaid, who is perhaps the best white arranger. Kincaid has the merit of writing arrangements in a style which is somewhat different from the usual. He likes clarinet ensembles and knows how to contrast them with the brass in an intelligent and sometimes imposing fashion. We owe to him a fine and agreeable orchestration of the famous *Boogie Woogie* of Pine Top Smith, excellently recorded by Tommy Dorsey.

Artie Shaw's orchestra, when in its heyday, i.e., towards the late thirties and the early forties, was swinging more than Dorsey's and Goodman's. But the best of the white bands was that of Woody Herman in the early and mid-forties. It had an amazing instrumental virtuosity and it could swing. But soon Woody Herman destroyed the quality of his music by using some "progressive" men and arrangements, and the band lost its spirit.

It is hardly necessary to mention Stan Kenton's orchestra in a book on real jazz, his pompous orchestrations being made under the "progressive" banner and sounding like a strange mixture of highbrowed, showy symphonies and Hollywood pseudo-jazz. That such a band could, at one time, have been taken as a "jazz" orchestra clearly shows how little the press and the public still know about the real jazz.

The fact that there have been no new big bands of importance during the last twelve years or so is strictly a matter of economics. Lack of well-paid bookings and nothing else was the cause of the decline of big bands. Otherwise there would be just as many, and probably more excellent big bands nowadays than twenty years ago. In fact, Quincy Jones (the most talented of young arrangers) formed a fine new big band in January of 1960, and it is still in doubt at this writing whether his orchestra will find enough bookings to survive.

16 jazz in recordings

To all those who love and wish to study jazz music, the record has a tremendous importance. It is the only means of preserving improvisations; the only means of hearing jazz musicians who are thousands of miles away; and especially the only means we have of preserving the work of those musicians who are dead, and those orchestras which have disappeared.

There is a current objection that a recording is inferior to direct audition. Certainly that is incontestable. Naturally it is preferable to hear musicians in the flesh rather than on a record, for one gets far more pleasure from an actual performance. But it is not always possible to hear a musician in person; and, alas, each time one of our favorite musicians dies, the record remains as our only resource—and how valuable it is then!

But many people—principally professional musicians—claim that a jazz musician cannot be judged from his recordings. They say that a musician cannot have the same liberty, ease, and carelessness in the cold atmosphere of a recording studio, and that he improvises and swings with a far livelier spirit in a night club [1] full of dancers and enthusiastic listeners. Briefly,

[1] Since this was written, jazz has been more and more featured in concert halls, and less in night clubs and dance halls. This is regrettable, as the solemn atmosphere of concert halls is not too favorable to such a spontaneous music as jazz. Nine times out of ten, musicians

they claim that a musician cannot give his best in a recording.

Of course, it is true that musicians—especially the very nerv-ous ones—may have difficulty in playing as well in a recording studio. But I still believe that, as a general rule, one can judge a musician just as accurately from a recording as from an actual performance, and these are my reasons:

Naturally the musician who records for the first time is nerv-ous, and this added to the coldness of the studio will prevent him from relaxing and letting himself go. This discomfort will continue during his second and third recording sessions. But if he records frequently, he will become accustomed to his sur-roundings and eventually will feel relatively at ease. Therefore, one must carefully abstain from judging a musician by a single record or even by three or four. On the other hand one can make a good estimate of his worth by hearing a great number of his recordings.

Then there is the claim that a musician can never reach the same heights in a recording as he does in a night club. But I beg you to consider the actual value of the judgments made at a dance. If you know jazz music, you know very well that almost all great musicians are subject to heights and depths, that on certain days they play marvelously and on others they are very short of inspiration. As a result this little story is often repeated.

A fan goes to hear an orchestra five or six times. He is struck by this trombonist or that saxophonist, whereas the pianist seems, justly enough, quite mediocre, because he is not in form that day. At the seventh performance the pianist plays in a dazzling fashion, but our fan isn't there. The next day, the

---

will play better for a dance than for a concert. Yet jazz concerts, like all "live" music, generally tend to be warmer than performances in the recording studio.

fan meets a friend who has heard that seventh performance. Both are dumbfounded to compare their completely different opinions of the pianist. Yet each has actually judged correctly in the light of what he heard. The ironical note will be the fact that a record may first reveal to these two people the pianist's great value. From my own experience I can say that I have heard some musicians in person who revealed themselves far more capable than I had supposed from their recordings. But just as frequently I have heard musicians in the flesh and found that they did not reveal the same inspiration as they had in their recordings. Moreover I have heard a musician twenty different times in various night spots and have judged him insignificant, and have been amazed upon hearing him the twenty-first time to discover that he is a musician capable of reaching the greatest heights.

All of this only goes to prove that it is just as difficult to judge a musician correctly after many direct auditions as after many recordings.

Naturally a musician is normally more at ease in a cabaret than in a recording studio. But nine times out of ten he will play better with a good orchestra at the studio than with a poor orchestra at a night club. And frequently the recording companies assemble a number of brilliant musicians who are rarely brought together in a night club orchestra. Moreover, a musician playing in a cabaret will take no pains to play well if he is feeling out of sorts, whereas in a recording studio he never fails to concentrate and force himself to give his best.

I heard recordings by Louis Armstrong and Duke Ellington as well as many others, long before hearing them in person. But I found that I had gotten a very exact idea of the grandeur of those musicians—of Louis' superiority to other trumpet players, of Duke's over other orchestras. How could I have made an accurate estimate if the records had not faithfully reflected the respective values of these musicans and orchestras?

In all truth one can say that the case for the record has been proven and that one can rely upon it in the majority of cases without fear.

As a matter of fact I would like to devote several pages to a discussion of the many brilliant orchestras which were either organized for recording purposes only, or which have been disbanded for many years and can now be heard only in recordings.

I will discuss first those excellent orchestras who made recordings in a pure New Orleans style—records which all those who sincerely appreciate jazz should hear.

King Oliver's was the earliest of these orchestras. It played in Chicago in 1922, 1923, and 1924, and recorded at that time. The orchestra included King Oliver and Louis Armstrong (trumpet), Honoré Dutrey (trombone), Johnny Dodds (clarinet), Lil Armstrong (piano), John St. Cyr (banjo), Bill Johnson (string bass), and Baby Dodds (drums), and was, in my opinion the best small orchestra in the history of jazz.

Most of the interpretations played by this orchestra were made up of ensembles. Two trumpets state the melody, with King Oliver playing the first trumpet. At the same time Johnny Dodds embroiders in the upper registers of the clarinet, while the trombone plays a bass part typical of the pure New Orleans style. The ensembles are cut, here and there, by a break and more rarely by an entire chorus or two played as a solo by one of the musicians.

But the extraordinary thing about these interpretations is the perfect balance which the musicians achieve in improvisation, and the grace and melodic clarity which reign from the beginning to the end. Listen, for example, to the sublime

Canal Street Blues which is one of the masterpieces of the orchestra. Is there anything more moving than the singing of the two trumpets, enriched by the singing counterpoint of Johnny Dodds' clarinet, all of which swings magnificently? Here is jazz in all its grandeur and purity; here it is free from all the external influences which later altered its primitive character. In fact the recordings made by King Oliver at that time are among the most beautiful jazz records—the immortal *Dipper Mouth Blues*, which contains the three famous chorus-solos played by King Oliver which have been extensively copied by other trumpets—*Jazzin' Babies Blues*, *Sweet Lovin' Man*, *New Orleans Stomp*, and *Camp Meeting Blues* as well as many others.[2]

A few years later, King Oliver made two other series of re-cordings, one for Brunswick-Vocalion (1926–1928), the other for RCA Victor (1929–1930). His band was not as great as it had been, but many of those performances give us a chance to hear King Oliver in long and well-recorded solos—a thing which hardly ever happened in the 1922–1924 discs. The style of the performances is very different from that of King Oli-ver's oldest records. There is little ensemble improvisation; instead, solos alternate with simple and melodious arrange-ments, often conceived by Joe Oliver himself: very swinging clarinet trios, nice brass ensembles. Among the best Bruns-wick sides, let us name *Aunt Hagar's Blues*, *Speakeasy Blues*, *I'm Watchin' the Clock*, *Every Tub*, *Showboat Shuffle*; among the RCA Victor sides: *I Must Have It*, *You're Just My Type*, *New Orleans Shout*.

Let us come now to the records made in Chicago by Louis

[2] Twelve of those unforgettable recordings can be found in the Epic LP LN-3208, a record which should be in the collection of anyone in-terested in jazz.

Armstrong and an orchestra organized especially for recording during the years 1925–1929.

The life of this group can be divided into two periods. During the first, up to the year 1928, Louis used the following musicians: Kid Ory on trombone, Johnny Dodds on clarinet, Lil Armstrong on piano, and John St. Cyr on guitar or banjo, to which were sometimes added Peter Biggs on tuba, Baby Dodds on drums, and Lonnie Johnson on guitar.[3] During the second period (1928–1929) Louis used Fred Robinson on trombone, Jimmy Strong on clarinet and tenor saxophone, Earl Hines on piano, Mancy Cara on banjo, and Zutty Singleton on drums, while Don Redman on alto saxophone was added for the last records.

The recordings of the first period are in the classic New Orleans style, similar to King Oliver's, though with two principal differences. First, there is less ensemble work and there are many more solos. Second, the collective improvisations are more exuberant and more daring in conception. Since Louis Armstrong was the only trumpet he did not have to adjust his playing to another trumpet as in King Oliver's orchestra. Therefore he gives free rein to his audacious initiative in these records. This in itself suffices to give these records an entirely different atmosphere from those of King Oliver.

Although all the records that Louis Armstrong made with this orchestra should be cited, I will only mention a few of the particularly unusual ones—*Gut Bucket Blues*, an admirable blues interpretation in a moderate tempo; *Cornet Chop Suey*, in which Louis plays in an indescribable fashion; *Muskrat Ramble*; *Heebie Jeebies*; *Struttin' with Some Barbecue*; *Put 'Em Down Blues*; *Alligator Crawl*; *Wild Man Blues*; and

[3] When there is a tuba to be heard, the trombonist is not Kid Ory (contrary to what was believed for years) but John Thomas.

several blues in a slow tempo such as *Gully Low Blues; Savoy Blues; I'm Not Rough;* and finally two recordings with enrapturing collective improvisations—*Willie the Weeper* and *Potato Head Blues.*[4] The wonderful rhythm and harmonic work of John St. Cyr must not be overlooked, for it has a great deal to do with the beauty of these recordings. In fact it is doubtful whether the records would have been as fine had he not been a member of the orchestra.

The recordings of the second period also belong to the New Orleans style but they are not strictly classic. The ensembles are no longer improvised but are sometimes arranged—actually in a very simple fashion. Solos dominate more than in the recordings of the preceding period, and are frequently reinforced by a harmonic background. Moreover the musicians turn toward tonal and pianissimo effects during certain ensembles in order to create good orchestral effects. This can be observed in *Basin Street Blues* and *St. James Infirmary.* Besides those magnificent interpretations, the following should also be cited— the sublime *West End Blues,* which is perhaps the most beautiful jazz record ever made; *Skip the Gutter, A Monday Date, No Papa No, Muggles, No One Else But You, Save It Pretty Mama, Tight Like This, Heah Me Talkin' To Ya.* In all these recordings, both Louis Armstrong and Earl Hines play the most moving and audacious solos. The meeting of these two giants of jazz who understand each other so perfectly, and the presence of Zutty who is the ideal drummer for Louis, give these interpretations a unique character.

Many have sought to compare these two series of recordings. Those who favor the original New Orleans style claim that the records with Johnny Dodds are more beautiful because they

[4] Most of these recordings have been reissued in *The Louis Armstrong Story* (four volumes, Columbia ML-54383/86).

are more spontaneous and do not seek special effects. But others find these older records too crude and prefer those recorded with Earl Hines because they are more finished. In reality these comparisons are futile. Both series of recordings are equally magnificent, and have an added interest in that they show Louis Armstrong in two rather different aspects, and moreover prove that jazz can give us many varied interpretations of equal beauty. For, without any doubt, these records of Louis Armstrong are, with those made by King Oliver, the most beautiful we possess.

The recordings which Louis Armstrong made next are equally fine, but since most of them feature Louis as a soloist accompanied by a band, instead of being band records in the proper sense of the term, they do not quite belong in the present chapter. However, several Louis Armstrong albums recorded during the fifties, such as *Louis Armstrong Plays Handy* and *Satch Plays Fats*,[5] with Trummy Young on trombone and Barney Bigard on clarinet, belonged again to the same small-band tradition of the twenties. The *Louis Armstrong at the Crescendo* album, of a different type, is one of the best examples of "live" recording ever done. It was made in a night club, not at a concert, and its informal atmosphere clearly establishes the superiority of the former.

I must also mention *Louis Armstrong—A Musical Autobiography* (four-LP album) as including some of the finest Armstrong music ever recorded.

Another group of recordings in the New Orleans style were made between 1926 and 1929 under the direction of the great pianist, Jelly Roll Morton. For each session, he brought together musicians of great ability. The most interesting sessions

[5] Labels and catalogue numbers of those records—as well as many others—will be found in the Appendix.

were those held in Chicago in 1926 and 1927. The orchestra was formed in this way: George Mitchell on cornet, Kid Ory on trombone, Omer Simeon on clarinet, John St. Cyr on banjo and guitar, John Linsay on string bass, André Hilaire on drums, and Jelly Roll Morton at the piano. This group produced the following remarkable interpretations: *The Chant, Black Bottom Stomp, Smoke-House Blues, Steamboat Stomp, Sidewalk Blues, Dead Man Blues, Doctor Jazz, Original Jelly Roll Blues, Cannon Ball Blues, Grandpa's Spells.*

Another session, with a different group of musicians, was almost as successful, and produced *The Pearls, Beale Street Blues, Jungle Blues, Wild Man Blues, Hyena Stomp, Billy Goat Stomp.* These were recorded with George Mitchell on trumpet, George Bryant on trombone, Johnny Dodds on clarinet, Stomp Evans on alto saxophone, Bud Scott on guitar, Quinn Wilson on tuba, Baby Dodds on drums, and Jelly Roll Morton at the piano.

Finally I want to mention a session which took place in New York some time later. Among others it recorded the splendid *Kansas City Stomps, Boogaboo,* and *Georgia Swing.* The orchestra during this last session included Ward Pinkett on trumpet, Geechy Fields on trombone, Omer Simeon on clarinet, Lee Blair on banjo, Bill Benford on tuba, Tommy Benford on drums, and Jelly Roll Morton on piano.

In some ways these records resemble Louis Armstrong's earliest, because of the orchestral balance traditional of New Orleans style (clarinet-trumpet-trombone) and because of the alternation of collective improvisations and solos. But there are also some notable differences. Here almost all the numbers were composed by Jelly Roll Morton. These compositions are original and charming, and full of the melodic spirit of New Orleans style. Their characteristic accent differentiates them from the records made by other orchestras. Parenthetically I should note here that Jelly Roll is one of the most interesting composers jazz has produced. A number like *The Pearls* is unique in jazz music; while *Turtle Twist*, *Wolverine Blues*, *Shoe Shiner's Drag*, and many others, denote a melodic sense of freshness and ingenuity. Moreover, Jelly Roll's influence dominates the interpretation. Certain ensembles, instead of being improvised,were carefully prepared in advance. I have every reason to believe that even several solos, like the clarinet chorus in the *Original Jelly Roll Blues* and the high-register clarinet solo of *Grandpa's Spells*, were dictated by Jelly Roll rather than improvised by Omer Simeon. Be that as it may, these records are remarkable for their uniformity, the perfection of their style, the breath of inspiration which pervades all the numbers. Next to King Oliver's and Louis Armstrong's, they are the most beautiful recordings in the New Orleans style.

Almost ten years before Benny Goodman, Jelly Roll Morton made several remarkable recordings with a trio (clarinet-piano-drums), *Wolverine Blues*, *Mr. Jelly Lord*, with Johnny Dodds and Baby Dodds; *Shreveport* with Omer Simeon and Tommy Benford; *Turtle Twist* and *Smilin' the Blues Away* with Barney Bigard and Zutty.

At various times during 1928 and 1929 the clarinetist Johnny Dodds brought together small recording groups. He recorded at Victor with the following musicians: Natty Dominique on trumpet, Honoré Dutrey on trombone, Johnny Dodds on clarinet, Charlie Alexander on piano, Bill Johnson on bass, Baby Dodds on drums or washboard. We owe to this orchestra some marvelous blues played in the purest New Orleans tradition, some in slow tempo like *Bucktown Stomp*, *Weary City*, *Goober Dance*, and some in fast tempo like *Bull*

Fiddle Blues and *Blue Washboard Stomp.* Here the understanding between the musicians in the improvised ensembles
is truly marvelous.

Johnny Dodds also made some recordings for Brunswick
with a somewhat different group. This orchestra contained a
banjo and guitar (played by Bud Scott), instead of a bass, and
two trumpets instead of one. To some extent the interpretative style of this group recalls King Oliver's orchestra. *Joe
Turner Blues, When Erastus Plays His Old Yazoo, Come On
and Stomp Stomp Stomp* belong to this series.

Under the names "New Orleans Wanderers" and "New
Orleans Bootblacks," Johnny Dodds also made several records
with an orchestra almost identical to that used by Louis Armstrong in 1926. This group included George Mitchell on trumpet, Kid Ory on trombone, Lil Armstrong at the piano, John
St. Cyr on banjo, and Joe Walker on alto sax. The interpretations are largely made up of improvised ensembles with few
nuances, but their power and captivating melodies remind
one of the primitive New Orleans orchestras more than almost
any other. The numbers recorded were *Gate Mouth, Perdido
Street Blues, Papa Dip, Too Tight, Flat Foot, Mad Dog, I
Can't Say,* and *Mixed Salad.*

The records made by Jimmie Noone and his orchestra are
very different from all the preceding. His is a group which was
organized not for recording but for work in various Chicago
night clubs in 1927 and later years. Jimmie Noone created a
unique orchestral balance. There is no trumpet or trombone—
simply a clarinet and alto saxophone with the usual rhythm
section. The musicians were Jimmie Noone on clarinet, Joe
"Doc" Poston on alto sax, Earl Hines at the piano, Bud Scott
on banjo or guitar, Johnny Wells on drums, and occasionally
Lawson Buford on tuba.

In this orchestra, the alto saxophone carries the role of the trumpet to a certain extent; it states the melody, leading the ensembles, while the clarinet embroiders freely around it or plays in harmony with it. Since these two instruments are not ordinarily heard together, the tonal balance obtained is quite surprising and in fact very agreeable to the ear.

The best records made by Jimmie Noone include *Sweet Sue, Every Evening, Four or Five Times, Forevermore, Ready for the River, Apex Blues, Sweet Lorraine, Blues My Naughty Sweety Gives to Me.* But the orchestra was changed after these recordings were made. Earl Hines, Bud Scott, and Buford were replaced respectively by Alex Hill, Junie Cobb, and Bill Newton. And though his group lost some of its merit, Jimmie Noone still produced some very beautiful interpretations, notably *I Got a Misery* and *Chicago Rhythm.* I want to mention one other recording, *My Daddy Rocks Me,* played with an extra trumpet and trombone, and with Zinky Cohn at the piano instead of Alex Hill.

The exceptional value of these interpretations rests principally on the perfect understanding which rules between those two incomparable musicians, Jimmie Noone and Joe Poston, as well as on the admirable contrast of the singing and melodic parts of the two reed instruments against the compact rhythm section which swings with suppleness. Earl Hines frequently detaches himself from the group to improvise dazzling countermelodies which give an incisive quality to the executions. Without any doubt, records like *Sweet Sue, Forevermore, Every Evening, Four or Five Times,* and *Apex Blues* can be numbered among the most beautiful that jazz has given us.

The recordings we have just discussed bring us to the year 1929. But from 1930 on, for reasons mentioned in the fourth chapter, practically no recordings were made in the New Orleans style. However the year 1932 was an exception. At that time six excellent numbers were recorded by "Ladnier's and Bechet's New Orleans Feetwarmers," a small group which played for a time at the Savoy in New York. The orchestra was made up of Tommy Ladnier on trumpet, Sidney Bechet on soprano sax and clarinet, Ted Nixon on trombone, Hank Duncan on piano, Wilson Myers on bass, and Morris Morand on drums. *Maple Leaf Rag, I've Found a New Baby, Shag, Lay Your Racket* are very rapid, fiery, and exuberant executions—in fact almost too much so. This is to a great extent due to Bechet's ardent and dynamic playing. Only *Sweetie Dear* is a clear and well-ordered interpretation, though it too has the same power.

From that time on, only rare and isolated attempts were made to record numbers in New Orleans style. The few attempts that were made produced no results, for the musicians forced themselves to copy the old executions to the letter, instead of impregnating themselves with the spirit. Consequently these interpretations seem more like caricatures of the older records than anything else.

During the thirties only the white clarinetist Mezz Mezzrow succeeded where others failed. Because of his rare intelligence he was able to make the spirit of New Orleans live in new and varied forms. Thus in 1934, as leader of a mixed Negro and white orchestra, he recorded three remarkable works—*35th and Calumet, Apologies,* and *Sendin' the Vipers.* He brought together Max Kaminsky, Reunald Jones, and Chelsea Qualey on trumpet, Floyd O'Brien on trombone, Benny Carter on alto sax, Bud Freeman on tenor sax, Willie "The Lion" Smith on piano, John Kirby on bass, and Chick Webb on drums, while Mezzrow himself played clarinet. The basic construction of these interpretations was this: The part formerly carried by two trumpets in King Oliver's orchestra was adapted for the entire brass section; the clarinet embroidered around the ensemble. Toward the middle of the record a place was given for solos, which were soberly and powerfully supported by rhythmic figures played by the ensemble. As a matter of fact the title, *Apologies*, signifies "Apologies to King Oliver and Louis Armstrong for using some of their ideas," for there is a certain resemblance here to the famous *Dipper Mouth Blues*.

The attempt was a complete success. The magnificent clarinet part which Mezz develops against the phrases of the brass section evokes the spirit of Johnny Dodds' embroideries around the two trumpets, King Oliver and Louis Armstrong. Yet Mezz's results are completely new in form.

In 1938 Mezz did even better. He again directed three recording sessions during which the New Orleans style lived once more in pure improvisation.

For the first session, the orchestra was composed of Tommy Ladnier and Sidney De Paris (trumpet), Mezzrow (clarinet), James P. Johnson (piano), Teddy Bunn (guitar), Elmer James (bass), Zutty (drums). The interpretations, *Comin' On with the Come On* (in two parts) and *Revolutionary Blues*, were made up almost entirely of improvised ensembles. The two trumpets did not play in harmony like King Oliver and Louis Armstrong but improvised independently. For the recording of *Comin' On with the Come On*, Mezz had an excellent idea. He had the two parts recorded *without interruption* which meant that the good start the musicians got on the first half was carried right over to the second part which they attacked with a vivacity and fire which had never before been achieved on a record. Consequently *Comin' On with the Come On* is a unique recording in the history of jazz—in spite of certain imperfections at the close of the second part. The style of *Revolutionary Blues* is so pure that one seems here to have returned to the old music of New Orleans.

During the second session the orchestra was made up of Tommy Ladnier on trumpet, Milton Mezzrow on clarinet and tenor sax, Sidney Bechet on soprano sax and clarinet, Cliff Jackson at the piano, Teddy Bunn on guitar, Elmer James on bass, and Manzie Johnson on drums. This session produced two masterpieces—*Really the Blues* and especially *Weary Blues* which has a perfect tempo and swings in an indescribable manner. Here an excellent effect is obtained by the two clarinets (Mezz and Bechet) playing first in harmony with the trumpet, then improvising with it in the last chorus.

For his third and last session Mezz used only four musicians—Tommy Ladnier on trumpet, Teddy Bunn on guitar, "Pops" Foster on bass, and Manzie Johnson on drums. In the alternating ensembles and solos, Tommy Ladnier and Mezz reveal an astonishing fecundity in their improvisations and a perfect understanding of each other. The notable records made during this session include the imposing blues played in a slow tempo, *If You See Me Comin'*; two blues in fast tempo, *Royal Garden Blues* and *Gettin' Together*; and a remarkable interpretation, *I Ain't Gonna Give Nobody None of My Jelly Roll*.

In the years 1945 and 1947 Mezz made new series of beautiful New Orleans records with the great Sidney Bechet.

In 1945, the sessions produced moving slow blues (the themes of which were composed by Mezz) : *Gone Away Blues, Out of the Gallion, Bowin' the Blues*; and powerful fast numbers such as *Old School, Ole Miss, De Luxe Stomp, Jelly Roll, Perdido Street Stomp*. In all, Mezz's clarinet and Bechet's soprano sax blend in a way which is a treat to the ear, both improvising together with admirable understanding and perfectly backed by the three-man rhythm section: Fitz Weston on piano, Pops Foster on bass, and Kaiser Marshall on drums.

The 1947 records were made with the same group, except that Sammy Price is at the piano instead of Fitz Weston. Here also, Mezz composed and produced wonderful slow blues: *Tommy's Blues*, dedicated to the late Tommy Ladnier and full of his musical spirit, *I Want Some, I'm Going Away From Here*.

Finally, Mezz made some of his most important records in France, where he settled in 1951, some with a band which included two great New Orleans jazzmen: Lee Collins on trumpet and Zutty Singleton on drums; some with Jimmy Archey on trombone and the young trumpet player from New Orleans, Wallace Davenport (*Serenade to Paris, Moonglow, Reverend Blues* were among the products of this session); and a session which was titled *Mezz at the Schola Cantorum*, with two trumpet players—Peanuts Holland (at his greatest!) and Guy Longnon, the young Canadian pianist Milton Sealey, and Kansas Fields on drums: *Blues Avec Un Pont* and *Mineur Avec Un Pont* (each number taking a whole 12-inch side). These are among the best jazz performances ever released on LP as they have the warmth, the spontaneity of "live" jazz: the musicians sound as if they had been recorded without knowing it while playing for their own pleasure in a night club.

During the forties Kid Ory, the greatest New Orleans trombone player, who had been musically inactive for some years, formed a band again which turned out to be the greatest and purest New Orleans-style band since the old days. No wonder, as Kid Ory had the perfect men: Mutt Carey on trumpet, Buster Wilson on piano, Bud Scott on guitar, Ed Garland on bass, and Minor Hall on drums, while the clarinet players were

alternatively Omer Simeon, Darnell Howard, and Barney
Bigard, all first-class New Orleans men. The records Ory made
in 1944–1946, such as *Panama, Weary Blues, Oh Didn't He
Ramble, Maple Leaf Rag, Bill Bailey Won't You Please Come
Home*, are among the best New Orleans-style performances
ever waxed.

Because some of his musicians died soon afterward, Ory's
records of the late forties and of the fifties were not as close to
perfection. But most of them were excellent, especially those
made with the remarkable Teddy Buckner on trumpet. Also,
it must be observed that most of the "Good Time Jazz" Ory
records (early and mid-fifties) offer the best recorded New
Orleans drumming (by Minor Hall) there is.

I shall turn now to the recording orchestras which do not
play in the New Orleans style.

One of the most important is the group directed by Fats
Waller under the name of "Fats Waller and His Rhythm."
This orchestra made innumerable records from 1934 until
1942. Fats attempted to use, insofar as possible, the same
musicians throughout. Consequently the orchestra is as uni-
fied as a permanent orchestra. In fact after several years Fats
did use his recording orchestra for engagements in night clubs.
It is curious indeed to find a small recording group thus becoming a permanent orchestra.

Generally Fats' orchestra was made up of Herman Autrey
on trumpet, Gene Sedric on tenor sax and clarinet, Fats at the
piano, Al Casey on guitar, Cedric Wallace on string bass, and
Slick Jones on drums. In the earliest records Billy Taylor
played bass and Harry Dial drums, but though there were
several later changes it is unnecessary to note them here.

The simple formula for the interpretations almost never
varies. Fats plays the first chorus on the piano, and sings the

second (vice versa); then his soloists improvise; finally he sings the last chorus or has it interpreted by the entire orchestra in collective improvisations. There are also a few records in which Fats doesn't sing.

While the records discussed in the preceding pages have interested only musicians and those who appreciate real jazz, Fats' recordings have had a wide popular success and have been disregarded by most connoisseurs as "commercial." These people claim that Fats is too much of a clown in his vocal choruses, and that he forces the "yes, yes" and other cries far too much in his recordings. It is true that most of Fats' vocal choruses are comical—one of the main reasons for his wide success with the general public. But that comedy in no way hinders his vocals from being remarkable from a purely jazz viewpoint. Unlike Louis Armstrong, Fats is not a singer of genius nor does he have a particularly beautiful voice, but he has an excellent feeling for the style of vocal suitable to jazz. His direct manner is stripped of all pretense and he swings with vitality and abundance. Here again one finds that same perfect tempo which is so striking in his piano. Moreover the comic note he introduces in his vocal choruses is certainly well justified in view of the stupid lyrics written for the majority of songs. In truth I cannot understand the objections leveled against Fats. Isn't it far more entertaining and pleasant to hear such exasperating phrases as "love nest," "moon," and other dull clichés ridiculed with an exaggeratedly emphatic tone or by humorous remarks, than to hear them sung in an unbearably solemn manner? As Madeleine Gautier aptly expressed it: Fats has "a way of singing the most tender melodies with a bantering air which ridicules the shopworn sentimentalism which is crushing the real heart of the world."[6]

[6] *Jazz Hot*, July-August, 1939.

Fats often sings these lyrics with a poker face. "He can mouth these lyrics with all the verisimilitude in the world and then in one bar he'll tear the glorious edifice down with a crushing satirical twist."[7] Shouldn't we be grateful to Fats for this reaction against the sentimental foolishness which so often spoils jazz?

As for the reproach against the "yes, yes" and the "ha, ha" these expressions are in fact altogether natural. When Negro musicians and audiences are enthusiastic they frequently cry out with such exclamations. Therefore I don't see that Fats is showing bad taste by introducing the expressions which are usually used in a night club into his recordings.

The exceptional value lies not so much in the individual performance of this or that musician as in the unique spirit which rules. Throughout Fats' recordings, there is an ease and relaxation never found in other records. In fact these are almost the only recordings where the musicians play with the same spirit as they would in a night club. This is due in part to the fact that this little group has recorded so many times that it has come to feel as free in the recording studio as elsewhere. Moreover Fats' own calm and ease has meant that he could play in a studio with perfect freedom and confidence. Then too, as I mentioned earlier, Fats is an orchestral pianist whose power, ease, and clarity give the maximum to those with whom he works. Finally the technical equipment and conditions were such that the records are vitally alive.

And if someone were to ask me what recordings reflect most sincerely jazz as it is heard in the flesh, I would immediately reply, the records of "Fats Waller and His Rhythm."

Almost all of Fats' records are equally good. I will cite several which I feel are particularly effective—*Christopher Co-*

[7] Stanley Nelson, in the *Melody Maker*, November 27, 1937.

lumbus, Paswonky, Bach Up to Me, Hallelujah, Things Look Rosy Now, Nero, One in a Million, Honeysuckle Rose, The Meanest Thing You Ever Did Was Kiss Me, Spring Cleaning, Baby Brown, Dream Man (both sides recorded with Bill Coleman on trumpet), *You're Not the Only Oyster in the Stew, Sweetie Pie, Serenade for a Wealthy Widow*—the last three were recorded with the unusual presence of Milton Mezzrow on clarinet and Floyd O'Brien on trombone.

Who's Afraid of Love and *Sposin'* are perfect examples of the genial way in which Fats mocks sentimental songs. By his intelligent piano style and his amusing vocalizing, he succeeds, with few transformations, in making an effective melody from an insipid one.

The rhythm section, which is magnificently led by Fats, is one of the best and most homogeneous ever recorded. In Albert Casey and Slick Jones, Fats found a guitarist and drummer ideal for recording with him. During his vocal choruses Fats uses Casey in a very original way. He has Casey improvise a countermelody *with chords*, which creates a mobility which draws the rhythm section on and thereby creates a singing background. Listen, for example, to the guitar part during the first vocal chorus of *Dream Man*.

But whatever the quality of Al Casey's part and Sedric's tenor solos, Fats' part is above all the thing which makes these records so exceptional. His animation and vitality never cease for a minute; he constantly stimulates the musicians by his powerful and fascinating basses; consequently one listens to the piano support with more pleasure than to the solos themselves. The irresistible joy of his playing is communicated to the other musicians in such a way that his records never have that lassitude and dryness which make so many recordings dull and boring—as for instance many of those made under the direction of the pianist, Teddy Wilson, which are withal recorded by very good musicians.

Another musician who took charge of a series of remarkable recordings is Lionel Hampton. Unlike Fats, Lionel used different musicians at every session; consequently his records do not have as well-defined a style. Nevertheless when he is playing the vibraphone, drums, or piano, Lionel's personality is so powerful that it gives a characteristic expression to the majority of these recordings.

In general, these interpretations are made up of a series of solos framed by rather simple arrangements. Lionel's dynamic quality, which inspires the other musicians enormously, is largely responsible for the fire and warmth. In all, the value of these recordings varies considerably with the musicians employed. For example, the recordings made with some members of Benny Goodman's orchestra are only mediocre, with the exception of *Jivin' the Vibes.*

Probably the most interesting session directed by Lionel was that which produced *Whoa Babe, Buzzin' Around with the Bee,* and *Stompology.* The orchestra for this session included an impressive number of stars—Cootie on trumpet, Lawrence Brown on trombone, Johnny Hodges on alto sax, Milton Mezzrow on clarinet, Jess Stacy on piano, Allan Reuss on guitar, John Kirby on bass, Cozy Cole on drums, and Lionel on vibraphone. The solos have the greatest inspiration, and the ensembles have a terrific "punch."

A session which was almost as successful was made up of Harry James on trumpet, Benny Carter on alto sax and clarinet, Dave Matthews on alto sax, Herschel Evans and Babe Russin on tenor sax, Billy Kyle on piano, John Kirby on bass, Jo Jones on drums, and Lionel on vibraphone. This group recorded two masterpieces—*Shoe Shiner's Drag* and *I'm in the*

Mood for Swing. The charming arrangements for these numbers were written by Benny Carter, and are superbly executed
by the orchestra. Moreover the solos are equally fine.

Another session worthy of mention is that which produced
Rhythm, Rhythm, and an especially beautiful version of *On
the Sunny Side of the Street*. The orchestra was made up of
Johnny Hodges on alto sax, Buster Bailey on clarinet, Jess
Stacy at the piano, Allan Reuss on guitar, John Kirby on counterbass, Cozy Cole on drums, and Lionel again at the vibraphone.

Finally I want to cite *Drum Stomp* with Lionel on drums
and Jonah Jones on trumpet; *Sweethearts on Parade;* and
Denison Swing, recorded with "Chew" Berry on tenor sax at
his greatest.

As for Hampton's big-band recordings, which came later,
I have discussed them in the previous chapter. But I must
mention here Hamp's greatest studio-group LP recordings of
the fifties, which he made while in Paris—some of them with
the French tenor sax player Alix Combelle, Hamp's amazing
guitarist Billy Mackel, and trumpet player Walter Williams
(*Free Press Oui, Walkin' at the Trocadero,* etc.), which have
an excitement and fire seldom caught on records; and some
with a small unit including Mezz Mezzrow on clarinet (*Blues
for The Hot Club De France, Serenade to Nicole's Mink
Coat,* etc.), a session during which Hamp also recorded one
of the greatest drum solos ever: *Crazy Hamp*.

Another series of noteworthy recordings were those made
by some of the musicians from Duke Ellington's orchestra.
Some were made under Barney Bigard's direction, others under Johnny Hodges', Cootie's, or Rex's. For each session the
composition of the orchestra varied slightly. These records
have the characteristic atmosphere of Duke Ellington's or-

chestra, except that an arrangement for a small group of seven or eight musicians cannot have the harmonic ampleness of one written for a large orchestra. With the large orchestra in mind, moreover, the ensembles seem a little empty. But the atmosphere of improvisation which reigns in all these records gives them a seductive lightness.

Probably the most successful were the four made under Rex's direction—*Swing Baby Swing* (also known as *Love in My Heart*), *Shim Sham Shimmy*, *Tea and Trumpets*, *The Back Room Romp*. For this session, Rex composed melodies of excellent workmanship which swing admirably because of light touches in the arrangement. The perfect tempo adopted, Rex's and Johnny Hodges' splendid solos, and Duke's beautiful work on the piano make these records eminently satisfying.

The recordings made under the leadership of Barney Bigard included some first-class performances, such as *Stompy Jones*, *Caravan* (the original version of this celebrated number), *Clouds in My Heart*, *Jazz a la Carte*.

Among Cootie Williams' most successful waxings were *I Can't Believe That You're in Love with Me*, *Mobile Blues*, *Delta Mood*, *Boudoir Benny*.

But the most proficient of all was Johnny Hodges. From 1938 to 1941 he headed more recording sessions than any of the Duke's other men, and some of his fine performances became very popular, such as *Jeep's Blues*, *The Jeep Is Jumpin'*, and *Things Ain't What They Used to Be* (it was the original version of this famous number, later rechristened *Time's A-Wastin'*). But other records, not so well known, such as *Rent Party Blues* and *The Rabbit's Jump*, are equally superb.

Later on, in the early fifties, when he had left Duke and become the leader of one of the best small groups of the time, Johnny Hodges made another fine series of recordings, including *Sideways, Who's Excited, Duke's Blues,* and *Johnny's Blues.* After returning to Duke, Johnny Hodges kept on making fine records under his name with a part of Duke's band (or even the whole band)—records which are amazing by reason of their consistently high level. *Snibor, You Got Mit Coming,* and *Duke's Jam* are among the best, but many other titles could be noted. In fact, Johnny Hodges' name on a label has become synonymous with good, singing and swinging jazz. And just by the *sound* of his alto sax, in the ensembles as well as in solos, Hodges gives his own unforgettable stamp to the performances.

Numerous recordings were made by studio groups during the forties and fifties. Many are worth listening to, but few offer any real orchestral work. Most of the time they consist of a succession of solos, everyone taking his chorus in turn just as at the jam sessions which used to take place in some cabarets; in fact, some of those records have been titled or subtitled "Jam Session." With the invention of the LP, there was a tendency for these recordings to be uneven, because in such long performances weak soloists can make the whole thing tiresome to listen to. That is why only first-class soloists (and playing in the same musical spirit) should be assembled on such occasions. Unfortunately, this seldom happens, as many of those in charge of the recording sessions do not know enough about jazz music and make serious mistakes, such as mixing poor soloists with excellent ones or—worse—mixing jazzmen with boppers.

One of the very best LP series in this vein is the Buck Clayton jam sessions (recorded by Columbia), which almost invariably had swinging rhythm sections and first-class soloists. *The Huckle-Buck, Robbins' Nest, Lean Baby, Don't Be That Way, Broadway,* and *Don't You Miss Your Baby* are about the best products of this series, which includes other good performances.

Another great series of the fifties is that by the great singer Jimmie Rushing, around whom were assembled some of the finest studio groups of the time. The session (recorded for Vanguard) which produced, among others, *How Long Blues* and *Goin' to Chicago* with a band featuring Buddy Tate on tenor sax, Sammy Price on piano, Walter Page on bass, and Jo Jones on drums; the session with almost the same band but with Pete Johnson on piano instead of Sammy Price, which gave us *Every Day* and *See See Rider*; and the one (with, among others, Marlowe Morris at the organ and Roy Gaines on guitar) which produced *My Friend Mr. Blues, If This Ain't the Blues,* and *I Can't Understand,* all three can be numbered among the best LP's of the fifties.

Of course there are many other records worth mentioning. For instance, certain small regular groups such as John Kirby's, an unbelievably smooth and refined group (yet a swinging one), made remarkable records in the late thirties and during the forties, and Louis Jordan's straightforward combo waxed stupendous performances of the blues. But to mention all good jazz records would lead us far beyond the scope of this book.

17 jazz today

As I write this, in 1960, the situation of jazz is a strange one.

The music itself is just as healthy as ever; and there are hundreds of first-class musicians, of all ages, who can create beautiful jazz—if they are given a chance.

But it is seldom that they are given the chance. Of course, I'm not speaking of celebrities such as Louis Armstrong, jazzmen who are so well known that they get more offers than they can accept. But very few are in such a position. Most jazzmen either are out of work most of the time, or find themselves obliged to play music of an uncongenial sort.

Of course, there have been other crises in the history of jazz. But the situation has been tougher during the fifties than ever before. There are not as many night clubs as in the old days; and dance jobs, which were the mainstay of most jazzmen, have become fewer. Taxes on cabarets have caused many musicians to lose steady, profitable jobs.

Since jazz is a collective music—I mean a music that can only be created collectively (except in the case of some great piano soloists, or when a blues singer accompanies himself on his own guitar)—lack of jobs has meant a decrease in creation. No big band can be held together when well-paid jobs are lacking. In the early thirties (not a prosperous period at that), there were six or seven colored big bands around Kansas City.

Today one could not find as many in New York and Chicago put together.

Even small bands have been hard put to survive. We have come into an era of trios, quartets, and all kinds of small groups which by no stretch of the imagination can be really considered as bands. And except where the musicians are outstandingly gifted, it is more difficult to create first-class jazz within such limitations.

Of course, there have been some wonderful small units. The Jo Jones Trio, with Ray Bryant on piano and Tom Bryant on bass, has produced music of a sort that one can listen to for hours without tiring. The Jonah Jones Quartet has been playing fine jazz since 1955. The Wild Bill Davis Trio with Floyd Smith on guitar and Chris Columbus on drums has proved to be one of the most exciting small units in the whole history of jazz. And one could name a few others.

But how many colored big bands have been continuously active during the fifties? Only four: Duke Ellington, Count Basie, Lionel Hampton, Buddy Johnson. The rest had only a spasmodic existence.

Small bands have hardly done better. Louis Armstrong's All Stars; Wilbur De Paris' "New New Orleans Band" (which, with Sidney De Paris and/or Doc Cheatham on trumpet, Sonny White on piano, Wilbert Kirk on drums, and some others has been one of the greatest bands in recent years); Kid Ory's band; and a few other bands more or less in the New Orleans style (such as Teddy Buckner's) were the only successful ones, along with what have come to be known as "rhythm and blues" groups, the best of which were Roy Milton's band (with Camille Howard on piano), one of the most swinging small bands of the fifties; Earl Bostic's group; Bill

Doggett's; and, in more recent years, Cozy Cole's with George Kelly on tenor sax, later replaced by Eddie Chamblee.

Now, it is a shame to notice that those "rhythm and blues" groups (or "rock 'n roll" groups as they are sometimes called) are dismissed as bad or unimportant bands by self-appointed critics—critics concerned only with progressive musicians or groups (such as Miles Davis, Chet Baker, or Ornette Coleman, who, in fact, have nothing to do with jazz).

Let us make one thing clear: I am not speaking here of the horrible stuff that most of the time is given to the public under the name of "rock 'n roll." But there is no reason ever to confuse the good music that was originally produced under the "rock 'n roll" label with the bad stuff (the commercial exploitation). "Rock 'n roll" first designated the kind of jazz based on the permanent use of "shuffle rhythm" and a strong afterbeat, which are strict jazz devices: the accented afterbeat was used by New Orleans bands and, even earlier, it was the hand-clapping of the people in churches and camp meetings. Shuffle rhythm is nothing other than a kind of boogie-woogie rhythm, which was used not only by the earliest blues pianists but also by the oldest blues guitarists who played before the orchestral music known as jazz was actually born.

Consequently, no one with the slightest knowledge of jazz music can pretend that real, honest "rock 'n roll" does not belong to jazz. It *was* jazz *before* getting this name. In fact, it is the same story as for the word jazz itself: a lot of false, commercialized music was given the same label as the real thing.

One of the main reasons for the success of "rock 'n roll" (the bad version, unfortunately, more often than the real thing!) lies in the boisterous way certain club owners, managers, and newspaper men insisted in imposing on the public the pseudo "modern jazz" (bop, cool, progressive), for had this boring music been left to find its own way, it would have died in no time. But the persistent boost that was given to it brought a strong reaction, and what happened was this: tired of such complicated, cold music, which was not even danceable, the public cried for simple, plain music—and along came "rock 'n roll"!

The sad thing is that most good jazzmen were then left in the cold between conflicting extremes. Of course, they could have made good music out of "rock 'n roll" if the product had not been so badly commercialized. But guitarists had to get piercing sounds with noisy amplification; tenor saxists had to growl, scream, and honk all the time; and musicians playing trombone or even trumpet were seldom given a chance to make themselves heard in such groups. Many could not stand it, which is hardly surprising. As a result, they were often out of work.

Thus the public who liked good, real jazz was denied it most of the time. There were just as many excellent jazzmen as ever before, and they were eager to play, but there were very few places where they could be heard.

Paradoxically, and for the first time in jazz history, some jazzmen had more chances to play the music they liked in recording studios than in night clubs. In the early fifties (beginning in 1953, to be precise), at the instigation of John Hammond and George Avakian, wonderful musicians such as Buck Clayton, Vic Dickenson, Jimmy Rushing, Jo Jones, and some others were put in charge of noncommercial recordings and cut fine, successful performances on LP's.[1] Norman Granz, by his many recording sessions with Johnny Hodges, Ben Webster, Art Tatum, Roy Eldridge, Illinois Jacquet, and others, helped several great jazzmen to make

[1] The best ones are listed in the Appendix.

themselves heard during the fifties. But there was, comparatively, so little of this music on records that in the late fifties
it took an English writer and critic, Stanley Dance, to record
some first-class musicians who had been long left in the cold
and thereby gave a new impulse to what in many circles has
come to be called "mainstream jazz"—a name as good as any
if it is understood the right way: "mainstream jazz" includes
all post-New Orleans jazz. Bob Weinstock, since the late
fifties, has also been helping several jazzmen get their chance
by recording them on LP's.

The irony of the situation is this: in Europe, many a jazz
lover took a liking to records by Buck Clayton, Jimmy Rushing, Rex Stewart, Tiny Grimes, and others, made with all-
star studio bands. But when these enthusiasts took a trip to
the land of jazz and tried to locate the places where this wonderful jazz was played, they could not find it—because it is
nowhere to be found. The only regular band currently playing
in New York which performs good jazz like that on the above-
mentioned records is Buddy Tate's swinging group, which has
been heard for several years at the "Celebrity Club" in Harlem
but which is so little publicized by the so-called "jazz critics"
that most people do not even know it exists—or do not know
where to find it.

I have heard it said that there is nothing to do in such a situation and that the public is given what it wants. This is absurd.
The public does not know what it wants until it hears it. If
the listener is not presented with the musicians and orchestras he would like, what can he do about it? It took about
25 years for Jonah Jones to get a chance to make himself heard
by a large public. He had been playing *exactly* the same way
for a long time so, logically, he should have been recognized
years ago as he is now. But when the connoisseurs, who knew

his worth, tried to get managers, bookers, and agents interested
in him, they were given the usual answer: "You've got to give
the public what it wants!" Now, there are dozens of other
great jazzmen still waiting for a similar chance, and not being
given one.

The critics and the press should help in making those musicians known to the public. But they seldom do. They are too
busy trying to build up "progressive" musicians—which would
be all right if they would refrain from calling them "modern
jazz" musicians. Their efforts would cause no difficulty if they
had enough sense to make the necessary distinctions. But by
pretending that the music progressive musicians are playing
is jazz music, that it is improved jazz, more "serious" and
"artistic" than what was done before, those critics are helping
progressive musicians to take the places that belong to the
real jazzmen.

There is, among most so-called jazz critics, a way of looking at the music which is incompatible with the understanding of jazz. Those critics keep on stating that "progressive"
men are making more serious music than what was created
earlier. Any colored musician who conforms to the behavior
of white classical musicians is greeted as a real artist, full of
dignity; while the one who remains himself and acts as an
entertainer in a club or on stage is despised as a clown or, even
worse, as being "Uncle Tom."

By presenting as dogma such erroneous perspectives, these
critics confuse many a young colored musician, who gets to
thinking that it would be better to adopt the white people's
ways, including the kind of music that gets write-ups. Those
young musicians do not realize that the real "Uncle Tomism"
lies in rejecting their own natural music, their way of living,

their congenital reactions in order to conform to the ways of the white folks. By doing so, they cease to be themselves, they lose their own personality, crush and twist their natural gifts, and they have to live on attitudes. Louis Armstrong, who is a great observer and has a penetrating eye, wonderfully described such youngsters:

"What they're playing ain't jazz. . . . They're posing, heard some stories, and so they're trying to be something they're not. Look, you don't pose, never. That's the last thing you do, because the minute you do you're through as a jazz-man. Maybe not as a musician, but jazz is only what you are."[2]

This is the point I have always wanted to make clear: progressive men might be fine musicians of their kind, but they are certainly not jazzmen. Some of those who, at first, did not realize it when listening to the Parker-Gillespie disciples are beginning to wonder what is happening now that they are faced with such sounds as Ornette Coleman's, who brought to its ultimate consequence the stream of music that was started by Charlie Parker and developed by Miles Davis and others of the same bent. (Parker, unlike his disciples, had roots in jazz.)

It is highly comical to watch the reactions of many of those "critics" to Ornette Coleman's playing. Some try to follow through and state that he is the new great man; but the very way they express themselves shows how embarrassed they are. Others just give up and reject Ornette Coleman's sounds, saying that it is not jazz any more. But they should have said the same of Miles Davis and others, and for the very same reasons. As the great trumpet player Roy Eldridge so aptly

[2] *The Reporter*, May 2, 1957; quoted by Stanley Dance in *Jazz Journal*, August 1957.

said, speaking of trumpet players: "That lifeless tone so many cats produce these days—I don't think it's the way it should be. Jazz isn't supposed to be a sad thing—even the blues, the sad blues, there must be feeling in it. But a straight tone with no vibrato always reminds me of a brass band cornet player: no warmth, no feeling. . . . I can't get with that straight sound on no kind of horn. It's for brass bands, but it ain't for jazz."[3]

And here is what Roy Eldridge has to say about Ornette Coleman: "I heard that group and I know one thing: they're the bravest people I ever seen! I went three nights in a row, sober at that, and never got the message. You have to hear them in person and then you *really* can't understand it. I went with some young, modern musicians, took Paul Chambers with me; 'You explain to me what's happening,' I said. But he said: 'Man, I don't understand it either.' The group start out with something, play a riff on the first chorus, then they leave everything and just blow. No melody, no kinda way. You can't say it's the blues nor *How High the Moon*—or nothin'. . . . Course, everybody (back home) is afraid to say anything about it, because it's new and it might be good, y'know. . . ."[4]

Roy Eldridge's last sentence very sensibly refers to that superstition of our time: NEW. People are so imbued with the "being new" superstition that they no longer realize that something new, whether music or anything else, is not automatically or necessarily good or beautiful and can just as well be bad or ugly. You hear people say how "new" a musician is— I have even heard some say, "You've got to be new to be good," while it should be the other way round: "You've got

[3] "In my opinion," interview of Roy Eldridge by Sinclair Traill in the English magazine *Jazz Journal*, June 1960.
[4] Same article.

to be good to be new." A man's desire to create something new never will give him the ability for it if he has not the creative gift in him. But if he has the gift, by just being himself he will automatically be new. When Louis Armstrong started, he listened and studied in order to play the very same kind of music played by Joe Oliver and some great New Orleans men, and that discipline in just trying to do it made him create more new jazz than anybody else. He did not want to be original, he was original and just could not help being so. As the philosopher Friedrich Nietzsche so well said: "The requisite for beauty is not the desire but the capacity."[5]

That is the reason why all the current literature about how new a musician is or is not, is plain nonsense. Music is good or bad, that is all.

Now, let nobody pounce upon this last sentence to claim that if music is just good or bad, there is no point in carping about whether it is jazz or not. The answer is only too easy: jazz is a collective music, and one simply cannot get good results by blindly mixing together musicians who do not express themselves in the same idiom. Jazzmen and boppers should never be associated in concerts, recording dates, or TV programs. However, despite this evidence, the trick has been played on jazzmen on innumerable occasions, when they had to play with a bop section behind them, thus irremediably spoiling the music.

To conclude, I wish long life to that beautiful cry of jazz music, a cry of joy, sorrow, and love. May it be taken as it is, heard where it comes from—for there is no way to distort it without destroying it. It is beautiful and will remain so, whether the cry was uttered thirty years ago or two days ago. It comes from everyday life, from the soul of a people.

[5] *The Wanderer and His Shadow*, Aphorism 336.

Only God knows what tomorrow's cry will be. But let us not miss today's cry, which will tomorrow be yesterday's. That is why, today, I dare say to all who love real jazz music and musicians: stop, look, and listen.

selection
of the best
jazz lp's
available

APPENDIX:

In the following pages the reader will find a carefully selected list of jazz LP's. I wish that all jazzmen of first importance could be represented in that list, but it is impossible, because the record companies have not yet reissued most of the great recordings made between 1923 and 1945, which were the golden years for many great jazzmen, some of whom died as early as 1931; and some of the few good reissues made have been cut out from the catalogues soon after their release. It would be of little service to readers to list hard-to-get or unavailable records. So I have decided that the wisest thing to do is to present a selection of all *the best* LP's currently available. Of course, this policy means that some artists are represented by two, three, or even more records, while others (equally good) are not represented at all. But this is unavoidable. And I have not thought it advisable to list a bad LP simply for the sake of a couple of minutes of solos by a good musician, lost among very poor music.

So I list here only the first-class LP's, under the names of the artists arranged alphabetically. It would take too much space (in a book of this sort) to list the names of all the musicians in the orchestras on the records selected; but when one or several musicians are especially important to the value of a record, their names are given, even if they are sidemen only.

H. P.

CAT ANDERSON (Trumpet)

Cat on a Hot Tin Horn (U.S.: Emarcy MG-36142; England: Mercury MMB-12006). With his orchestra, including JIMMY FORREST on tenor sax and GEORGE DUVIVIER on bass.

LOUIS ARMSTRONG (Trumpet and Vocal)

The Louis Armstrong Story, Vol. I (U.S.: Columbia ML-54383; England: Philips BBL-7134). 1925–1927 performances, with KID ORY on trombone, JOHN ST. CYR on banjo.

The Louis Armstrong Story, Vol. II (U.S.: Columbia ML-54384; England: Philips BBL-7189). 1927 recordings with JOHNNY DODDS on clarinet.

The Louis Armstrong Story, Vol. III (U.S.: Columbia ML-54385; England: Philips BBL-7202). 1928 recordings with EARL HINES on piano, ZUTTY SINGLETON on drums.

The Louis Armstrong Story, Vol. IV (U.S.: Columbia ML-54386; England: Philips BBL-7218). 1929–1931 recordings with various orchestras.

Satchmo's Collectors' Items (U.S. only: Decca 8327). 1935–1941, with various groups.

Satchmo Sings (U.S.: Decca 8126; England: Brunswick LAT-8243). 1945–1953, with various groups.

Louis Armstrong Plays W. C. Handy (U.S.: Columbia CL-591; England: Philips BBL-7017). 1954, with his small all-star group including TRUMMY YOUNG on trombone and BARNEY BIGARD on clarinet.

Satch Plays Fats (U.S.: Columbia CL-708; England: Philips BBL-7064). 1955, same group as on *Louis Armstrong Plays W. C. Handy*.

Louis Armstrong at The Crescendo, two volumes (U.S.: Decca DL-8168/69; England: Brunswick LAT-8084/5). 1955, same group as above, live recording at The Crescendo Club in Hollywood.

Satchmo—A Musical Autobiography, four volumes (U.S.: Decca DXM-155; England: Brunswick LAT-8211/14). 1956–1957, with his own small group, sometimes enlarged but always including TRUMMY YOUNG on trombone and BILLY KYLE on piano.

Louis and The Good Book (U.S.: Decca DL-8741; England: Brunswick LAT-8270). 1958, spirituals.

Louis Armstrong Meets Oscar Peterson (U.S.: Verve MG-V-8322; England HMV CLP-1328). Probably 1958, with just the OSCAR PETERSON rhythm section.

Satchmo Plays King Oliver (U.S. and England: Audio-Fidelity AFLP-1930). 1959, with his own all-star group, including BILLY KYLE on piano.

LA VERN BAKER (Vocal)

La Vern Baker Sings Bessie Smith (U.S.: Atlantic 1281; England: London LTZ-K-15139). Accompanying band includes BUCK CLAYTON on trumpet, NAT PIERCE on piano, JOE MARSHALL on drums, and, in some tracks, VIC DICKENSON on trombone.

COUNT BASIE (Piano) and His Orchestra

Count Basie (U.S.: Brunswick 54012; England: Brunswick LAT-8589).

Count Basie and His Orchestra (U.S.: Decca 8049; England: Brunswick LAT-8028).

Count Basie Classics (U.S.: Columbia CL-754; England: Fontana TFL-5077).

Basie's Back in Town (U.S. only: Epic LN-3169).

Lester Leaps In (U.S.: Epic LG-3107; England: see *Lester Young Memorial Album*, below).

Let's Go to Prez (U.S.: Epic LN-3168; England: see *Lester Young Memorial Album*, below).

Basie—One More Time (U.S.: Roulette R-52024; England: Columbia SX-1183).

Lester Young Memorial Album, two volumes (U.S.: listed separately as *Lester Leaps In* and *Let's Go to Prez*, above; England: Fontana TFL-5064 and TFL-5065).

Except *Basie—One More Time*, which features the Basie band of the late fifties playing good QUINCY JONES arrangements, all the other records belong to the late thirties and early forties and feature the incomparable rhythm section composed of FREDDIE GREEN on guitar, WALTER PAGE on bass, JO JONES on drums, and of course, Basie himself on piano. Among the famous soloists featured in those records are BUCK CLAYTON and HARRY EDISON on trumpet, DICKIE WELLS on trombone, HERSCHEL EVANS, LESTER YOUNG, BUDDY TATE, DON BYAS on tenor sax.

SIDNEY BECHET (Soprano Sax and Clarinet)

Jazz Classics, Vol. I (U.S. only: Blue Note 1201).

Sidney Bechet Memorial Album (England only: Fontana TFL-5087). With "Clarence Williams Blue Five"—LOUIS ARMSTRONG plays trumpet on most of the tracks.

CHEW BERRY (Tenor Sax)

Chu (U.S.: Epic LG-3124; England: Philips BBL-7054).

EUBIE BLAKE (Piano)

The Fabulous Piano of Eubie Blake (U.S.: see *The Wizard of the Ragtime Piano*, below; England: Top Rank JKP-2008 and 2040). With PANAMA FRANCIS on drums and, in most tracks, BUSTER BAILEY on clarinet.

The Wizard of the Ragtime Piano (U.S.: 20th Fox 3003; England: listed as *The Fabulous Piano of Eubie Blake*, above).

EARL BOSTIC (Alto Sax)

Earl Bostic Plays Sweet Tunes of the Roaring 20's (U.S. only: King 620).

The Best of Bostic (U.S. only: King 395–500).

Earl Bostic For You (U.S. only: King 395–503).

Earl Bostic Plays Sweet Tunes of the Swinging 30's (England: Parlophone PMC-1117).

Earl Bostic Plays Tunes of the Fantastic 50's (England: Parlophone PMD-1074).

BIG BILL BROONZY (Vocal and Guitar—Blues)

Big Bill Broonzy Sings Country Blues (U.S. only: Folkways FA-2326).

The Blues—Big Bill Broonzy (U.S.: Emarcy MG-36137; England: Mercury MMB-12003).

Big Bill Broonzy (England only: Vogue LAE-12009, Philips BBL-7113).

RAY BRYANT (Piano)

Alone with the Blues (U.S. only: New Jazz 8213). Piano solos.

Ray Bryant Trio (England: Esquire 32–006).

MILT BUCKNER (Organ and Piano)

Rockin' Hammond (U.S.: Capitol T-722; England: Capitol T-722).

TEDDY BUCKNER (Trumpet)

Teddy Buckner and His Dixieland Band (U.S.: Dixieland Jubilee DI-504; England: Vogue LDE-175).

See also KID ORY.

BENNY CARTER (Alto Sax, Trumpet, Arranger)

Aspects (U.S.: United Artists UAL-4017; England: London LTZ-T-15169). With a big band.

Swingin' the 20's (U.S.: Contemporary M-3561; England: Contemporary LAC-12225). BENNY CARTER plays alto sax and trumpet, EARL HINES is at the piano.

Jazz Giant (U.S.: Contemporary C-3555; England: Vogue LAC-12188). BENNY CARTER plays alto sax and trumpet.

ALBERT CASEY (Guitar)

Buck Jumpin' (U.S. only: Prestige/Swingville 2007).

RAY CHARLES (Vocal and Piano)

Yes Indeed (U.S.: Atlantic 8025; England: London HA-E-2168).
Ray Charles (U.S. only: Atlantic 8006).
The Genius of Ray Charles (U.S.: Atlantic 1312; England: London LTZ-K-15190).
What'd I Say (U.S.: Atlantic 8029; England: London HA-E 2226).

CHARLIE CHRISTIAN (Guitar)

Charlie Christian with the Benny Goodman Sextet and Orchestra (U.S.: Columbia CL-652; England: Philips BBL-7172).

BUCK CLAYTON (Trumpet—Leading All-Star Studio Groups)

The Huckle-Buck Robbins' Nest (U.S.: Columbia CL-548; England: Philips BBL-7032). Band includes JOE NEWMAN on trumpet, HENDERSON CHAMBERS on trombone, JULIAN DASH on tenor sax, SIR CHARLES THOMPSON on piano, WALTER PAGE on bass, JO JONES on drums.
Rock-a-Bye Basie, Jumpin' at the Woodside, Blue and Sentimental, Broadway (U.S.: Columbia CL-701; England: Philips BBL-7087). Featuring, among others, RUBY BRAFF on trumpet, BENNY GREEN and DICKIE HARRIS on trombone, COLEMAN HAWKINS and BUDDY TATE on tenor sax, MILTON HINTON on bass.
All the Cats Join In (U.S.: Columbia CL-822; England: Philips BBL-7129). Featuring most of the same men as the two previous LP's.
Buckin' the Blues (U.S.: Vanguard VRS-8514; England: Vanguard PPL-11010). Featuring, among others, VIC DICKENSON on trombone, EARL WARREN on alto sax, JO JONES on drums.
Buck Clayton (England only: Vogue LAE-12032). Recorded in Paris. MEZZ MEZZROW on clarinet. SEDRIC on tenor sax and DON BYAS on tenor sax are featured on some of the records.
See also LA VERN BAKER, COUNT BASIE, JIMMY RUSHING.

COZY COLE (Drums)

Cozy Cole Hits (U.S. only: Love LP-500).
Cozy's Caravan (U.S.: Felsted 7002; England: Felsted FAJ-7002). Reverse, very good: EARL HINES.

WILD BILL DAVIS (Organ)

Wild Bill Davis at Birdland (U.S. only: Epic LN-3118).
Wild Bill Davis in Hollywood (U.S. only: Imperial 9015). Recorded with FLOYD SMITH on guitar and CHRIS COLUMBUS (JOSEPH MORRIS) on drums.

EDDIE "LOCKJAW" DAVIS (Tenor Sax)

Jaws (U.S. only: Prestige 7154).
Eddie Davis Trio + Joe Newman (U.S.: Roulette R-52007; England: Columbia SX-1117). With COUNT BASIE on piano.
Jazz with a Horn (U.S. only: King 395–526).
Modern Jazz Expressions (U.S. only: King 395–506).
    Most of the King performances have DOC BAGBY at the organ; the others, SHIRLEY SCOTT.

WILBUR DE PARIS (Trombone) and His Band

Wilbur De Paris and His New New Orleans Jazz (U.S.: Atlantic 1219; England: London LTZ-K-15024).
Wilbur De Paris at Symphony Hall (U.S.: Atlantic 1253; England: London LTZ-K-15086). Recorded at Boston's Symphony Hall, October 26, 1956.
Wilbur De Paris Plays Cole Porter (U.S.: Atlantic 1288; England: London LTZ-K-15156).
    In the three records, the band features SIDNEY DE PARIS on trumpet, OMER SIMEON on clarinet, SONNY WHITE on piano, WILBERT KIRK on drums.

WILLIE DIXON (Vocal and String Bass—Blues)

Willie's Blues (U.S. only: Prestige/Bluesville 1003). With MEMPHIS SLIM on piano, WALLY RICHARDSON on guitar, AL ASHBY on tenor sax, GUS JOHNSON on drums.

JOHNNY DODDS (Clarinet)

See LOUIS ARMSTRONG and KING OLIVER.

CHAMPION JACK DUPREE (Vocal and Piano—Blues)

Blues from the Gutter (U.S.: Atlantic 8019; England: London LTZ-K-15171).

ROY ELDRIDGE (Trumpet)

Dale's Wail (U.S.: Verve 8089; England: Columbia C-9005).

DUKE ELLINGTON (Piano) and His Orchestra

Early Ellington (U.S. only: Brunswick 54007). With BUBBER MILEY on trumpet in some numbers, COOTIE WILLIAMS in others; TRICKY SAM on trombone, BARNEY BIGARD on clarinet, JOHNNY HODGES on alto sax, WELLMAN BRAUD on bass.

At The Cotton Club (U.S.: Camden 459; England: Camden CDN-119). With the same musicians featured, except Bubber Miley.

In a Mellotone (U.S.: Victor LPM-1364; England: RCA RD-27134). Recordings of the early forties featuring, among others, REX STEWART on trumpet, TRICKY SAM on trombone, JOHNNY HODGES on alto sax, BEN WEBSTER on tenor sax, HARRY CARNEY on baritone sax, JIMMY BLANTON on bass.

The Duke Plays Ellington (U.S. only: Capitol T-477). Piano solos by Duke Ellington.

Ellington '55 (U.S. only: Capitol W-521). Featuring, among others, RAY NANCE and CLARK TERRY on trumpet, PAUL GONSALVES on tenor sax.

Royal Concert One (U.S.: Aamco 301; England: see *Historically Speaking*, below).

Historically Speaking (U.S.: listed as *Royal Concert One*, above; England: Parlophone PMC-1116).

Ellington at Newport (U.S.: Columbia CL-934; England: Philips BBL-7133). Featuring, among others, JOHNNY HODGES on alto

SAX, PAUL GONSALVES on tenor sax, RUSSELL PROCOPE on clarinet, RAY NANCE on trumpet.

Newport 1958 (U.S.: Columbia CL-1245; England: Philips BBL-7279). Featuring, among others, PAUL GONSALVES on tenor sax, CAT ANDERSON, HAROLD BAKER on trumpet, RAY NANCE on trumpet and violin, SAM WOODYARD on drums.

Festival Session (1959) (U.S.: Columbia CL-1400; England: Philips BBL-7355). PAUL GONSALVES on tenor sax and JOHNNY HODGES on alto sax; each has a special—and wonderful— feature number in this LP.

A Blues Serenade (England only: HMV DLP-1172). Recordings of the late thirties, featuring, among others, COOTIE WILLIAMS and REX STEWART on trumpet, TRICKY SAM on trombone, JOHNNY HODGES on alto sax, BILLY TAYLOR on bass.

See also JOHNNY HODGES.

ELLA FITZGERALD (Vocal)

Lullabies of Birdland (U.S.: Decca 8149; England: Brunswick LAT-8115).

Ella and Louis, three volumes (U.S.: Verve 4003, 4017, 4018; England: HMV CLP-1098, CLP-1146, CLP-1147). With LOUIS ARMSTRONG.

ERROLL GARNER (Piano)

Erroll Garner Plays for Dancing (U.S. only: Columbia CL-667).

Afternoon of an Elf (U.S.: Mercury MG-20090; England: Mercury MLP-6539).

The Most Happy Piano (U.S.: Columbia CL-939; England: Philips BBL-7282).

Erroll Garner (U.S. only: Columbia CL-535).

AL GREY (Trombone)

The Last of the Big Plungers (U.S. only: Argo LP-653). With some of the Count Basie musicians, including BILLY MITCHELL on tenor sax, EDDIE JONES on bass, SONNY PAYNE on drums.

TINY GRIMES (Guitar)

Callin' the Blues (U.S.: Prestige 7144; England: Esquire 32–092). With J. C. HIGGINBOTHAM on trombone, EDDIE DAVIS on tenor sax, RAY BRYANT on piano, WENDELL MARSHALL on bass, OSIE JOHNSON on drums.

JUANITA HALL (Vocal)

Juanita Hall Sings the Blues (U.S. only: Counterpoint (compatible) CPST-556). With DOC CHEATHAM on trumpet, COLEMAN HAWKINS on tenor sax, BUSTER BAILEY on clarinet, CLAUDE HOPKINS on piano, GEORGE DUVIVIER on bass, JIMMY CRAWFORD on drums.

LIONEL HAMPTON (Vibraphone, Drums, Piano)

The Hampton-Tatum-Rich Trio (U.S.: Verve MG-V-8093; England: Columbia CX-10045). With ART TATUM on piano, BUDDY RICH on drums.

Lionel Hampton and His Giants (U.S.: Verve MG-V-8170; England: Columbia CX-10063). With ART TATUM on piano, HARRY EDISON on trumpet.

Lionel Hampton '58 (U.S. only: Verve MG-V-8223). With OSCAR PETERSON on piano, RAY BROWN on bass, BUDDY RICH on drums.

Lionel Hampton (U.S.: Contemporary C-3502; England: Vogue LAE-1234). Recorded in Paris with a group including WALTER WILLIAMS on trumpet, AL HAYSE on trombone, ALIX COMBELLE on tenor sax, CLAUDE BOLLING on piano, BILLY MACKEL on guitar, CURLEY HAMNER on drums. Hamp plays piano in one of the numbers.

Hamp in Paris (U.S.: Emarcy MG-36032; England: Felsted EDL-87007/8). Recorded in Paris with a group including MEZZ MEZZROW on clarinet, ANDRÉ PERSIANY on piano, BUDDY BANKS on bass, CURLEY HAMNER on drums. Hamp plays piano and drums in some of the numbers.

Jivin' the Vibes (England only: Camden CDN-129). 1937–1939, by various all-star groups including, among others COOTIE WILLIAMS on trumpet, BENNY CARTER on alto sax and clarinet,

JOHNNY HODGES on alto sax, HERSCHEL EVANS on tenor sax, JOHN KIRBY on bass, COZY COLE on drums.

COLEMAN HAWKINS (Tenor Sax)

Coleman Hawkins Encounters Ben Webster (U.S.: Verve MG-V-8327; England: see *Blue Saxophones*, below).
Blue Saxophones (U.S.: listed as *Coleman Hawkins Encounters Ben Webster*, above; England: Columbia CX-10143).
The High and Mighty Hawk (U.S.: Felsted FAJ-7005; England: Felsted FAJ-7005).
The Big Sounds (U.S. only: Brunswick 54016).
See also JUANITA HALL and BUCK CLAYTON.

EARL "FATHA" HINES (Piano)

Earl's Backroom (U.S.: Felsted FAJ-7002; England: Felsted FAJ-7002). Reverse, very good: COZY COLE.
Earl "Fatha" Hines Solo (U.S. only: Fantasy 3238).
The Earl Hines Trio (U.S.: Epic LN-3501; England: Philips BBL-7222).
   The two latter albums are entirely piano solos accompanied by a rhythm section.
Piano Solos 1928-1932-1950 (England only: Philips BBL-7185).
Piano Solos and Band Performances (England only: Gala GLP-316).
See also LOUIS ARMSTRONG.

JOHNNY HODGES (Alto Sax)

Hodge Podge (U.S. only: Epic LG-3105). Recorded with a part of Duke Ellington's band, including COOTIE WILLIAMS on trumpet.
Castle Rock (U.S. only: Verve MG-V-8139).
The Blues (U.S. only: Verve MG-V-8151).
   The latter two with Johnny Hodges' fine small band of the early fifties.
Duke's in Bed (U.S.: MG-V-8203; England: Columbia CX-10098). Recorded with a part of Duke Ellington's band including

CLARK TERRY on trumpet, RAY NANCE on trumpet and violin, HARRY CARNEY on baritone sax, JIMMY WOODE on bass, SAM WOODYARD on drums.

Ellingtonia '56 (U.S.: Verve MG-8145; England: Columbia CX-10055). One side by the whole Ellington band, the other side by a part of it.

The Big Sound (U.S.: Verve MG-V-8271; Columbia CX-10136). With most of Duke Ellington's men, including SAM WOODYARD on drums.

Back to Back (U.S.: Verve MG-V-8317; England HMV CLP-1316). With a small group including HARRY EDISON on trumpet and DUKE ELLINGTON on piano. Here, Duke shows his genius as a piano player.

See also DUKE ELLINGTON.

JOHN LEE HOOKER (Vocal and Guitar—Blues)

I'm John Lee Hooker (U.S. only: Vee Jay 1007).

SAM "LIGHTNIN' " HOPKINS

Sam "Lightnin' " Hopkins (U.S. only: Folkways FS-3822).
Lightning Hopkins (U.S. only: Time T-70004).
The Rooster Crowed in England (England only: "77" LA-12-1).

HELEN HUMES (Vocal)

Helen Humes (U.S. only: Contemporary M-3571). Accompanied by a studio group including BENNY CARTER on trumpet.

MAHALIA JACKSON (Vocal)

The World's Greatest Gospel Singer (U.S. only: Columbia CL-644).
Bless This House (U.S. only: Columbia CL-899).
Great Gettin' Up Morning (U.S.: Columbia CL-1343; England: Philips BBL-7362).

ILLINOIS JACQUET (Tenor Sax)

Swing's the Thing (U.S. only: Verve MG-V-8023). With ROY ELDRIDGE on trumpet and JO JONES on drums.

BUDDY JOHNSON and His Orchestra

Rock and Roll with Buddy Johnson (U.S. only: Mercury 20209).

JAMES P. JOHNSON (Piano)

The Art of Jazz Piano (U.S. only: Epic LN-3295). The record features also ART TATUM, EARL HINES, and JOE SULLIVAN. It is indeed regrettable that there is not one LP available entirely devoted to such an important pianist as James P. Johnson.

PETE JOHNSON (Piano)

It is a shame that such a great pianist has no LP's available. But he can be heard to good advantage on RUSHING's Vanguard VRS-8505 and on TURNER's Atlantic 1234.

HANK JONES (Piano)

Have You Met Hank Jones (U.S.: Savoy MG-12084; England: London LTZ-C-15079). Piano solos.

JO JONES (Drums)

Jo Jones' Trio (U.S.: Everest LPBR-5023; England: Top Rank 35-039). With RAY BRYANT on piano and TOM BRYANT on bass.
Jo Jones Plus Two (U.S. only: Vanguard VRS-8525). Also with the BRYANT BROTHERS.
See also COUNT BASIE, ILLINOIS JACQUET, JIMMY RUSHING, BUCK CLAYTON.

JONAH JONES (Trumpet)

Swingin' at the Cinema (U.S.: Capitol T-1083; England: Capitol T-1083).

Jumpin' with Jonah (U.S.: Capitol T-1039; England: Capitol
T-1039).
Jonah Jones at The Embers (U.S. only: Groove LG-1001).

LOUIS JORDAN (Vocal and Alto Sax)

Somebody Up There Digs Me (U.S.: Mercury 20242; England:
Mercury MPT-7521).

B. B. KING (Vocal and Guitar—Blues)

Singin' the Blues (U.S. only: Crown 5020).
The Blues (U.S. only: Crown 5063).

TOMMY LADNIER (Trumpet)

Tommy Ladnier (U.S. only: "X" LVA-3027). With MEZZ MEZZ-
ZROW on clarinet. If, as I suspect, this LP has been cut out,
Tommy Ladnier can be heard in two tracks of *From Spirituals
to Swing*, Carnegie Hall LP's (U.S.: Vanguard VRS-8523/24;
England: Top Rank 35/064), which has some very good music
by Basie's men, Lips Page, and other fine musicians; some of
Tommy Ladnier's best recorded work might be in Fletcher
Henderson's LP's, which Columbia may release by the time
this book is published.

JOHNNY LETMAN (Trumpet)

Cascade of Quartets, two volumes (England only: Columbia SX-
1191 and SX-1218). Johnny Letman has two numbers in each
of these LP's.

JIMMIE LUNCEFORD and His Orchestra

Jimmie Lunceford and His Orchestra (U.S. only: Decca 8050).
Lunceford Special (U.S.: Columbia CL-634; England: Philips
BBL-7037). Band often includes SY OLIVER, trumpet and arranger, TRUMMY YOUNG on trombone, WILLIE SMITH on alto
sax, JOE THOMAS on tenor sax, JAMES CRAWFORD on drums.

MEMPHIS SLIM (Piano—Blues)

The Real Boogie Woogie (U.S. only: Folkways FG-3524). Piano solos.

At the Gate of Horn (U.S. only: Vee-Jay LP 1012). Memphis Slim sings and plays piano with a small band including MATTHEW MURPHY on guitar.

See also WILLIE DIXON.

MILTON "MEZZ" MEZZROW (Clarinet)

Mezz à la Schola Cantorum (U.S.: London TKL-93092; England: Ducretet Thompson TKL-93092). With PEANUTS HOLLAND and GUY LONGNON on trumpet, MILTON SEALEY on piano, KANSAS FIELDS on drums.

See also BUCK CLAYTON and LIONEL HAMPTON.

JELLY ROLL MORTON (Piano)

Mr. Jelly Lord (U.S. only: Riverside RLP-12-132). Piano solos.

The King of New Orleans Jazz—Jelly Roll Morton (U.S.: RCA Victor LPM-1649; England: RCA RD-27113). With a New Orleans style band including in most numbers GEORGE MITCHELL on trumpet, KID ORY on trombone, OMER SIMEON on clarinet.

JOE NEWMAN (Trumpet)

Soft Swingin' Jazz (U.S.: Coral CRL 57.208; England: Coral LAV 9106).

JIMMIE NOONE (Clarinet)

Jimmie Noone Apex Club (U.S.: Brunswick BL-58006; England: Coral LRA-10026). With EARL HINES on piano. This LP is probably cut out but there is no other LP entirely devoted to the greatest of all jazz clarinet players. Jimmie Noone can also be heard in a couple of numbers in the King Oliver Creole Jazz Band, Epic LP (see KING OLIVER).

JOE "KING" OLIVER (Trumpet)

King Oliver (U.S.: Epic LN-3208; England: Philips BBL-7181).
  With the greatest of New Orleans bands, including LOUIS
  ARMSTRONG on second trumpet, and JOHNNY DODDS on clarinet
  —replaced by JIMMIE NOONE on some tracks.

KID ORY (Trombone)

Tailgate (U.S.: Good Time Jazz 12022; England: Good Time
  Jazz LAG-12104). 1944-1945, one of the purest New Orleans-
  style LP's.
Creole Jazz Band—1954 (U.S.: Good Time Jazz 12004; England:
  Good Time Jazz LAG-12004). The band includes MINOR HALL
  on drums.
Creole Jazz Band—1956 (U.S.: Good Time Jazz 12016; England:
  Good Time Jazz LAG-12084). The band includes WELLMAN
  BRAUD on bass and MINOR HALL on drums.
Kid Ory Plays W. C. Handy (U.S.: Verve MG-V-1017; England:
  HMV CLP 1364). With TEDDY BUCKNER on trumpet.

LIPS PAGE (Trumpet and Vocal)

It is a shame that several years after the death of such an
important artist, none of his performances have been reissued
and put together on LP. However, one of his finest trumpet
recordings is available in the LP two-record album, *From
Spirituals to Swing* (U.S.: Vanguard VRS-8523/24; England:
Top Rank 35/064).

"MA" RAINEY (Vocal—Blues)

Blues (U.S. only: Riverside 12-108).

JIMMY REED (Vocal—Guitar—Harmonica—Blues)

I'm Jimmy Reed (U.S. only: Vee Jay 1004).

DJANGO REINHARDT (Guitar)

The Art of Django (England only: HMV CLP-1340).
The Best of Django Reinhardt, two volumes (U.S. only: Capitol TBO-10226).
Django (England only: HMV CLP-1249).

JIMMY RUSHING (Vocal)

These records are recommended not only for Rushing's vocals but for the wonderful studio groups whose instrumental work is heavily featured in most of the numbers.

Goin' to Chicago (U.S.: Vanguard 8518; England: Vanguard PPT-12002). Band includes PAT JENKINS on trumpet, BUDDY TATE on tenor sax, SAMMY PRICE on piano, WALTER PAGE on bass, JO JONES on drums.

Listen to the Blues with Jimmy Rushing (U.S.: Vanguard VRS-8505; England: Vanguard PPT-12016). Band includes EMMETT BERRY on trumpet, BUDDY TATE on tenor sax, PETE JOHNSON on piano, JO JONES on drums.

If This Ain't the Blues (U.S.: Vanguard VRS-8513; England: Vanguard PPL-11008). Band includes VIC DICKENSON on trombone, BUDDY TATE on tenor sax, MARLOWE MORRIS on organ, ROY GAINES on guitar, JO JONES on drums.

The Jazz Odyssey of James Rushing, Esq. (U.S.: Columbia CL-983; England: Philips BBL-7166). With various studio groups headed by BUCK CLAYTON on trumpet.

CHARLIE SHAVERS (Trumpet)

Charlie Digs Dixie (U.S. only: MGM E 3809).
Girl of My Dreams (U.S. only: Everest LPBR 5070).

HAL SINGER (Tenor Sax)

Blue Stompin' (U.S. only: Prestige 7153). Band includes CHARLIE SHAVERS on trumpet, RAY BRYANT on piano.

BESSIE SMITH (Vocal)

The Bessie Smith Story, four volumes (U.S.: Columbia CL-855/58; England: Philips B-07002/05-L). LOUIS ARMSTRONG, trumpet, is featured in Vol. I; JOE SMITH, trumpet, is featured in Vol. III; JAMES P. JOHNSON, piano, is featured in Vol. IV.

STUFF SMITH (Violin)

Stuff Smith (U.S.: Verve 8206; England: Columbia CX-10093). *Sweet Swingin' Stuff* (U.S. only: Fox 3008). With JOHNNY LETMAN on trumpet.

WILLIE "THE LION" SMITH (Piano)

The Legend of Willie the Lion Smith (U.S.: Grand Award GA-33-368; England: Top Rank RX-3015). *The Lion Roars* (U.S. only: Dot DLP-3094). *Accent on Piano* (U.S. only: Urania UJ-1207). In this LP, some numbers are played by a studio group; *Perdido* is the best recorded example of CECIL SCOTT's tenor sax playing.

REX STEWART (Trumpet)

Rendez-Vous with Rex (U.S.: Felsted FAJ-7001; England: Felsted FAJ-7001). By a studio group including GEORGE KELLY on tenor sax, WILLIE "THE LION" SMITH on piano, ARTHUR TRAPPIER on drums. *Henderson Homecoming* (U.S. only: United Artists UAL-4009). Recorded at the L.I. South Bay Festival, with a big band, including BUDDY TATE on tenor sax, HILTON JEFFERSON on alto sax, TAFT JORDAN on trumpet.

ROOSEVELT SYKES (Vocal and Piano—Blues)

The Return of Roosevelt Sykes (U.S. only: Prestige/Bluesville 1006).

BUDDY TATE (Tenor Sax)

Rock 'n Roll (U.S. only: Baton BL-1201). Reverse by FRANK CULLEY's orchestra. *Swinging Like Tate* (U.S.: Felsted FAJ-7004; England: Felsted FAJ-7004).

Tate's Date (U.S. only: Prestige-Swingville 2003).
   These three records have been made by Buddy Tate's regular
   band, except for a few changes in the two last LP's.
Cascade of Quartets, two volumes (England only: Columbia SX-
   1191 and SX-1218). Buddy Tate has two numbers in each of
   these LP's.
See also COUNT BASIE, BUCK CLAYTON, JIMMY RUSHING, REX STEWART.

ART TATUM (Piano)

The Art of Tatum (U.S. only: Decca 8715).
The Genius of Art Tatum, Vols. III, V, VI, and XI (U.S. only:
   Verve 8038, 8040, 8055, 8095).
The Greatest Piano of Them All (U.S. only: Verve 8323). This LP
   has the most beautiful photo of any jazz musician, by Phil
   Stern.
Art Tatum Discoveries (U.S.: Fox 3029; England: Top Rank
   35/067).
Presenting . . . The Art Tatum Trio (U.S.: Verve 8118; England:
   Columbia C-9039). With a trio including JO JONES on drums.
Art Tatum (England only: Columbia C-9033, CX-1053). Piano
   solos.
Here's Art Tatum (England only: Coral LVA-9047).
See also LIONEL HAMPTON and BEN WEBSTER.

CLARK TERRY (Trumpet)

Duke with a Difference (U.S. only: Riverside RLP-12-246). With
   PAUL GONSALVES on tenor sax, JOHNNY HODGES on alto sax, SAM
   WOODYARD on drums.
See also DUKE ELLINGTON, JOHNNY HODGES.

SISTER ROSETTA THARPE (Vocal and Guitar)

Gospel Train (U.S.: Mercury MG-20201; England: Mercury MPL-
   6529).
Gospel Train . . . Sister Rosetta Tharpe (U.S.: Decca DL-8782;
   England: Brunswick LAT-8290). With the SAM PRICE trio.
The Gospel Truth (U.S. only: Mercury SR 60080).

JOE TURNER (Vocal)

Joe Turner (U.S. only: Atlantic 8005). This LP includes the famous and wonderful number *Shake, Rattle and Roll.*

Rockin' the Blues (U.S.: Atlantic 8023; England: London HA-E-2173).

Big Joe Is Here (U.S.: Atlantic 8033; England: London HA-E-2231).

The Boss of the Blues (U.S.: Atlantic 1234; England: London LTZ-K-15053). This one with PETE JOHNSON on piano.

EDDIE VINSON (Vocal)

Cleanhead's Back in Town (U.S. only: Bethlehem BCP-5005).

FATS WALLER (Piano and Vocal)

Fats, two volumes (U.S. only: RCA Victor LPT-6001).
Ain't Misbehavin' (U.S. only: Victor LPM-1246).
Handful of Keys (U.S. only: Victor LPM-1502).
The Real Fats Waller (England only: Camden CDN-131).
Fats Waller (England only: RCA RD-27047).
Fats Waller (England only: RCA RC-24004).
> GENE SEDRIC (tenor sax and clarinet), HERMAN AUTREY (trumpet), AL CASEY (guitar), SLICK JONES (drums) and some other good musicians appear on these records.

LITTLE WALTER (Vocal and Harmonica—Blues)

The Best of Little Walter (U.S. only: Chess 1428).

ETHEL WATERS (Vocal)

Ethel Waters (U.S. only: Vik LX-999).
The Favorite Songs of Ethel Waters (U.S. only: Emarcy MG-20051).

MUDDY WATERS (Vocal and Guitar—Blues)

The Best of Muddy Waters (U.S.: Chess 1427; England: London LTZ-M-15152).

BEN WEBSTER (Tenor Sax)

Ben Webster—King of the Tenors (U.S. only: Verve MG-V-8020).
The Art Tatum–Ben Webster Quartet (U.S.: Verve MG-V-8220;
England: Columbia CX-10137).
See also COLEMAN HAWKINS.

DICKY WELLS (Trombone)

Trombone Four-in-Hand (England: Felsted FAJ 7009). With
three other trombones (VIC DICKENSON, BENNY MORTON,
GEORGE MATTHEWS).

COOTIE WILLIAMS (Trumpet)

Cootie Williams in Hi-Fi (U.S. only: RCA Victor LPM-1718).
Very good for Cootie's trumpet solos, but not for the band
with him—not his own but an indifferent studio group.
See also DUKE ELLINGTON.

SONNY BOY WILLIAMSON (Vocal and Harmonica— Blues)

Down and Out Blues (U.S. only: Checker LP-1437).

JIMMY WITHERSPOON (Vocal)

*Wilbur De Paris Plays and Jimmy Witherspoon Sings New Orleans
Blues* (U.S.: Atlantic 1266; England: London LTZ-K-15150).
Here is some of the finest music put on records by the Wilbur
De Paris band, especially for SIDNEY DE PARIS trumpet work and
OMER SIMEON clarinet.
Jimmy Witherspoon at the Monterey Jazz Festival (U.S. only:
Hifijazz J-421). Featured, among others, are EARL HINES on
piano, COLEMAN HAWKINS and BEN WEBSTER on tenor sax.

LESTER YOUNG (Tenor Sax)

The Lester Young–Buddy Rich Trio (U.S. only: Verve 8164).
With KING COLE on piano.

Tenor Sax, Vol. I (U.S.: Aladdin 801; England: Vogue LAE-12194).

The two "Lester Young Memorial" albums are listed under COUNT BASIE.